Easy Model Railroad Wiring

SECOND EDITION

Andy Sperandeo

KALMBACH
BOOKS

Printed in the United States of America

99 00 01 02 03 04 05 06 07 08   10 9 8 7 6 5 4 3 2 1

Visit our website at http://books.kalmbach.com
Secure online ordering available

Publisher's Cataloging-in-Publication
(Provided by Quality Books, Inc.)

Sperandeo, Andy.
    Easy model railroad wiring / Andy Sperandeo. — 2nd ed.

    p. cm.
    Previous edition published under title Your guide to easy model railroad
    wiring. Includes bibliographical references and index.
    ISBN: 0-89024-349-2

    1. Railroads—Models—Electric equipment. I.
Sperandeo, Andy. Your guide to easy model railroad wiring.
II. Title.

TF197.S629 1999   625.1´9
                                                         QBI98-1526

Book design: Mark Watson
Cover design: Kristi Ludwig

Contents

Introduction

You've built the benchwork, you've laid the track and wired it, and now, finally, you're ready to run your trains. You flip the switch, and . . . nothing, your trains remain still, as motionless as they were the day you plucked them off the hobby shop shelf. Chances are this has happened to you, and chances are the problem could be traced to faulty wiring. This book makes finding and correcting such problems easier than ever. Better yet, it helps you avoid common—and not so common—wiring errors that keep your trains from doing what they're supposed to.

Easy Model Railroad Wiring tells you how to wire your layout for satisfactory, flexible, and reliable operation. This invaluable book covers every dimension of basic model railroad wiring, from choosing a power pack to deciding what type of turnout to use to installing and, yes, fixing layout wiring. If it has to do with wiring track and getting trains operating, then you'll find it in this book.

Basic model railroad electricity

CHAPTER ONE

This chapter is a basic introduction to electrical operation of scale model trains. If you've had experience with model railroad wiring you may want to skip ahead, although I've learned that there's often some elementary point that we think we know but really don't.

The Power Pack

The power and control package most often used to run scale model trains is called a power pack. Like the toy train transformer it plugs into a wall socket and connects to the track, but there are important differences. Figure 1-1 shows the inside of a typical power pack.

A power pack includes a transformer, a device that reduces the electrical power flowing from your house's wall outlet to a safer level for operating a model railroad. House current in the U. S. is typically between 110 and 120 volts (a volt is a unit of electrical force). This is too much current to pass safely through exposed rails on a layout; the transformer in a power pack reduces it to around 16 or 18 volts.

House current in the U. S. is alternating current (AC). The alternation referred to is in the direction of the current's flow; the 60-cycle AC we get from the wall socket actually reverses its direction of flow 60 times every second. This has some advantages—it's what makes electric clocks keep time—but it has important disadvantages for model railroading.

Lionel and other toy trains many of us are familiar with run on AC. That's why they have to use what's called sequence reversing. To change directions with sequence reversing you have to turn off the speed controller and stop the train, turn on the controller again, and turn it off again—the train doesn't move at this point in the sequence—and finally turn on the controller once more to move the train in the other direction.

While stopping any train before changing its direction is smart, you

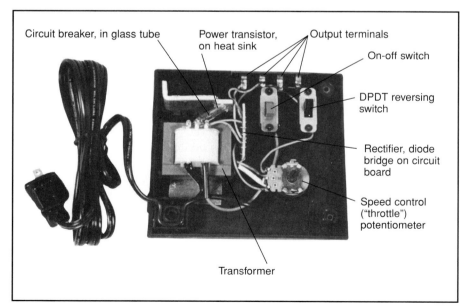

Fig. 1-1. INSIDE A POWER PACK. A typical basic power pack—this one is the MRC Railpower 1200, rated for N and small HO scale locomotives—includes a transformer to reduce house current, a circuit breaker for overload protection, a rectifier bridge to convert AC to DC, a throttle or speed control (here a potentiometer and power transistor), and a reversing switch.

Circuit breaker, in glass tube
Power transistor, on heat sink
Output terminals
On-off switch
DPDT reversing switch
Rectifier, diode bridge on circuit board
Speed control ("throttle") potentiometer
Transformer

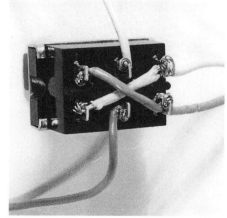

Fig. 1-2. DPDT REVERSING SWITCH. This is the back side of a double-pole, double-throw toggle wired for reversing. The two wires coming into one end of the switch are from the speed control, and the two wires on the center terminals connect to the track and train. The crossed wires connecting the end terminals of the switch provide the reversing action, as fig. 1-3 will show.

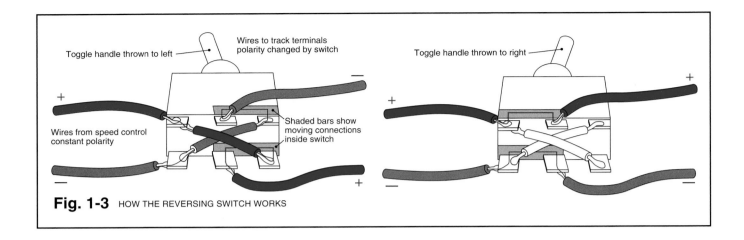

Fig. 1-3 HOW THE REVERSING SWITCH WORKS

Toggle handle thrown to left

Wires to track terminals polarity changed by switch

Wires from speed control constant polarity

Shaded bars show moving connections inside switch

Toggle handle thrown to right

can see how sequence reversing might slow down your yard switching. Another important disadvantage is that sequence reversing makes it hard to tell which way a train will move when you first start it. There's also the possibility that a momentary interruption of power will reverse the train without your control. The final disadvantage is that the locomotives have to carry reversing relay equipment—the Lionel E-unit—that we'd

rather not have to accommodate in smaller scale models. For these and other good reasons scale model trains run on direct current (DC). Direct current flows in only one direction at a time, which means with DC motors we can reverse our locomotive's direction simply by reversing the current flow. The rectifier device in the power pack converts AC into DC. Together the transformer and rectifier turn high-voltage, AC

house power into low-voltage, DC train power.

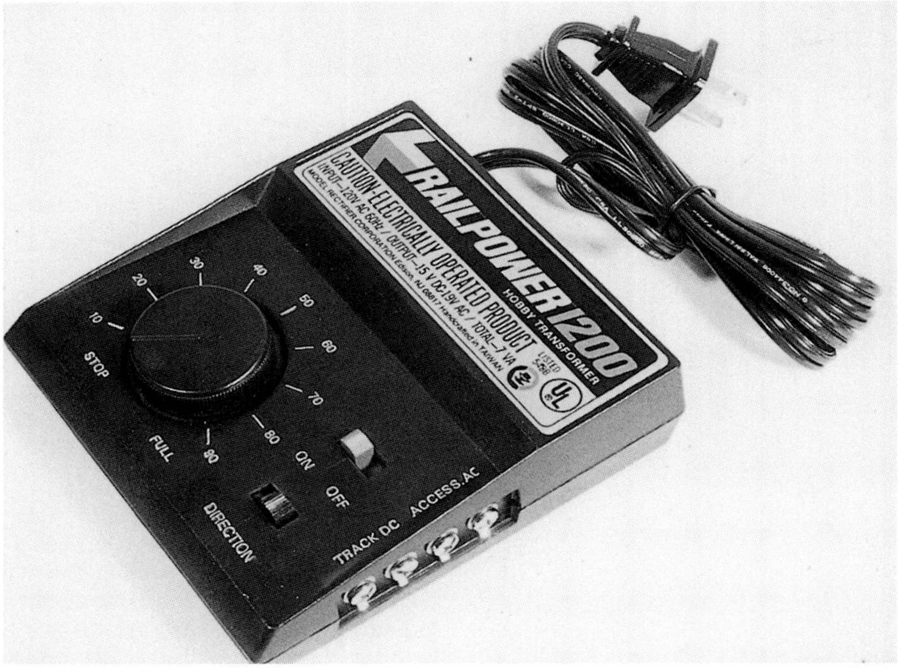

Speed Control

Model railroaders like to call the speed control on a power pack the "throttle," because it's similar in function to the throttle of a real locomotive. It's a handy general term because the throttle in a power pack may be one of several different kinds of electrical devices. The one shown in fig. 1-1 is a potentiometer, which controls the transistor that controls the voltage. Chapter 2 will tell more about this and other throttles and how they work.

All throttles serve the same purpose: to control the speed of a train by varying the voltage flowing to the locomotive's motor. Increasing the voltage makes the train run faster; lowering it slows the train down. The maximum voltage allowed is 12 to 18VDC (Volts Direct Current), according to National Model Railroad Association (NMRA) standard S9.

Model railroaders speak of using "12-volt motors" and prefer locomotives to reach their fastest speed when running on 12 volts, but the NMRA standard allows a bit more. On the other hand, the maximum voltage delivered by most power packs is close to the low end of the S9 range. You'll remember that we were getting 16 to 18VAC (Volts Alternating Current) out of the transformer, but losses in the rectifier, speed control,

Fig. 1-4. POWER PACK TERMINALS. The four screws along the right side of this power pack are its output terminals. You can see how they are clearly labeled for DC track power and AC accessory power.

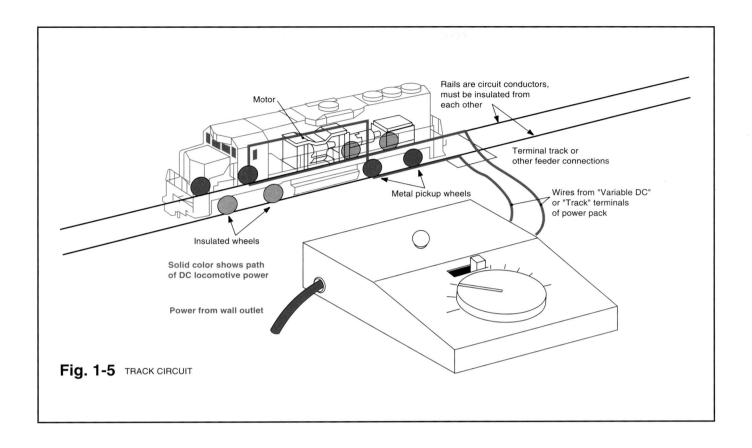

Motor

Rails are circuit conductors,
must be insulated from
each other

Terminal track or
other feeder connections

Metal pickup wheels

Wires from "Variable DC"
or "Track" terminals
of power pack

Insulated wheels

**Solid color shows path
of DC locomotive power**

Power from wall outlet

Fig. 1-5 TRACK CIRCUIT

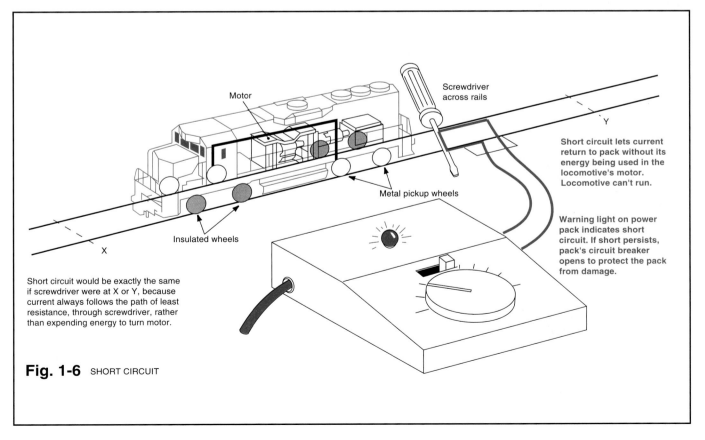

Motor

Screwdriver
across rails

Y

**Short circuit lets current
return to pack without its
energy being used in the
locomotive's motor.
Locomotive can't run.**

Metal pickup wheels

**Warning light on power
pack indicates short
circuit. If short persists,
pack's circuit breaker
opens to protect the pack
from damage.**

Insulated wheels

X

Short circuit would be exactly the same
if screwdriver were at X or Y, because
current always follows the path of least
resistance, through screwdriver, rather
than expending energy to turn motor.

Fig. 1-6 SHORT CIRCUIT

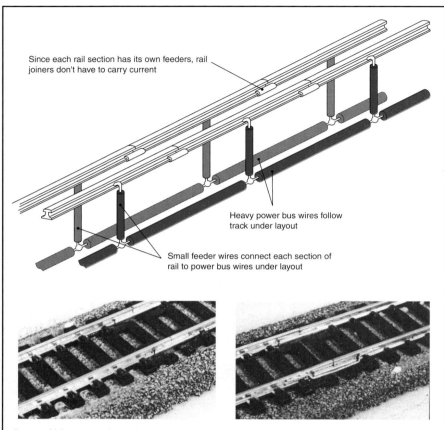

Since each rail section has its own feeders, rail joiners don't have to carry current

Heavy power bus wires follow track under layout

Small feeder wires connect each section of rail to power bus wires under layout

Loose rail joiner connections can cause open circuits and power loss. The left photo shows the simplest way to avoid such troubles: The joiner is soldered to the two rails it connects. In the second photo, the same effect is achieved by the light-guage "bond wire" soldered to the rails on each side of the joint. The drawing shows how parallel feeders to each length of rail can be used to eliminate any need for electrical connections at rail joints.

Fig. 1-7 RAIL JOINT CONNECTIONS

and from other causes usually keep the voltage going to the motor down to something less.

Direction Control

The power pack's reversing switch is the device you use to reverse the DC flow, and so reverse the direction of the train. It is a double-pole, double-throw (abbreviated DPDT) switch wired as in fig. 1-2.

Later in this book we'll refer to many kinds of electrical switches in terms of poles and throws. "Pole," as used to describe switches, means a connection or wire that the switch can change. "Throw" means a position that a pole can be changed to.

Thus "double pole, double throw"

means that two connections can be changed to either of two positions. Figure 1-3 shows how this works to reverse the current flow.

The direction of current flow is expressed in terms of positive and negative "potential," often indicated with "+" and "−" signs. In a DC flow, electrons move from an area of negative potential toward an area of positive potential, but we don't really have to concern ourselves with electrons. For our purposes positive and negative potential are just reference points to help us keep our connections straight.

Circuit Breaker and Terminals

Finally, almost all power packs include some sort of circuit breaker

to protect the pack against overloads. The most common types reset themselves automatically, and better power packs include a warning light to let you know that the breaker is open. Remember that the circuit breaker only protects the pack and not your locomotives or accessories. It's up to you to protect these through careful use.

On the outside of your power pack you'll find output terminals. These are generally marked to help you connect them correctly. Power packs usually have at least two pairs of terminals and sometimes more—see fig. 1-4. The terminals marked "Variable DC," or more obviously "Track," deliver the train power, while those marked "AC" or "Accessories" are for remote control switches and other devices that operate on AC. Consult the manufacturer's directions regarding other terminals and markings. The most important thing to remember is that you should never connect AC terminals to your track, because AC will do damage to DC motors.

The Rails

In model railroading we use the track rails as conductors to carry the power to the train. The rails form the sides of a "circuit," or current path connecting the power pack with the locomotive motor, as in fig. 1-5.

The two rails must be kept "insulated" or electrically separate from each other, which is why we use plastic, wood, or other insulating materials for track crossties. You can find out what happens if the rails aren't insulated by bridging across the rails with a metal screwdriver blade while the train is running. (Caution: Be sure your power pack has a circuit breaker before making this experiment.)

As fig. 1-6 shows, the current takes the path of least resistance, which is through the screwdriver blade where it doesn't do any work such as turning a motor or lighting a headlight. The train stops because it isn't getting any current, and the circuit breaker shuts off the power pack because the load on the pack is too great. This condition is called a "short circuit," or "short" for short.

If you've tried setting up anything but the simplest of layouts, you've already seen that turnouts (track switches), crossings, and such provide lots of opportunities for shorts between the two sides of our track circuit. You'll learn how to keep the circuit working through all kinds of trackwork in Chapters 3 and 4.

Since the rails conduct power to our trains, they should form a nearly continuous current path. Anything less means imperfect operation, annoying hesitation and stalling, and in general models that don't act like real trains. Here are two important considerations:

Rail joints can be the source of many conductivity problems; therefore, the best rule is simply not to trust the typical folded sheet metal rail joiner to carry current on its own. With sectional track layouts that you want to change you can make some improvement by crimping loose joiners with pliers, but a permanent model railroad deserves something better. Figure 1-7 shows three ways of getting current around the rail joiner.

My favorite method is soldering the joiners to the rails, which also makes the rail alignment permanent. This can cause problems with expansion and contraction on layouts subject to great temperature changes; if you're concerned about this you may want to use the bond-wire method.

The bond wires, so called because they're like the prototype wire connections of the same name used to carry signal circuits around rail joints, can be light gauge because they're so short. When the track is painted and weathered their appearance is acceptable in HO and larger scales. If you're working in N or Z scale, or using light rail in HO, you'll probably prefer the bus-and-feeder method.

This last approach uses feeder wires to every length of rail with connections to heavy-gauge bus wires below the layout ("bus" is the electri-

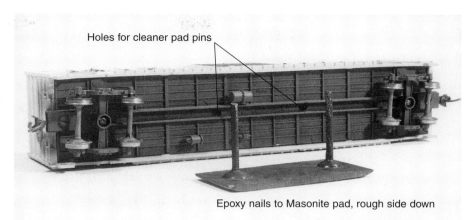

Holes for cleaner pad pins

Epoxy nails to Masonite pad, rough side down

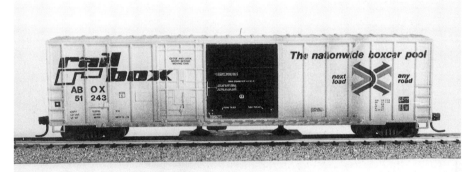

Fig. 1-8. JOHN ALLEN'S TRACK CLEANER. A simple Masonite pad with rough side down converts any boxcar or other "house" car into a track cleaner. The pads are unobtrusive and practically invisible on the layout. Two large nails are cemented to the top of the pad with epoxy, and the nails ride in loose-fitting holes drilled in the car floor. The ends of the pad are beveled to ride over any slight irregularities in the track.

cal term for a single wire or other conductor carrying a number of connections). The bus-and-feeder method is reliable and gives the rails freedom to expand and contract, but it's also the most work.

Clean rails are necessary for smooth running, because the contact area of a typical model locomotive is small and just a little crud can cause a lot of trouble. The type of rail you use can make a big difference.

Brass rail comes with most HO train sets, and many modelers stick with it because it's inexpensive. Brass oxidizes easily, however, especially in humid climates, and its oxide does not conduct electricity.

The best way to clean heavily oxidized brass rail is with an abrasive rubber track-cleaning block like the

Bright Boy sold by Wm. K. Walthers. You want to avoid doing too much of this, however, because it scratches the rails and gives them a "tooth" that will collect more dirt.

A good way to clean lightly oxidized brass rail is with a liquid contact cleaner such as De-Ox-Id, sold by the GC Electronics Division of Hydrometals Inc., Rockford, IL 61101, available in electronic parts and supply stores (check your local Yellow Pages). This is sold in electronics parts stores for cleaning moving contacts. Put a little on the rails a few inches ahead of a locomotive, and let the engine's wheels spread it around your layout.

To avoid the problems of brass most modelers prefer to use nickel silver rail. Nickel silver is used almost

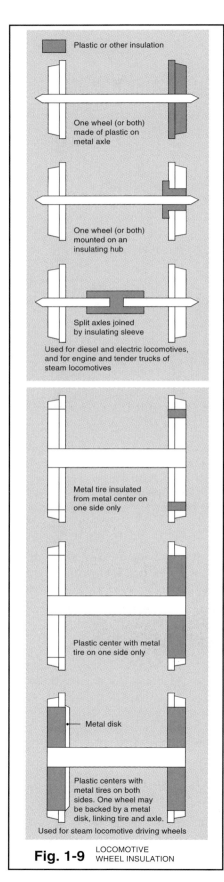

Plastic or other insulation

One wheel (or both) made of plastic on metal axle

One wheel (or both) mounted on an insulating hub

Split axles joined by insulating sleeve

Used for diesel and electric locomotives, and for engine and tender trucks of steam locomotives

Metal tire insulated from metal center on one side only

Plastic center with metal tire on one side only

Metal disk

Plastic centers with metal tires on both sides. One wheel may be backed by a metal disk, linking tire and axle.

Used for steam locomotive driving wheels

Fig. 1-9 LOCOMOTIVE WHEEL INSULATION

exclusively in N and Z scales, where even a little oxidation is a serious matter. It's also popular with experienced modelers in HO and larger scales. Like brass, nickel silver oxidizes, but its oxide is still a conductor. Although it has nothing to do with its electrical properties, nickel silver also has an advantage in appearance over brass because its silver color is more like steel.

Steel has been used for O scale rail for many years, and the weight of standard gauge O scale trains means that many potential contact problems just never show up. Some lines of HO sectional and train set track now use steel rail, and it appears to work well.

Of course, when steel oxidizes you get rust, but I was unable to make a sample of HO steel track rust even after soaking it in salt water. Steel sectional tracks appear to have a zinc coating to protect the steel rail. I don't know of any HO layouts that have operated for a long time with steel sectional track, but for our purposes it does appear to be a better material than brass.

(By the way, there is no electrical reason why you should not combine two or three different kinds of rail on one layout.)

Keeping Track Clean

Even nickel silver won't solve all contact problems, so model railroaders continue to look for better ways to clean track. Most experienced modelers agree that the best way to keep the track clean is to run the trains frequently. Few of us have time to run our model railroads as often as we'd like, however, so here are two suggestions.

John Allen used track cleaner cars like the one in fig. 1-8 on his famous Gorre & Daphetid RR. The Masonite pad slides along the rails under its own weight, and rises and falls easily over slight irregularities. The pads should be cleaned before each operating session by sanding them lightly to remove the black streaks that will

build up. Run the track cleaner cars in regular trains. The extra drag of the pad makes these cars the equivalent of two ordinary cars when you're figuring train tonnage, but other than that you treat them as ordinary cars.

The beauty of these track cleaners is their simplicity—they're easy to make and work well when cleaned regularly. Anything I've seen done to "improve" them, like adding weight to the top of the pads or saturating them with oil or cleaning fluid, just makes them less effective.

Every few years the idea of oiling the railhead to improve its conductivity seems to be rediscovered, and this can help if done sparingly. Oil is especially good for reducing arcing, the sparking between wheels and rail that puts tiny pits in both and makes them grab dirt more readily. Both hair-clipper oil and kerosene can accomplish the job, and as with contact cleaner you put small amounts on the rail and let a locomotive spread it around.

One problem with oiling track is that doing so can actually accumulate dirt on the railhead if the oil is used too heavily, especially if your railroad is in a dusty environment or you're working on scenery. Some modelers have expressed concern over oil's effect on traction, but if you had enough oil to make the rails slippery you'd have a lot of dirt in the oil.

Overall the merits of oiling track are by no means certain. If you're having contact problems and nothing else seems to work, you might want to try just a little bit of oil.

Locomotive Pickup Wheels

Locomotive wheels pick up current from the rails, so they must be insulated to avoid shorting out the circuit. This insulation can take many forms, fig. 1-9. To identify the pickup wheels on your locomotive, look for all-metal wheels running in metal frames, or wheels with metal tires contacted by wipers or sliders.

There isn't much standardization

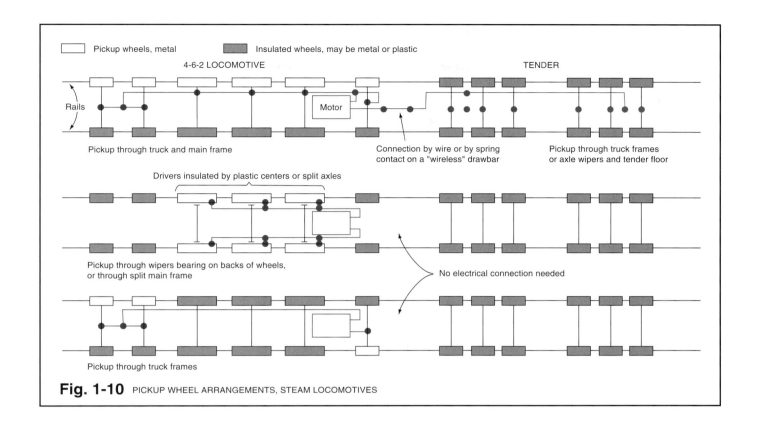

□ Pickup wheels, metal   ▨ Insulated wheels, may be metal or plastic

4-6-2 LOCOMOTIVE

TENDER

Rails

Motor

Pickup through truck and main frame

Connection by wire or by spring contact on a "wireless" drawbar

Pickup through truck frames or axle wipers and tender floor

Drivers insulated by plastic centers or split axles

Pickup through wipers bearing on backs of wheels, or through split main frame

No electrical connection needed

Pickup through truck frames

Fig. 1-10 PICKUP WHEEL ARRANGEMENTS, STEAM LOCOMOTIVES

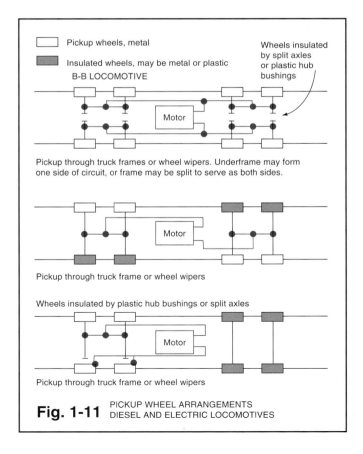

□ Pickup wheels, metal

▨ Insulated wheels, may be metal or plastic

B-B LOCOMOTIVE

Wheels insulated by split axles or plastic hub bushings

Motor

Pickup through truck frames or wheel wipers. Underframe may form one side of circuit, or frame may be split to serve as both sides.

Motor

Pickup through truck frame or wheel wipers

Wheels insulated by plastic hub bushings or split axles

Motor

Pickup through truck frame or wheel wipers

Fig. 1-11 PICKUP WHEEL ARRANGEMENTS DIESEL AND ELECTRIC LOCOMOTIVES

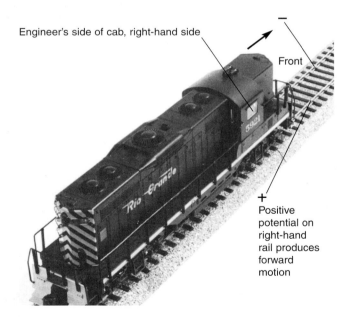

Engineer's side of cab, right-hand side

−

Front

+

Positive potential on right-hand rail produces forward motion

Fig. 1-12. THE RIGHT-HAND RULE. If we imagine that this Geep is set up to run short-hood forward, and that we're therefore looking over the engineer's shoulder as he sits on the engine's right-hand side, it's easy to see the meaning of the right-hand rule in NMRA standard S9. The rail under the near side of the locomotive is the right-hand rail; positive polarity on that rail should make the locomotive go forward.

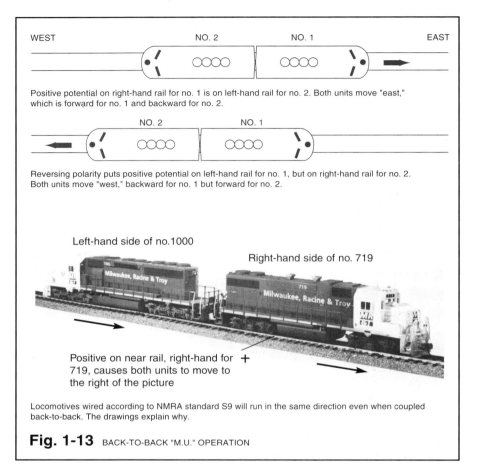

Positive potential on right-hand rail for no. 1 is on left-hand rail for no. 2. Both units move "east," which is forward for no. 1 and backward for no. 2.

Reversing polarity puts positive potential on left-hand rail for no. 1, but on right-hand rail for no. 2. Both units move "west," backward for no. 1 but forward for no. 2.

Positive on near rail, right-hand for 719, causes both units to move to the right of the picture

Locomotives wired according to NMRA standard S9 will run in the same direction even when coupled back-to-back. The drawings explain why.

Fig. 1-13 BACK-TO-BACK "M.U." OPERATION

in the arrangement of pickup wheels on model locomotives, but however they're arranged their job is always to provide a steady, uninterrupted flow of power to the motor. Although no standard is in place, there are some fairly common systems. Figure 1-10 shows the configurations most often found on steam locomotive models. The top illustration, with pickup from the right-hand engine wheels and the left-hand tender wheels, shows the most common arrangement on domestic kit and imported brass locomotives.

Diesel locomotives come in three basic arrangements, fig. 1-11. These are also used for electric locomotive and interurban and streetcar models, which are usually not wired for overhead pickup as sold off the shelf.

Although the merits of the pickup schemes depend somewhat on how individual models are designed, there

is one common value for us to consider. If you compare two otherwise similar locomotives in performance on a layout, the one with the most wheels picking up current will work best. It's a simple statistical fact that the more pickup wheels an engine has, the less chance there is that the current path will be interrupted.

The Right-Hand Rail Rule

One standard that does apply to pickup wheels and the way they're connected to the motor governs the direction in which the trains run. NMRA standard S9 states that for equipment using polarity reversing, positive potential on the right-hand rail shall produce forward motion.

Figure 1-12 shows what this rule means. The "right-hand rail" is the rail on your right if you look along the line of the track over the front of the engine, or if you imagine yourself in

the engineer's position in the model. When this rail is positive, all model locomotives that conform to the NMRA standard will move forward.

This standard has two main advantages. One is that you can always be sure which way a locomotive will move before you start it. The other is that you can couple two or more locomotives together, as for double-heading or multiple-unit (m.u.) operation, and count on having them all move the same way.

One point that might not be obvious is that the engines will move the same way on the track even if they are facing different directions. Say we have two diesel A units, units 1 and 2, coupled back to back for m.u. operation, fig. 1-13. If we apply positive potential to the rail indicated, unit 1 will move forward because the right-hand rail is positive in relation to the way it is facing. But unit 2 will move in reverse, that is, right along with unit 1, because the positive potential is on the left-hand rail relative to the way unit 2 is facing.

If you have two locomotives that run in opposite directions when placed on the track together, one of them is wrong and should be changed to conform to the standard. You can use an ammeter, an instrument that measures current flow, to determine the polarity on the track, fig. 1-14. The ammeter won't give a reading when its positive terminal is connected to negative potential, so you can flip the reversing switch and watch the meter to see which rail is positive.

How you adjust a locomotive going the wrong way depends on the design of the model. If the wheels are insulated on one side and the circuit goes through the truck or locomotive frames, you can reverse the wheels to effectively reverse the way the motor is wired to the track. If all wheels pick up, or if the pickup is through wipers bearing on the wheels, you'll have to reverse the wiring to the motor.

As with track, it's important to have an uninterrupted current flow within your locomotives. If you have a locomotive that runs erratically even though the rails are clean and continuously powered, make sure the pickup wheels are clean. If they are, or if cleaning them doesn't help, consider one or more of the following ways to improve locomotive pickup:

Pickup shoes are sliding contacts that rub along the tops of the rails, as shown in fig. 1-15. Because a shoe has a flat surface in contact with the rail, it has a larger contact area than even several wheels. Also, the sliding motion helps to wipe dirt out of the way and makes the shoe a more efficient contact than a rolling wheel. Shoes are unobtrusive when the locomotive is on the track, and usually one shoe wiping each rail is enough to ensure continuous contact. For HO scale locomotives, ready-to-install shoes are available from Taurus Products, P. O. Box 6534, Orange, CA 92667, and Tomar Industries, 9520 East Napier Ave., Benton Harbor, MI 49022.

Wheel and axle wipers can help if contact through the axle bearings seems inadequate, or if you want to pick up from insulated metal wheels or wheels in a plastic truck. Spring brass or phosphor-bronze wire makes effective wipers. Figure 1-16 shows how these wipers may be arranged.

Hard-wiring the current path helps when sliding contact, such as between truck and body bolsters, is unreliable. The wire should be light, 28 gauge or smaller, and stranded for flexibility. Tone-arm wire used for flexible phonograph connections is ideal.

Although we've been talking strictly about locomotives, the wiring for lighted cars, or cars that need to pick up current for any reason, is essentially similar. Figure 1-17 shows a typical arrangement. Axle wipers and hard-wiring are also useful for improving car contact; shoes aren't as well suited for car pickups unless the cars are unusually heavy.

Motors

A motor converts electrical energy into mechanical energy. It does this

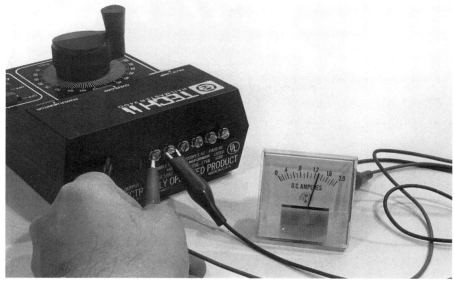

Fig. 1-14. DETERMINING POLARITY WITH A METER. The clip leads connect the ammeter's positive and negative terminals to the power pack's variable DC terminals. The pack is on and the speed control is turned up. When the needle deflects to the left of the scale as in the photo at left, meter positive is connected to negative on the pack. When the needle moves up the scale as in the photo on the right, meter positive is connected to positive on the pack.

by using the magnetic field created when current flows through a wire, and by taking advantage of magnetic attraction and repulsion to create motion. The theory of electric motors is of little concern to us, but knowledge about their basic parts and function can help later on. Figure 1-18

shows a typical permanent-magnet motor as used in model locomotives.

Let's start with the brushes. These are spring-loaded wiping contacts that carry current from the wheels and other pickups into the motor. When I mentioned reversing the wiring to the motor as a means of

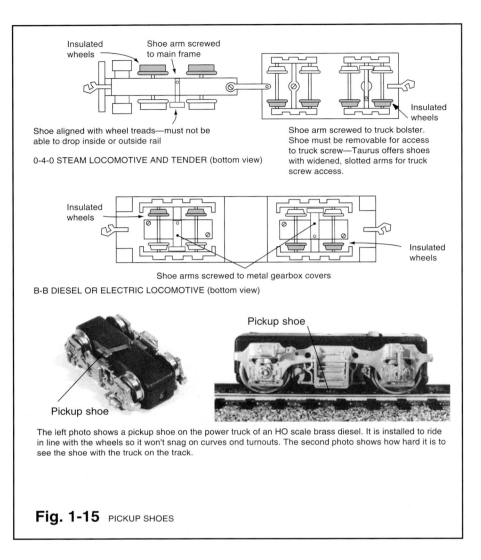

Insulated wheels

Shoe arm screwed to main frame

Insulated wheels

Shoe aligned with wheel treads—must not be able to drop inside or outside rail

0-4-0 STEAM LOCOMOTIVE AND TENDER (bottom view)

Shoe arm screwed to truck bolster. Shoe must be removable for access to truck screw—Taurus offers shoes with widened, slotted arms for truck screw access.

Insulated wheels

Insulated wheels

Shoe arms screwed to metal gearbox covers

B-B DIESEL OR ELECTRIC LOCOMOTIVE (bottom view)

Pickup shoe

Pickup shoe

The left photo shows a pickup shoe on the power truck of an HO scale brass diesel. It is installed to ride in line with the wheels so it won't snag on curves ond turnouts. The second photo shows how hard it is to see the shoe with the truck on the track.

Fig. 1-15 PICKUP SHOES

standardizing direction, I was referring to the two wires connected to the brushes.

The brushes wipe on the commutator, a segmented drum or plate that acts as a switch to energize the electromagnetic coils of the armature. When current is applied to the motor, the armature coils are magnetized so as to be set turning by their attraction to and repulsion from the permanent field magnet. As the armature turns, the commutator switches the polarity of the armature coils so they are always being drawn to or pushed away from the poles of the field magnet.

For model railroad use the desirable characteristics in an electric motor, besides the obvious one of small size, are low starting voltage, smooth turning motion (torque) at low speeds, and low current requirements. We want a low starting voltage to give us the greatest possible control range, while smooth low-speed torque helps a locomotive to start and stop smoothly and run steadily at slow speeds.

The current requirements of motors are expressed in amperes—"amps" for short, or abbreviated "A"—which are units of current flow. We want motors whose requirements are within the capacity of our power supplies, and which will leave reserve capacity for other uses like headlights and car lights. Another expression used for the power requirements of motors is "current drain,"

which accurately portrays the relationship of motor and power supply.

A motor draws a given amount of current, or amperage, when doing a given amount of work. As long as this amperage is less than the power pack's capacity everything is okay. If the current drain is more than the power pack can supply, the pack is overloaded and the circuit breaker should open. The power pack doesn't "pump" power into the motor; the motor drains the power it needs from the pack.

Kinds of Motors

Voltage and amperage are easy to measure with appropriate meters, but smooth, low-speed torque is harder to get a handle on. One helpful rule of thumb is the number of electromagnet poles in a motor armature (it's common to describe motors as "three-pole," "five-pole," and so on). In general more poles mean smoother torque at low speeds, because there's less tendency for the motor to "cog" or hesitate in turning as if waiting for a gear tooth to push it.

Three poles is the practical minimum for a functional motor, and it's hard to avoid cogging with a three-pole motor. Five poles are common in the better model railroad motors; occasionally seven-pole motors are available.

In addition to checking the number of poles, you can judge motors by the width of the slots between poles: The smoothest motors will have the narrowest slots. Skewed armatures, with the poles and slots set at an angle to the motor shaft, provide the most even torque.

We need to be aware of the several types of motors used in model railroading. Figure 1-19 shows the three main ones, open frame, can, and coreless motors.

The open frame motor has existed the longest and is still common. It usually has a permanent magnet at one end, or sometimes off to one side, with iron pole pieces extending to each side of the armature. The

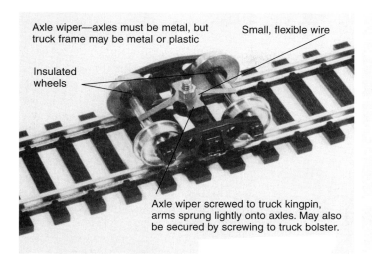

Axle wiper—axles must be metal, but truck frame may be metal or plastic

Small, flexible wire

Insulated wheels

Axle wiper screwed to truck kingpin, arms sprung lightly onto axles. May also be secured by screwing to truck bolster.

Wheel wiper screwed to truck bolster, arms sprung lightly onto back (or treads) of wheels

Small, flexible wire

Wheel wiper—only pickup wheels must be metal

Insulated wheels

Fig. 1-16. The left photo shows axle wipers made by Model Die Casting and used on Roundhouse HO locomotive tenders. The right photo shows a homemade wheel wiper screwed in place on the underside of the truck bolster.

armature is visible, hence "open frame," and has an iron or steel core wound with wire coils. This can still be a good motor, although it tends to draw more current and run less smoothly than the two newer types.

The can motor is completely enclosed, with a ring magnet surrounding an armature similar to an open-frame motor. Can motors draw less current and produce smoother torque than open frame motors; therefore, they are more desirable for powering model locomotives. They are also more robust than coreless motors, with thrust bearings and a generally greater capacity for taking abuse.

The coreless motor, also called a micro motor or instrument motor,

looks much like a can motor externally, but is quite different inside. It has a central drum-shaped magnet surrounded by a cup-shaped wire coil armature (with no steel or iron core, hence "coreless"), all enclosed in a ring of magnetically conductive material. Coreless motors typically draw the least current for a given power output, and they run smoothly at slow speeds. Some coreless motors have bearings that cannot take thrust loads. This means they can't be used with some of the simpler model locomotive drive trains, which transmit thrust to the motor. Nevertheless, coreless motors are especially popular with modelers who use locomotive sound systems (see Chapter 2) because they produce

little electronic "noise" to be picked up and amplified through a speaker.

You may also encounter a few hybrid types. Probably the most common is the Athearn HO motor, which is not completely enclosed but does have a ring magnet. Another common variation is the flat can motor, with a flat-sided enclosure and two semicircular magnets instead of one ring magnet. As you might expect, these in-between types combine advantages of the better motors with disadvantages of the lesser ones.

Fortunately, we can think of all these motors as being the same electrically. Where special considerations apply I'll be sure to mention them.

Remotoring locomotives is more of a mechanical project than an

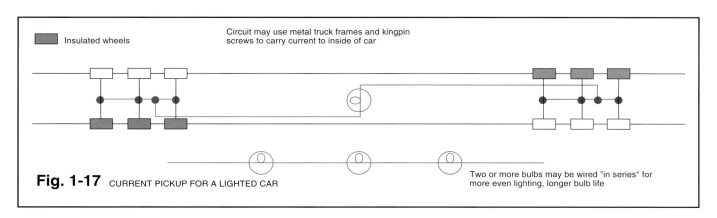

Insulated wheels

Circuit may use metal truck frames and kingpin screws to carry current to inside of car

Fig. 1-17 CURRENT PICKUP FOR A LIGHTED CAR

Two or more bulbs may be wired "in series" for more even lighting, longer bulb life

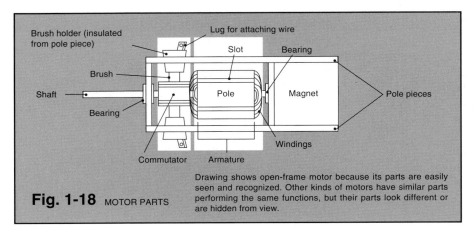

Brush holder (insulated from pole piece)

Lug for attaching wire

Slot

Bearing

Brush

Shaft

Pole

Magnet

Pole pieces

Bearing

Windings

Commutator

Armature

Drawing shows open-frame motor because its parts are easily seen and recognized. Other kinds of motors have similar parts performing the same functions, but their parts look different or are hidden from view.

Fig. 1-18 MOTOR PARTS

Fig. 1-19. MOTOR TYPES. Three common model railroad motors. On the left is an open-frame motor, here with a worm on its shaft to mate directly with the worm gear of a steam locomotive model. In the center is a modern ring-magnet "can" motor. These may have shafts extending from both ends and may also have flat sides for installation in the narrow hoods of model diesels. At right is a "coreless" or "iron-less rotor" motor, which is externally indistinguishable from the motor in the center but different internally.

electrical one If you're tempted to improve an engine's performance by installing a better motor, you'll find articles on how to do it in MODEL RAILROADER Magazine. I'll just say that you should be sure a real advantage will be gained by repowering a locomotive. It's a waste of effort to replace an open frame motor that's working well just because can motors are fashionable.

Motor Safety

Motor safety is both an electrical and a mechanical consideration, so I'll close this chapter by mentioning some things to watch for. Every motor has a maximum safe current rating within which it's designed to operate. Unfortunately not all manufacturers publish this information, but if you can find it, it's the best way to be sure your locomotives are operating properly.

If you can't find the manufacturer's rating, locomotive reviews in MODEL RAILROADER's product reviews department state current drains for the models tested. If you have a similar model that gives a vastly higher read-ing, that's a signal that something might be wrong.

The danger in having a motor draw too much amperage comes from the heat generated by the passage of electrical current. Motors are designed to handle a certain amount of heat, but when they draw more current than they should they can get too hot. The most common heat-related failure occurs when the insulation in the armature windings melts down, causing the coils to short out. The result is a burned-out motor. A practical test is to touch a motor you suspect of running hot: If you can't hold your fingers against it, it's probably in trouble.

Though the effect of overloading is felt electrically, the cause is almost always mechanical: binding in the mechanism preventing the motor from turning freely; excessive weight for the motor and gear-train combination; or anything that makes the motor work harder than it should (as shown by too high a reading on an ammeter).

The need for a free-running mechanism is obvious, but the problem with weight may not be. Many modelers add weight to their locomotives to increase traction and pulling power. As long as the motor isn't overloaded that's fine. The maximum safe weight for a locomotive is one at which it can slip its drivers when held stationary without exceeding the safe current rating of its motor.

More than that is asking for trouble, as is running a locomotive with a load that keeps it partially slipping all the time. In many years of model railroading I've seen a few motors burned out, and I've ruined more than my share of motors. I can say honestly that I've never seen a motor burn out that was not in some way being abused. To put it more optimistically, if you take a few simple precautions, motor safety is nothing to worry about.

Choosing a power pack

CHAPTER TWO

You have several choices to make in selecting power packs for your railroad. All model railroad power supplies are supposed to serve the same purpose—delivering a controlled DC voltage to the locomotive motor. You can achieve this in several ways, and some options can add to your enjoyment.

Current Capacity

The first question to ask about any power pack is whether it supplies enough power, measured in amperes ("amps"), to run your train. Since a locomotive's power requirements vary with its size, weight, and load, modeling scales provide a rule-of-thumb guide to power needs. Figure 2-1 is a table of current requirements for the three most popular scales.

These ratings are conservative and allow for the most power-hungry motors you're likely to encounter. The current drain of similar locomotives can vary widely depending on their motors, particularly if you compare an engine with an open-frame motor to one with a high-efficiency can or coreless motor. You may be able to get along well with less power, but it's better to err on the high side.

Notice that fig. 2-1 states the ratings in terms of powered units, so if your locomotive is a three-unit diesel consist with no dummies (units without motors), you'll need a power pack with three times the capacity you'd need to handle a single powered unit. In addition, the requirements in fig. 2-1 apply only to power packs used to run one train at a time. If you want to run more than one train from a single pack, again multiply the power requirements by the number of powered units.

Light bulbs draw power too, not much but enough to add to the overall current drain while running a train. A typical miniature bulb used for a locomotive headlight or for lighting a passenger car draws .02A to .03A. An engine headlight by itself draws so little current compared to the motor that it's not worth worrying about. Suppose, however, you have a five-car passenger train illuminated by two bulbs in each car. Figure 2-2 shows that you'd need .3A for the train lights in addition to whatever current the locomotive was drawing. That could be half or more of the motor's requirement, especially in the smaller scales, and that can be another good reason for picking a power pack with extra capacity.

Remember, though, it's current drain we're concerned with. A power

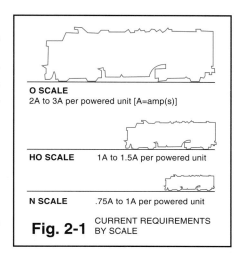

O SCALE
2A to 3A per powered unit [A=amp(s)]

HO SCALE
1A to 1.5A per powered unit

N SCALE
.75A to 1A per powered unit

Fig. 2-1 CURRENT REQUIREMENTS BY SCALE

Fig. 2-3. ACCESSORY TERMINALS. The terminals labeled "ACCESSORIES AC" on this power pack deliver a constant 16.5VAC to operate accessories like switch machines and lights.

Locomotive with headlight 1.5A	Passenger cars with two bulbs each .03A X 2 = .06A	.06A	.06A	.06A	.06A
			Locomotive current: 1.5A Car lighting current: 5 X .06A = +.3A		
Fig. 2-2 CURRENT FOR TRAIN LIGHTING (HO scale example)			Total current for train: 1.8A		

Fig. 2-4. ACCESSORY POWER SUPPLY. This is a 12VDC power supply sold by Radio Shack (catalog no. 22-127). Use it to power switch machines and other accessories so the full output of your power packs can be used to run trains.

Fig. 2-5. DC ACCESSORY TERMINALS. The terminals that are labeled "FIXED DC" on this power pack deliver a constant 20VDC, which may be used for accessories but can also power an add-on throttle.

pack with several times the current capacity needed by your locomotives won't make them pull any more or run any faster or smoother. Enough power is what we're after, with just a bit in reserve.

When you start looking at power packs, you'll find that power capacity is labeled on most power packs in terms of "VA," which simply means "volts x amps." There's an easy way to convert this into the ampere ratings model railroaders use.

Suppose a pack is labeled for an output of 7VA. You divide 7 by 12, which gives you .58. That means that the pack is rated for an output of .58 amp at its full voltage of 12 volts. You'll always divide the VA number on the power pack by 12 to give you the output in amps. It's that simple. (Leave the question of why to the mathematicians.)

Throttles

The next consideration is how the power pack controls the train's speed. That means you want to know what kind of electrical device it uses to control voltage, or in model railroad terms, what kind of throttle it has.

Rheostats are the simplest throttles and are generally used in less-expensive power packs. A rheostat is an electrical device known as a resistor, which limits current flow and

drops voltage. More specifically, a rheostat is a variable resistor: You can increase and decrease its resistance by turning a knob.

A rheostat varies the constant voltage put out by the power pack's transformer and rectifier by wasting excess voltage as heat in its resistance coils. When you turn a rheostat to its lowest speed setting, you're actually turning up its resistance, which wastes more voltage and causes the train to run slower. To make the train run faster you turn down the resistance, allowing more voltage to reach the train and speed it up.

The voltage wasted by a rheostat is always proportional to the load, the amount of current being used. This means that for use as a throttle, a rheostat must be closely matched to the current drain of your locomotive motors. The less current a motor draws the higher must be the rheostat's maximum resistance, measured in units of resistance called ohms.

It's customary to describe power packs with rheostat throttles as N, HO, or O scale packs depending on the maximum resistance of their rheostats. Typically that's 70 to 100 ohms for N scale, 40 to 50 ohms for HO, and 20 to 30 ohms for O. These resistance ratings work well for motors close to the maximum current drains for each scale as shown in fig.

2-1, but they may not do so well with today's low-current motors.

A very efficient motor will not draw enough current to provide a load sufficient to let a rheostat control the voltage the motor receives. For example, an HO power pack with a 50-ohm rheostat might not be able to control or even stop a locomotive whose coreless motor draws .2A or less. With the resistance turned all the way up the engine could still race along at high speed, its motor receiving 10V or 12V because it's using so little current. This is the reason that N scale locomotives can't be started and stopped smoothly with an inexpensive HO power pack.

The solution is to use a throttle that controls voltage directly. Some of these will be described in the next few paragraphs. If you're using inexpensive, mass-produced locomotives as they come you're not likely to have any trouble with rheostat throttles, though newer off-the-shelf plastic locomotives contain more efficient motors. If you replace original-equipment motors with more efficient types, or use brass locomotives with low-current motors, you probably won't be satisfied with a rheostat throttle.

Variable transformers do control voltage directly; thus, they make better throttles than rheostats. When you turn the knob of a variable transformer, you change the point on the low-voltage or secondary winding where the transformer's output is connected, and so vary the output voltage.

A variable transformer doesn't depend on the load to control voltage; therefore, it can control any motor that doesn't exceed its current capacity. It also gives smoother control than a rheostat, because its voltage output won't vary when the load changes—as many times happens suddenly when a model locomotive initially starts to move.

Model railroaders who build their own power packs have been using variable transformers for a long time, though you may hear them called "Variacs," for a popular brand of variable transformers made by General Radio Co. Variable transformers have been available in some power packs, but they have not been popular as throttles with power pack manufacturers. Perhaps this is because variable transformers are usually bulkier, heavier, and more expensive than rheostats.

Transistor throttles are the most up-to-date voltage controls for model railroading. Like variable transformers they control voltage directly, providing smooth performance with a wide range of motors. They are made with modern electronic components that are small, light, and inexpensive.

Briefly, in a typical transistor throttle the knob you turn controls a potentiometer, a special voltage-dividing variable resistor commonly used as a volume control in audio amplifiers. In much the same way as it works in a radio, the potentiometer, or "pot," controls a small voltage flowing to a power transistor. That transistor conducts an output voltage to the track in proportion to the control voltage from the pot.

All we have to understand is that transistor throttles do a good job of controlling model trains, and because they take advantage of modern electronics, they can include a variety of special features. Power pack manufacturers offer several styles of transistor-throttle packs—often called "solid state" power packs to emphasize their up-to-date electronics.

You may find that power packs with transistor throttles or variable transformers are not classified in terms of modeling scales. That's because the current drain doesn't make any difference to throttles that control voltage directly, as long as it's within the pack's capacity. Transistor throttles don't have to be matched to the load the way rheostats do.

On the other hand, there are special voltage requirements in the smallest and largest scales now being offered commercially, and you will see modern power packs specifically for Z and G scale trains. The small motors used in Z scale are rated for a maximum of 8V; the voltage controls of Z scale packs are limited to that maximum. G scale trains have husky motors rated for 21V; G scale packs are built to supply that voltage. A few power packs have a selector switch that lets you choose 8V, 12V, or 21V maximums. If you use one of these be careful not to "zap" a low-voltage motor with too high an output.

SCR throttles are a special solid-state voltage control that use silicon-controlled rectifiers (SCRs) instead of transistors. Although transistor throttles provide a constant but variable voltage, SCR throttles deliver voltage in pulses that furnish good slow-speed control for switching.

SCR throttles aren't widely available in power packs, though they are offered in some add-on throttles you can use with a regular power pack or other power supply. They have also been popular do-it-yourself electronic projects for model railroaders. I'll have more to say about them later, when I explain "pulse power."

Power Pack Options

The current capacity and type of throttle are the basic points on which to judge whether a power pack is suitable for running your trains, but a

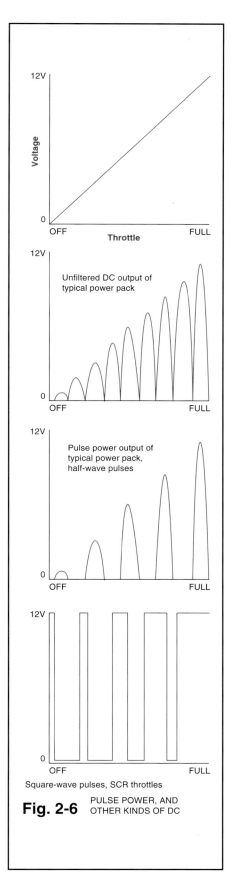

Unfiltered DC output of typical power pack

Pulse power output of typical power pack, half-wave pulses

Square-wave pulses, SCR throttles

Fig. 2-6 PULSE POWER, AND OTHER KINDS OF DC

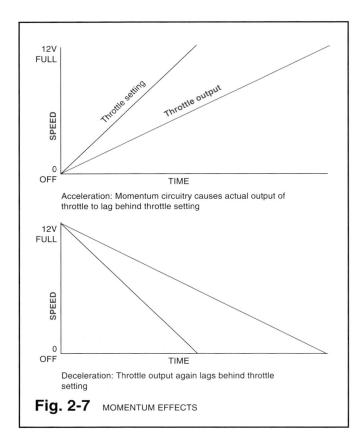

Acceleration: Momentum circuitry causes actual output of throttle to lag behind throttle setting

Deceleration: Throttle output again lags behind throttle setting

Fig. 2-7 MOMENTUM EFFECTS

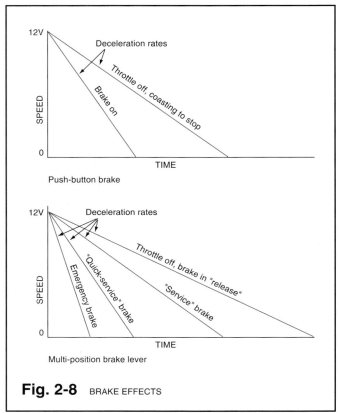

Push-button brake

Multi-position brake lever

Fig. 2-8 BRAKE EFFECTS

power pack can perform other functions. Depending on how you want to use your power pack, and how you want to run your trains, these additional features can be important.

Accessory power terminals come on most power packs, fig. 2-3. Usually they supply a constant 16 to 18VAC (Volts Alternating Current) right from the pack's transformer to be used for remote control turnouts (switches), layout lighting, and operating accessories.

The accessory terminals draw power from the same source, the transformer, that the power pack uses to run the train. Most power packs have only one transformer, and whatever part of its capacity you use for accessories isn't available for locomotives.

Use accessory power with care. Conceivably you could put enough of a load on a power pack through its accessory terminals that you could not run a train at all. What happens most often, though, is a near overload when you throw a remote turnout: The turnout mechanism ("switch machine") draws so much power that the train momentarily slows or even stops.

When you're only running a simple layout it's convenient to use the accessory terminals on your power pack. That way you have a single power source for all purposes. Providing separate power supplies for accessories, however, is best in the long run. If you buy a nicer power pack for running trains, for example, save your old pack for accessory power. Or you can purchase or build a separate accessory power supply, fig. 2-4.

One other caution to remember about AC accessory power or alternating current from any source: Don't connect it to your track. Your locomotive will move out at high speed and you'll have no control over its speed or direction. That's one obvious possibility for damage, but

there's another that's not so obvious. AC can reduce the power of a DC motor magnet, causing the motor to draw more current and develop less power. This damage occurs instantly and is permanent unless you can have the motor remagnetized.

Some power packs have DC accessory terminals as well as AC, fig. 2-5. Few accessories need DC; these terminals are mostly used to supply power to additional throttles. I'll have more to say about this under the heading "multiple throttles." Remember, though, that fixed DC power comes from the same source as variable DC train power and is subject to the same limitations as AC accessory power.

Pulse power is a series of short bursts—pulses—of voltage, supplied either instead of or along with a steady voltage, fig. 2-6. Its purpose is to furnish better slow-speed performance by giving the motor armature a series of short "kicks." This is effective with most motors, supplying armatures the extra impulse they need to overcome variations in mechanical resistance and turn steadily at low rates of rpm. Usually, however, it's not effective with three-pole motors, and flywheel mechanisms may tend to cancel its effect.

Pulse power is controlled differently with different types of throttles. Rheostat and variable transformer power packs that have this feature usually contain an on-off switch to start and stop the pulses. When the switch is on the pack adds "half-wave" pulses to its output, so called because the pulses are actually part of the alternating wave cycles in AC house current. This won't damage motor magnets, by the way, because it's only half the AC wave and doesn't reverse polarity like ordinary AC.

Pulse power is only helpful at slow speeds; it makes motors run hotter and noisier at high speeds. If it's controlled with a switch, though, you can't shut it off after the train picks up speed without having the train jump ahead. Shutting it off gradually is possible if it's controlled with a rheostat instead of a switch, but this control isn't available on power packs.

With transistor throttles, pulse power may be controlled automatically by the electronics inside the power pack. In its simplest form there's no separate control for the pulses. The throttle circuit provides pulse power at low voltages and phases it out as voltage increases. This is the ideal way to use pulse power, since you have it when you need it but not when it serves no purpose.

Transistor-throttle packs with pulse power may use half-wave pulses or may generate their own pulses electronically. More sophisticated throttles may contain adjustment devices to let you vary the shape or amplitude of the pulses, and the voltage levels at which they phase in and out.

SCR throttles provide short, high-voltage pulses all the time. The motor turns faster or slower depending on the frequency and duration of the pulses. The more often the pulses

Fig. 2-9. METER INDICATIONS. The top photo shows meter indications for normal operation: The voltmeter on the left shows the voltage set by the throttle, and the ammeter on the right shows normal current being drawn by the motor. The middle photo shows meters indicating an open circuit: The voltage is there, but no current is flowing. The bottom photo shows a short circuit indication: Voltage drops, and current is abnormally high.

start (the more pulses per second) and the longer they last, the higher the speed. Because of their full-time pulse output, SCR throttles are sometimes thought of as switching or yard throttles, although some designs include circuitry to smooth out the pulses for higher speeds.

As I said earlier, motors run hotter and noisier on pulse power than on normal DC. The heat is nothing to worry about as long as your locomotives are in good shape and performing well. If an engine has mechanical problems, pulse power will further abuse the motor, and the cumulative effect could overheat and damage the motor. The noise can range from a quiet hum to a distinct, though usually soft, buzz. Whether it's

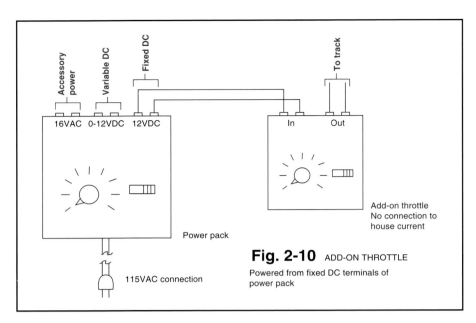

Fig. 2-10 ADD-ON THROTTLE
Powered from fixed DC terminals of power pack

Accessory power
Variable DC
Fixed DC
To track

16VAC 0-12VDC 12VDC

In   Out

Power pack

Add-on throttle
No connection to house current

115VAC connection

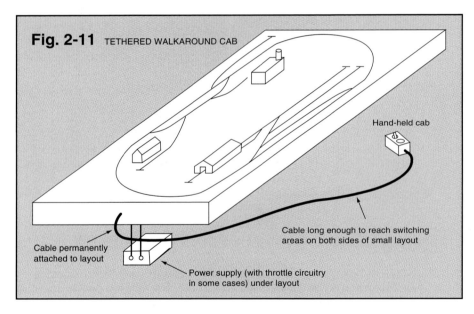

Fig. 2-11 TETHERED WALKAROUND CAB

Hand-held cab

Cable long enough to reach switching areas on both sides of small layout

Cable permanently attached to layout

Power supply (with throttle circuitry in some cases) under layout

objectionable is a matter of personal preference.

While on the subject of pulses, it's worth noting that even so-called normal DC has a bit of a pulse effect from our 60Hz (hertz, cycles per second) AC house power. Although you can filter this out with a capacitor, the resulting pure DC is the least desirable current for good low-speed performance with model trains.

Momentum and brake effects are available with transistor and SCR throttles. These features are intended to reproduce the action of real trains by means of electronic circuitry. With momentum effects the track voltage doesn't rise or fall just as fast as you turn the throttle knob. As fig. 2-7 shows, if you turn the throttle quickly to top speed, the voltage delivered to the track increases only gradually to give the effect of a heavy train slowly gathering speed. When you turn the throttle down or off, the voltage drops gradually again, and the train seems to coast.

The idea is to compensate for the relatively little inertia model trains have compared to their big, heavy prototypes. Momentum circuits are often called electronic flywheels; in fact, the electronic version can be more effective than any mechanical flywheel in a small scale model.

Brake circuits enable you to stop the train with more control than simply coasting to a stop but still with variable rates of deceleration, fig. 2-8. Again, the idea is to mimic prototype action, and even with the best air brakes a train weighing thousands of tons can't be stopped on a dime. Momentum is a function of the throttle, but for brake effects you get a separate control, either a button, a switch, or—most like the real thing—a multi-position lever.

These effects aren't for everyone, or for every operating situation. On a model railroad where several trains are running at once, a throttle with momentum and brakes may demand too much attention when there are other things to look out for. Switching can be frustrating when you have to manipulate extra controls and can't be sure where your engine will stop. Most throttles with momentum and brake effects have a switch or a brake position for "direct drive." This lets you turn off the simulated inertia when you'd rather not have it.

One annoying quirk of some momentum circuits is a delay of several seconds between turning the throttle on and the train starting to move. Slow acceleration response is one thing, but when there seems to be no response to the throttle you start to wonder if something hasn't gone wrong. The best momentum throttles don't have this delayed response, so you can enjoy the momentum effects without waiting for them to start.

Meters are useful power pack options because they help you monitor the performance of both your locomotives and your railroad (we've already seen the importance of measuring voltage and current in checking motor performance). There are two types, the voltmeter and the ammeter. As fig. 2-9 shows, meters can help troubleshoot on the layout by indicating whether the train isn't running because the circuit is open (current path not continuous), or because it's shorted (current path completed without a load).

Ideally the scales of the meters should closely match the quantities you want to measure: 0 to 12 or maybe 18 on the voltmeter, and 0 to the power pack's capacity in amps on the ammeter. The smaller the scale, the more precise the reading.

If the power pack you want isn't available with meters, it's not hard to add them. Chapter 11, which deals with control panels, tells how.

Multiple throttles are available on some power packs, usually two and sometimes three. It may be obvious to some, but if you're new to model railroading don't be misled into thinking that all you need is more than one throttle to run more than one train. There's more to it than that, as you'll learn in Chapter 5.

I don't think multiple-throttle power packs are a good deal. They may save a little money over two or three single-throttle packs, but their disadvantages offset this slight advantage.

The multiple-throttle pack may be ideal if you want to run two or three trains all by yourself, but if you'd rather have an operator or "engineer" for each train you won't want to crowd them together over one power pack. If you decide to change your control scheme you may find a multiple-throttle pack inflexible, while single packs fit into all sorts of arrangements. If something goes wrong with a multiple-throttle pack it can take all throttles out of service.

Especially troublesome are those multiple-throttle packs that use a single transformer to power all their throttles. This means that they can't be used with the useful "common rail" wiring scheme described in Chapter 5, or with the popular Atlas wiring components—Selectors and Controllers—which also use com-

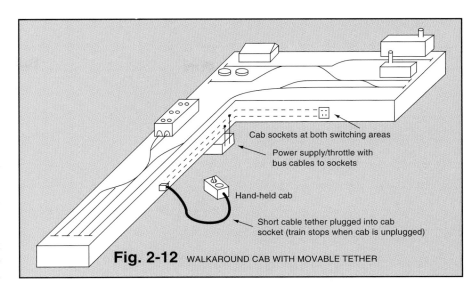

Cab sockets at both switching areas

Power supply/throttle with bus cables to sockets

Hand-held cab

Short cable tether plugged into cab socket (train stops when cab is unplugged)

Fig. 2-12 WALKAROUND CAB WITH MOVABLE TETHER

mon-rail wiring. Some multiple-throttle packs have a separate power supply for each throttle, but it's often difficult to tell when this is the case. For all these reasons you'll be happier with single-throttle power packs.

If you add another throttle powered from fixed DC terminals on a single-throttle pack, as in fig. 2-10, you'll have a multiple-throttle pack with a single power supply, still limited by its original power capacity. This is okay if your objective is to replace the original throttle with another type, a transistor throttle, say, instead of a rheostat, or a hand-held tethered throttle as I'll describe shortly under "walkaround control." As long as you don't use the old throttle, you can upgrade a power pack in this way without getting involved in the problems of multiple throttles.

Walkaround control is an arrangement of power pack and throttle components that enables you to move around your railroad with the train. The idea is to let you be on the spot for a switching move or a scenic part of the run, instead of being stuck at a fixed location several feet away from the action. With walkaround control you can imagine that you are traveling somewhere with a train, not just watching it make laps on your layout.

You can achieve walkaround control in many ways. I'll describe some

common ones that can be added to or that take the place of a regular power pack. I'll use the term "cab" to refer to a hand-held control box with at least a throttle and a reversing switch, and perhaps other controls as well. Usually the cab's power supply and perhaps some of its control circuitry must be mounted permanently under the layout, so the cab can be small and light enough for easy carrying.

• Tethered cab: The most basic form of walkaround control, with the hand-held unit on the end of a cable, or tether, fig. 2-11. The cable may be short or long, but it is permanently attached to the layout. Because its travel is limited by the length of the cable, the tethered cab is best suited to small layouts or parts of large ones, such as a yard or local switching district. A tethered cab may be added to any power pack, and several manufacturers offer hand-size cabs for this purpose.

• Movable tether: To get greater flexibility from a tethered cab, you can arrange to plug its cable into the layout at any of several points, fig. 2-12. This is good for a railroad of any size where you do lots of switching. You can run the train from one station to the next, unplug the cab and move to the new location, switch the new town, and proceed around the railroad by repeating this cycle. Any

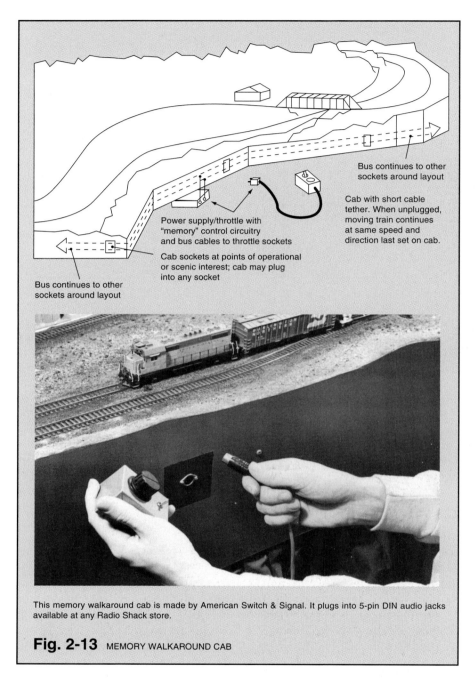

Bus continues to other sockets around layout

Cab with short cable tether. When unplugged, moving train continues at same speed and direction last set on cab.

Power supply/throttle with "memory" control circuitry and bus cables to throttle sockets

Cab sockets at points of operational or scenic interest; cab may plug into any socket

Bus continues to other sockets around layout

This memory walkaround cab is made by American Switch & Signal. It plugs into 5-pin DIN audio jacks available at any Radio Shack store.

Fig. 2-13 MEMORY WALKAROUND CAB

Fig. 2-14. This hand-held cab is not connected to the layout by a wire tether but by radio signals, giving the operator the greatest possible freedom of movement. The cab shown was built by Ken Thompson from a model airplane radio-control transmitter.

tethered cab may be set up with a movable tether by providing suitable plugs, sockets, and bus cables (a "bus" is a wire or cable that allows you to make the same connections at several locations).

• Memory walkaround: Uses circuitry that lets the train keep running while you move the cab, fig. 2-13. Even though you can take the movable tether anyplace around the railroad,

the train must be stopped while the cab is unplugged. If you don't first stop it deliberately, it will stop abruptly when you pull the plug! A memory walkaround throttle's stationary circuitry "remembers" the speed and direction setting when you unplug the cab, and keeps the train moving until you plug in again at a new location. This gives you the capability to follow a through train (one that doesn't stop

at every station) all over your railroad. Memory walkaround cabs need special circuitry and generally aren't just an addition to an existing power pack or tethered cab.

• Wireless walkaround: For the greatest possible freedom of movement you want a hand-held cab that doesn't have to be attached to the layout at all, fig. 2-14. Most often this is done with radio control transmitters like those used to fly model airplanes. The radio controls a fixed cab, and operates its throttle and reversing switch either electronically, directly from the radio signal, or through servo motors that respond to the radio signal. Some manufacturers have offered wireless cabs from time to time, but they have hardly become a staple item in hobby shops. Most wireless walkaround cab systems so far have been home built.

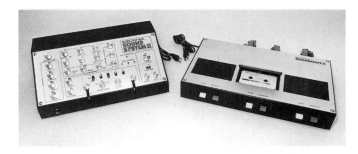

Fig. 2-15. The Pacific Fast Mail Sound System II sends steam-engine sound effects through the rails to a speaker carried in a locomotive. It also performs the functions of a power pack. The tape player on the right allows the system to use recorded sounds for special effects.

Fig. 2-16. WALKAROUND CAB WITH PUSH-BUTTON CONTROLS. This hand-held walkaround cab, built from an article in MODEL RAILROADER, uses push buttons to control speed and direction instead of the usual knobs and switches.

Sound effects for either steam or diesel locomotives are available with highly specialized power packs, fig. 2-15. Because the train power and control components amount to only a small part of the total package, these are called "sound systems" rather than power packs. They generate electronic locomotive sounds and play them out through a speaker installed aboard the locomotive. Controls let you blow the whistle and ring the bell while you run the train, and advanced systems include many other effects as well. Connecting a sound system to a layout is more involved than just hooking two wires to a power pack. Nevertheless, for the purposes of the wiring and control arrangements in most of this book, we can think of a sound system simply as another power pack.

Beyond Power Packs

You may also want to consider alternatives to power packs. These "command control" methods aren't features included in or added to power packs but replacements for them. One possibility is direct radio control. With this, you'd use a hand-held transmitter, as in wireless walkaround control, but with the radio receiver carried aboard the locomotive. Direct radio control appears to have many advantages: It makes the locomotives independent of each other as well as freeing their engineers from connections to the layout.

On the other hand, the locomotive must carry not just the radio receiver but also the throttle circuit and batteries to power the whole package, including the locomotive motor. In HO scale this has required a two-unit cab diesel packed with batteries and electronics and has been primarily an experiment or stunt. Still, in large scale applications, such as G scale used outdoors, direct radio control can be practical.

Carrier control is another way of making locomotives operate independently, but it sends control signals through the track instead of through the air. That means the receiver in the locomotive can be simpler and smaller, and power for the motor can come through the track as well.

Carrier control and direct radio control are both forms of command control, so called because you are in direct command of a locomotive. Carrier control has gained wider acceptance than direct radio control, both as a do-it-yourself project and commercially. Using command control to run a model railroad is so different from using power packs that it needs a special explanation of its own. You'll find that in Chapter 8.

Fig. 2-17. POWER PACKS WITH PULSE MOMENTUM. The MRC Railmaster 2400 on the left has a switch to turn its pulse power feature off, and circuitry to provide a jump-free transition from pulse to full-wave power. The MRC Loco-Motion 2500 on the right contains automatically controlled pulse power, momentum circuitry that may be switched on or off, and a spring-loaded brake switch that may be employed with momentum effects.

Two-rail wiring

CHAPTER THREE

When we looked at the rails as conductors in Chapter 1, I pointed out that the two rails of model railroad track must be kept insulated from each other. For ordinary track this is accomplished by using plastic, wood, or some other insulating material for the ties. At turnouts and crossings, however, the rails have to cross each other, and something more has to be done to maintain insulation. The set of measures we take to avoid short circuits in trackwork is known as two-rail wiring.

Two-rail wiring is easy enough, but you have the choice of doing it yourself or having it done for you. It all depends on the kinds of turnouts you choose. There are two types—all-live and power-routing. Before I examine these, however, you may want to review turnout terminology, fig. 3-1. You also should know that I use the term "turnout" for what real railroaders almost always call "switches." This common model railroad practice is especially helpful when talking about wiring, since it avoids confusion

between track and electrical switches.

• All-live turnouts have insulated frogs, jumper connections around the frogs between the corresponding closure and frog rails, and jumpers between corresponding closure and stock rails. (A jumper is a wire or other conductor that connects one rail to another.) The points are separately attached to insulated throw bars. All this keeps the two rails electrically separate at all points and keeps both routes through the turnout powered—hence the term "all-live." Most sectional track turnouts, including the popular Atlas Snap Switch and Custom Line brands, are all-live types. Figure 3-2 shows the important features of an all-live turnout.

• Power-routing turnouts are simply all rail with no insulation at the frogs and no jumper connections. The points need not be insulated at the throw bar or the hinges, and in fact they're often joined with metal bridles. As fig. 3-3 shows, only one route through this kind of turnout can be powered at a time—when both

rails under a locomotive are connected to the same potential, the effect is the same as if they were not connected to anything. That's why these are called "power-routing" turnouts, because they switch power as well as trains from one track to another.

Most turnouts sold for use with flexible track, such as the popular Shinohara line from Japan, are power-routing turnouts. So are most modelers' hand-laid turnouts; it's simpler and easier to build a turnout this way when you're doing it yourself.

Choosing Turnouts

All-live turnouts are simpler to wire as long as you're buying them ready-made. The combination of insulated frogs and jumpers, fig. 3-4, keeps the rails properly insulated and connected through all sorts of turnout arrangements, and the power-feed wires from the power pack, "feeders," can be connected anywhere.

Power-routing turnouts are another matter. Orienting these turnouts frog-to-frog, fig. 3-5, causes short

Fig. 3-1 TURNOUT TERMINOLOGY

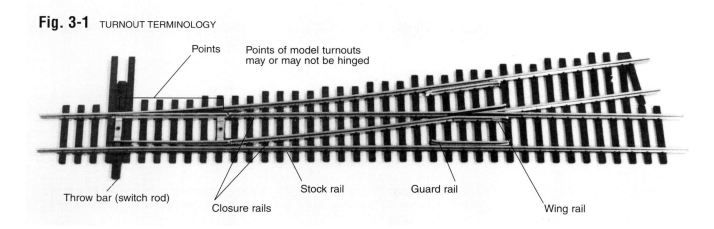

Points

Points of model turnouts may or may not be hinged

Throw bar (switch rod)

Closure rails

Stock rail

Guard rail

Wing rail

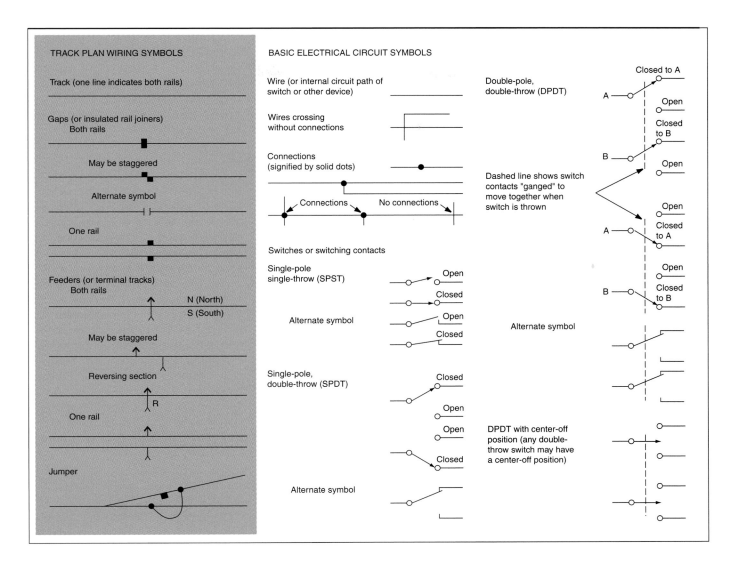

TRACK PLAN WIRING SYMBOLS

Track (one line indicates both rails)

Gaps (or insulated rail joiners)
Both rails

May be staggered

Alternate symbol

One rail

Feeders (or terminal tracks)
Both rails

N (North)
S (South)

May be staggered

Reversing section

One rail

Jumper

BASIC ELECTRICAL CIRCUIT SYMBOLS

Wire (or internal circuit path of switch or other device)

Wires crossing without connections

Connections (signified by solid dots)

Connections   No connections

Switches or switching contacts

Single-pole single-throw (SPST)
Open
Closed

Alternate symbol
Open
Closed

Single-pole, double-throw (SPDT)
Closed
Open
Open
Closed

Alternate symbol

Double-pole, double-throw (DPDT)

Closed to A
A
Open
Closed to B
B
Open

Dashed line shows switch contacts "ganged" to move together when switch is thrown

Open
A
Closed to A
Open
Open
B
Closed to B

Alternate symbol

DPDT with center-off position (any double-throw switch may have a center-off position)

circuits, as do feeder wires attached on the frog side of a power-routing turnout. To use these turnouts you have to insulate rails in certain places with gaps or plastic rail joiners, and be careful where you attach feeders. Most of this chapter will explain how to do this.

If you use all-live turnouts you can skip the rest of this chapter and go on to Chapter 4, although you might want to think about this: If power-routing turnouts are potential troublemakers and require extra care and work in wiring, why does anybody use them?

There are several answers, but the most common is that power-routing turnouts offer a control advantage precisely because they do

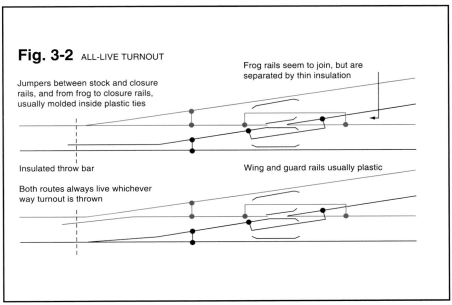

Fig. 3-2 ALL-LIVE TURNOUT

Jumpers between stock and closure rails, and from frog to closure rails, usually molded inside plastic ties

Frog rails seem to join, but are separated by thin insulation

Insulated throw bar

Both routes always live whichever way turnout is thrown

Wing and guard rails usually plastic

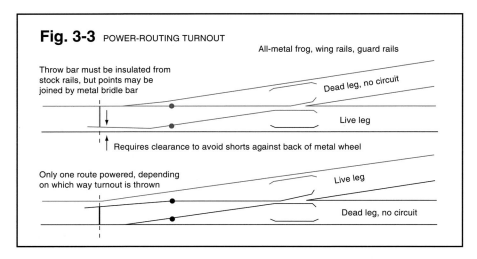

Fig. 3-3 POWER-ROUTING TURNOUT

All-metal frog, wing rails, guard rails

Throw bar must be insulated from stock rails, but points may be joined by metal bridle bar

Dead leg, no circuit

Live leg

Requires clearance to avoid shorts against back of metal wheel

Only one route powered, depending on which way turnout is thrown

Live leg

Dead leg, no circuit

best choice is to trade complexity of wiring for simplicity of control. It may require more work to wire a layout with power-routing turnouts, but that extra work will be worthwhile if it makes running your railroad easier and more enjoyable.

It is possible to wire a yard so the all-live turnouts automatically turn on the right track and turn off all the others. I'll show you how to accomplish it later in this book, but it takes still more complicated wiring. In many situations power-routing turnouts will need the simplest wiring overall to accomplish a given control scheme.

There's also the matter of appearance, although I don't mean to say that power-routing turnouts are necessarily better-looking than all-live turnouts. But suppose that you want to build an HO railroad with Code 70 rail, because you think it will look closer to scale size than the Code 100 rail commonly used in HO sectional track. You'll quickly discover that manufacturers offer only power-

route power. Figure 3-6 shows how power-routing turnouts alone can select which of several tracks in a yard is energized. To do the same thing with all-live turnouts would require insulated rail joints, more feeders, and electrical switches to turn the yard tracks on and off.

"Well," you might say, "more gaps and feeders here, more gaps and feeders there, it's all the same then."

Not quite. With power-routing turnouts you select which track is powered just by lining up the turnout points; with all-live turnouts you also have to turn on the power switch for that track, and make sure the other tracks are turned off.

This is the first of many instances in model railroad wiring where the

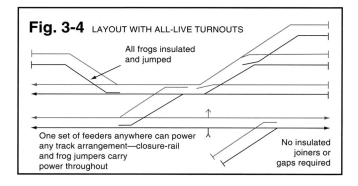

Fig. 3-4 LAYOUT WITH ALL-LIVE TURNOUTS

All frogs insulated and jumped

One set of feeders anywhere can power any track arrangement—closure-rail and frog jumpers carry power throughout

No insulated joiners or gaps required

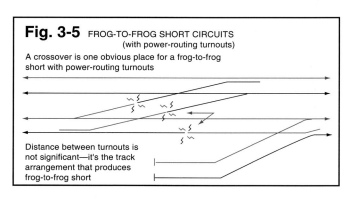

Fig. 3-5 FROG-TO-FROG SHORT CIRCUITS
(with power-routing turnouts)

A crossover is one obvious place for a frog-to-frog short with power-routing turnouts

Distance between turnouts is not significant—it's the track arrangement that produces frog-to-frog short

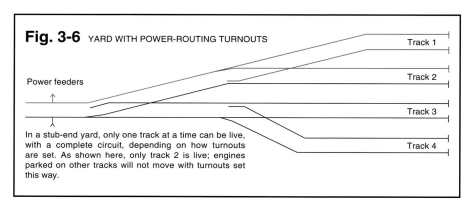

Fig. 3-6 YARD WITH POWER-ROUTING TURNOUTS

Track 1

Track 2

Track 3

Track 4

Power feeders

In a stub-end yard, only one track at a time can be live, with a complete circuit, depending on how turnouts are set. As shown here, only track 2 is live; engines parked on other tracks will not move with turnouts set this way.

routing turnouts with Code 70 rail. No mechanical or electrical reason dictates why this is so, it just is.

Many modelers end up using power-routing turnouts for this or other reasons of appearance, and if that's what you care about you need not let wiring concerns influence your choice. You'll discover that two-rail wiring is no big thing, even with power-routing turnouts.

Finally, if you are going to build

Fig. 3-7 RULE 1: Gap the rails between turnouts located frog-to-frog

Put gaps in both rails between turnout frogs in opposite rails

When both frogs are in the same rail, one gap in the frog rail is enough. Installing a gap at X won't hurt, however, and may help avoid mistakes.

X

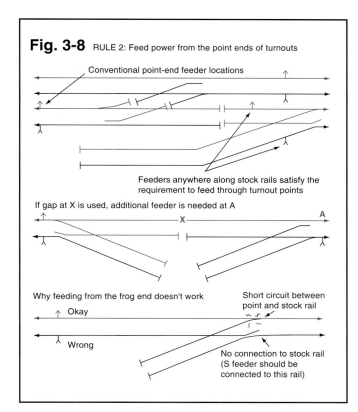

Fig. 3-8 RULE 2: Feed power from the point ends of turnouts

Conventional point-end feeder locations

Feeders anywhere along stock rails satisfy the requirement to feed through turnout points

If gap at X is used, additional feeder is needed at A

X   A

Why feeding from the frog end doesn't work

↑ Okay

⋏ Wrong

Short circuit between point and stock rail

No connection to stock rail (S feeder should be connected to this rail)

Fig. 3-9 USING TWO-RAIL WIRING RULES

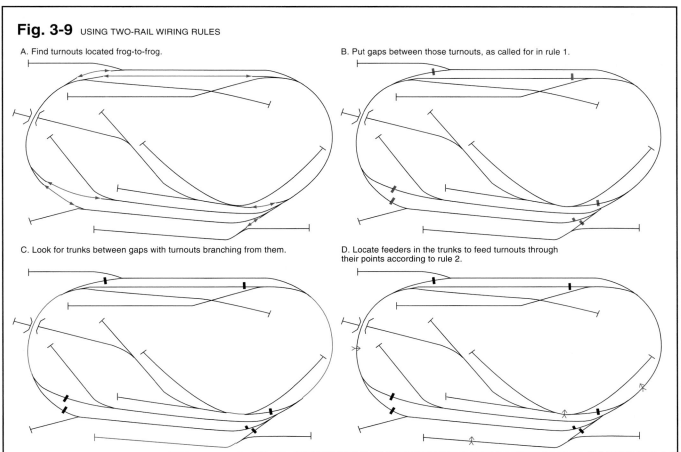

A. Find turnouts located frog-to-frog.

B. Put gaps between those turnouts, as called for in rule 1.

C. Look for trunks between gaps with turnouts branching from them.

D. Locate feeders in the trunks to feed turnouts through their points according to rule 2.

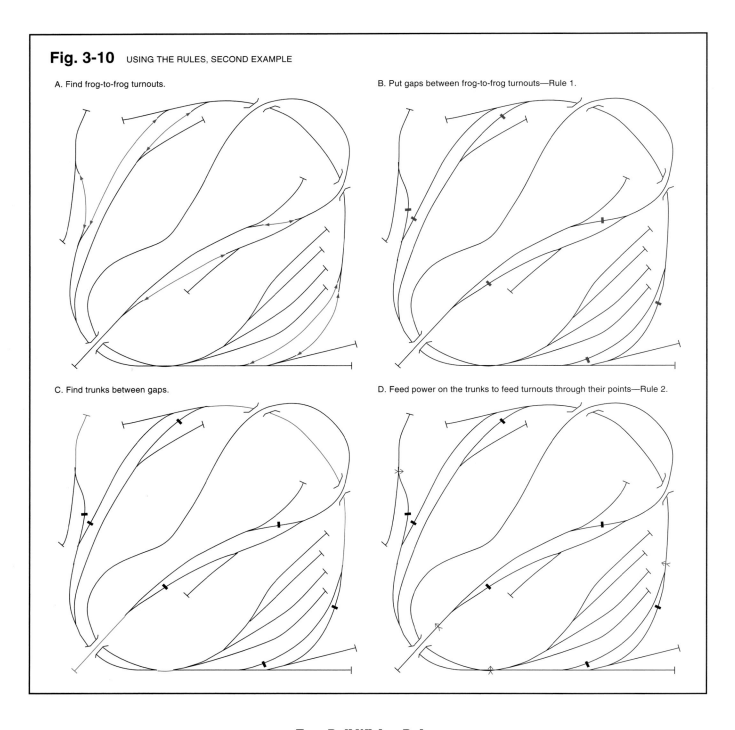

Fig. 3-10 USING THE RULES, SECOND EXAMPLE

A. Find frog-to-frog turnouts.

B. Put gaps between frog-to-frog turnouts—Rule 1.

C. Find trunks between gaps.

D. Feed power on the trunks to feed turnouts through their points—Rule 2.

your own turnouts from scratch, make them power-routing. The turnouts will be easier to make, and it would be more work to scratchbuild all-live turnouts than to install two-rail wiring for power-routing types. You won't have to do anything special: Just build a turnout from rail and it will be a power-routing turnout.

Two-Rail Wiring Rules

Basic two-rail wiring for power-routing turnouts is easy if you understand and apply just two simple rules:

1. Gap the rails between turnouts located frog-to-frog.

2. Feed power from the point ends of turnouts.

Figure 3-7 demonstrates rule 1.

Notice that it's related to rule 2 in that its purpose is to prevent feeding any turnout through the frog. Notice too that what is important is the arrangement of the turnouts, and not the distance between them.

Figure 3-8 shows why rule 2 is necessary, and what it means. Notice that feeders anywhere along the turnout stock rails satisfy rule 2. That's because the frog and the rails beyond it are still supplied with power only through the turnout points.

For comparison refer to fig. 3-2 to see why these rules aren't relevant to all-live turnouts. There's also the important matter of loops, wyes, and other turning tracks. These are not covered by the two basic rules. We'll address them in Chapter 4.

Applying the Rules

Figure 3-9 shows how to apply the rules. The track plan is Art Curren's Break The Rules RR, from the September 1980 MODEL RAILROADER, a 5 x 9-foot HO layout. We'll assume we want to wire it for commercial power-routing turnouts and flextrack. We start by scanning the plan for turnouts located frog-to-frog, fig. 3-9A. Remember, it's the arrangement and not the distance that counts. Following rule 1 we put a pair of gaps (or insulated rail joints) between each such pair of turnouts, fig. 3-9B.

Next we look for single-track trunks between gaps. If we located the gaps correctly, between sets of gaps or on spurs beyond gaps, there should be stretches of single track where any and all turnouts branch away from a central trunk. Figure 3-9C shows that there are four of these on the BTR RR, and that once more it's the arrangement of the turnouts and not the length of the trunk that counts. Put a set of feeders somewhere along each trunk, fig. 3-9D. That satisfies the requirement of rule 2—that every turnout be fed from its point end.

You'll notice in several places power will have to pass through one or more turnouts to get to the last turnout up a spur or along a section between gaps. That's okay so long as the points of every turnout in the chain are toward the feeders—if they aren't that way on your layout then you must have missed a frog-to-frog location. Put in another set of gaps, find and feed the new trunk,

Fig. 3-11 WIRING AROUND POWER-ROUTING TURNOUTS

SPDT auxiliary contacts on switch machine

and your railroad will be wired by the rules.

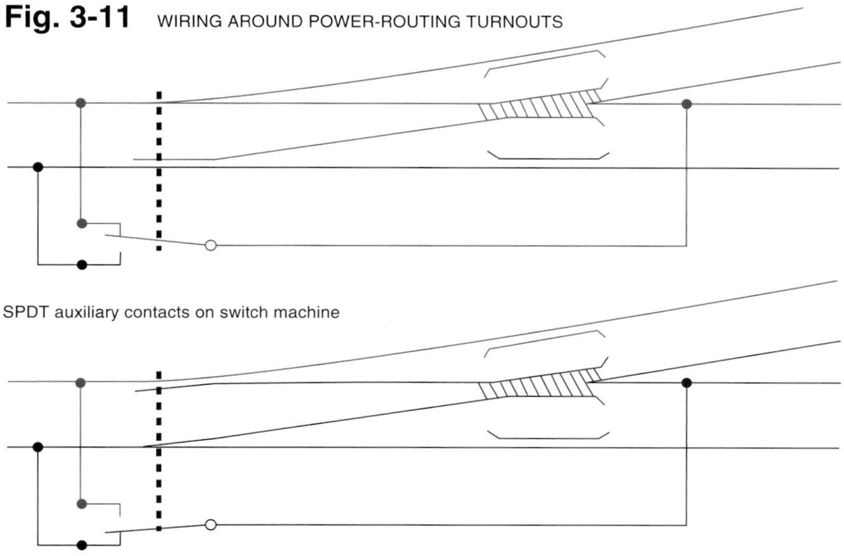

About now I can hear somebody asking, "What about that crossing between two spur tracks at the top of the plan? Doesn't that take special insulation?"

That's a good question. The answer is yes and no. The sides of our two-rail circuit can get all crossed up in a crossing, and that does take special insulation, which I'll explain later in this chapter. But remember that we're wiring the BTR RR for commercial turnouts and track. A ready-made crossing contains insulation and jumpers that make it just another piece of track as far as two-rail wiring is concerned. We can safely ignore the BTR's crossing for now, but you'll soon see how it works.

Before we go on to crossings and other special situations, however, let's look at another layout example. You want to be sure you understand how to apply these basic rules of two-

rail wiring with power-routing turnouts. Figure 3-10 shows Bob Lutz's Lake Shore Southern track plan from the January 1981 MR, a 4 x 4-foot N scale railroad.

Follow the same steps as before. First find the frog-to-frog turnouts (3-10A), then put gaps between them (3-10B). Next find the single track trunks (3-10C) and put feeders along them (3-10D). That's all there is to basic two-rail wiring. Now that you know how to do it you probably wonder why some people think it's so mysterious. Me too.

Two-rail wiring is a little more involved, of course. First of all, you'd probably find operating these railroads more convenient with a few more gaps and feeders than the figures show, although these are all you need to run one train at a time. Chapters 5 through 8 will explain how to run more than one train. Second, neither of these two examples has a turning track—as I've said,

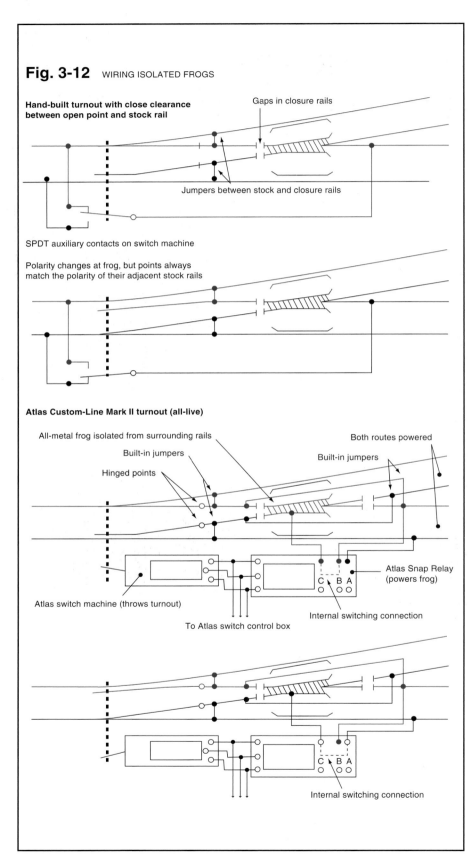

Fig. 3-12 WIRING ISOLATED FROGS

Hand-built turnout with close clearance between open point and stock rail

Gaps in closure rails

Jumpers between stock and closure rails

SPDT auxiliary contacts on switch machine

Polarity changes at frog, but points always match the polarity of their adjacent stock rails

Atlas Custom-Line Mark II turnout (all-live)

All-metal frog isolated from surrounding rails

Built-in jumpers

Hinged points

Both routes powered

Built-in jumpers

Atlas Snap Relay (powers frog)

C B A

Internal switching connection

Atlas switch machine (throws turnout)

To Atlas switch control box

C B A

Internal switching connection

these are covered in the next chapter.

Bigger and more complicated railroads than the BTR and LSS require more gaps and feeders, but it's still easy: Just apply the basic rules and step-by-step procedure.

Special Situations

The first special situation I'll describe isn't all that special, since it occurs at every power-routing turnout. I'm putting it first because it's basic, and the principle involved applies to some of the really special cases we'll get to shortly.

Wiring around power-routing turnouts. As we've seen, the points of a power-routing turnout conduct power from the stock rails, through the closure rails and frog, and on to the track. Points can be unreliable as electrical contacts, however. Dirt or a loose grain of ballast can easily interrupt the current path, even though the point might not be displaced enough to cause a derailment. This can be annoying, especially when power has to pass through a chain or ladder of several turnouts.

Figure 3-11 shows how to avoid the problem of poor point contact with power-routing turnouts. This is called "wiring around" the turnout because it provides an alternate current path that doesn't depend on the points. The switching contacts can be part of the switch machine, part of the switch machine control, or activated by a mechanical linkage—Chapter 9 will cover the use of switch machine contacts in detail. I like to wire around every power-routing turnout, whether it seems necessary or not, to be absolutely sure of having a continuous current path.

Wiring around can be useful for other reasons. Figure 3-12 shows a way of insulating and jumping a hand-built turnout so the points are the same polarity as the stock rails. One reason for doing this is to let the points lie close to the stock rails in their open positions. Model turnouts commonly move the open point

Fig. 3-13. COMMERCIAL CROSS-INGS. On these two examples of HO crossings (not crossovers—see fig. 3-16), from Atlas on the left and Shinohara on the right, you can see the plastic frog moldings that insulate the running and guard rails. What you can't see here, however, are the metal jumpers molded inside each crossing. Because the jumpers are in there, we can treat commercial crossings as ordinary pieces of track, and not worry about any additional wiring or insulation.

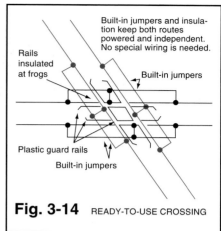

Built-in jumpers and insulation keep both routes powered and independent. No special wiring is needed.

Rails insulated at frogs

Built-in jumpers

Plastic guard rails

Built-in jumpers

Fig. 3-14   READY-TO-USE CROSSING

Fig. 3-15   WIRING ALL-RAIL CROSSINGS

A. Independent routes with 12 gaps and 4 jumpers, but no power to frogs or inside crossing. Suitable only for angles of 60 degrees and larger, and long-wheel base locomotives with many pickup wheels.

B. Independent routes with power to rails between frogs take 16 gaps and 6 feeders.

C. Only 2 dead frogs, 8 gaps, but routes are not independent. This is okay for a one-train railroad, or for command control.

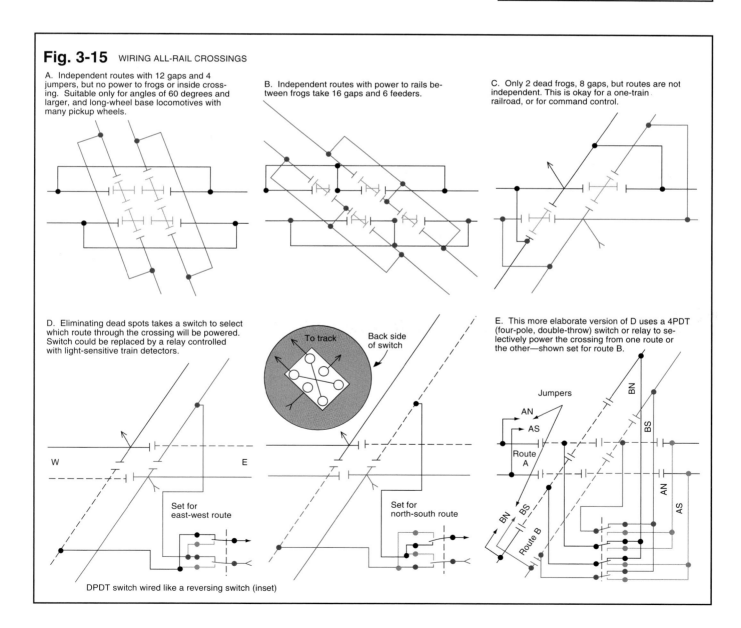

D. Eliminating dead spots takes a switch to select which route through the crossing will be powered. Switch could be replaced by a relay controlled with light-sensitive train detectors.

To track

Back side of switch

W   E

Set for east-west route

Set for north-south route

DPDT switch wired like a reversing switch (inset)

E. This more elaborate version of D uses a 4PDT (four-pole, double-throw) switch or relay to selectively power the crossing from one route or the other—shown set for route B.

Jumpers

BN

AN

AS

BS

Route A

BN

BS

AN

AS

Route B

much farther from the stock rail than the prototype. This avoids short circuits through the backs of wheels.

A turnout gapped and wired as in fig. 3-12 need only have flangeway clearance between the open point and the stock rail, and can therefore look more realistic. It must be wired around, though, because the insulated points don't power the frog. Also, if you use Atlas HO Custom-Line Mark 2 turnouts you may find it helpful to wire around them. These turnouts use a modified all-live design with a solid metal frog insulated from all the rails around it. The frog is not powered, so it's an interruption in the current path. Atlas offers an accessory called a Snap Relay for wiring around a Custom-Line Mark 2 turnout and powering the frog; it's designed for use with an Atlas remote switch machine. You can also wire around Mark 2 turnouts with other switch machines and controls (see Chapter 9).

Crossings. Also known as a railroad grade crossing or diamond, a crossing—fig. 3-13—obviously has the potential to cause short circuits.

If you simply build a crossing from rail with no gaps or insulation, you've got dead shorts between both rails of both routes.

As we saw in wiring the BTR RR, however, ready-to-use crossings are made with insulated frogs and jumper connections, fig. 3-14. Not only are the rails in both routes insulated from each other, but the two routes are insulated from each other as well. For two-rail wiring, commercial crossings can be treated as just so much track. If you build a crossing by hand, wiring gets more complicated. You could make the frogs out of plastic or other insulating material, add jumpers, and end up with a crossing that works just like the store-bought kind. If you'd rather make your crossing out of rail, you'll need gaps, and either feeders, or jumpers, or both.

Figure 3-15 shows several ways of wiring a homemade, all-rail crossing. For clarity the diagrams show only the running rails, not the guard rails,

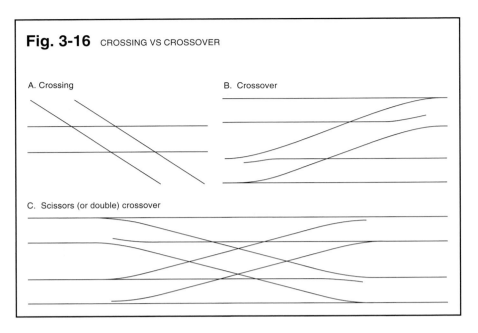

Fig. 3-16 CROSSING VS CROSSOVER

A. Crossing

B. Crossover

C. Scissors (or double) crossover

which also will need gaps around the central diamond. The wiring of 3-15D or 3-15E provides the best train performance because the current path for the chosen route is continuous.

Figure 3-15D mentions controlling the crossing with a relay—an automatic electrical switch activated by an electromagnetic coil called a solenoid—and light-sensitive detectors—photocells or "electric eyes." Circuitron manufactures detection and relay circuits which can be used for this job.

A piece of advice: Unless you have compelling reasons for doing otherwise, use commercial crossings. Unlike power-routing turnouts, all-rail crossings have no operational advantage to outweigh the complications of wiring them.

Double crossovers. A double or scissors crossover is a combination of two crossovers with a crossing in the middle, and this is as good a time as any to straighten out some often confusing terms. A crossing is a place where two railroad tracks cross at the same level, fig. 3-16A. A crossover is an arrangement of two turnouts to let a train cross between parallel—sometimes only roughly parallel—tracks. See fig. 3-16B.

So far so good. Notice that a crossover always creates a frog-to-frog situation, which requires gaps to follow Rule 1 for two-rail wiring with power-

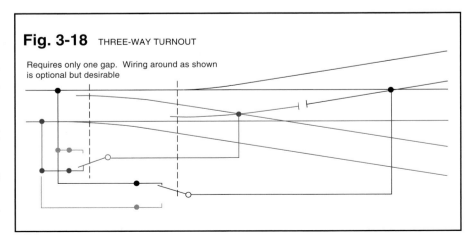

Fig. 3-18 THREE-WAY TURNOUT

Requires only one gap. Wiring around as shown is optional but desirable

Fig. 3-17 WIRING SCISSORS CROSSOVER

A. Wiring scissors crossover with ready-to-use crossing (single-line schematic as in track plans)

Gaps in outer rails at X and Y are optional, but if used require an additional N feeder at A and an S feeder at B

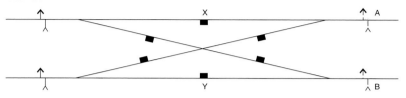

B. How it works
Internal gaps and jumpers of ready-to-use crossing not shown

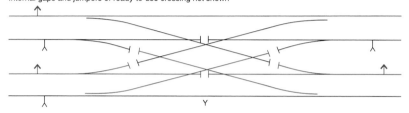

As set for one crossover route. Wiring works just as well if both crossover routes are set, though obviously both routes can't be used simultaneosly!

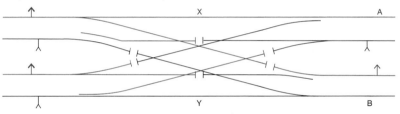

C. Wiring to scissors crossover with all-rail frogs in crossing

All crossing frogs isolated. Center frogs have their own permanent N and S feeders

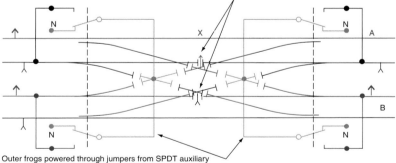

Outer frogs powered through jumpers from SPDT auxiliary contacts on switch machines (contacts N have no connections)

With one crossover route set, outer frogs are correctly powered through auxiliary contacts. Turnout controls MUST be arranged so that only one crossover route at a time can be set to avoid short circuits through outer frogs.

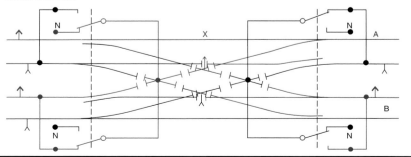

routing turnouts. Now, if we put two crossovers together so that they cross in the middle, we get a double crossover, fig. 3-16C.

Figure 3-17 shows where to put gaps in a double crossover, assuming a commercial or similarly wired crossing. The essential point is to keep all four turnout frogs insulated from each other.

You can even use an all-rail crossing in a double crossover, fig. 3-17C, if you route power to the crossing frogs by wiring around through auxiliary switch machine contacts. Allowing only one crossover route to be set up at a time keeps the wiring relatively simple. Besides, that's all you can use at once.

Three-way turnouts. These are more properly called lapped turnouts, because they're formed by two ordinary turnouts overlapped into a little more than the length of one. As fig. 3-18 shows, one gap will prevent shorts through the central frog.

Slip switches. A slip switch is a combination crossing and multiple turnout. The rarely seen single slip, fig. 3-19A, offers a choice of three routes instead of the two of a crossing, while the double slip, fig. 3-19B, offers four. Double slips are sometimes called "puzzle switches." It is easy to understand how they route trains if you think of them as double crossovers collapsed in on themselves—with the important difference that the two "parallel" routes cannot be employed at the same time.

For all their complexity of construction and appearance, slip switches are easy to wire, as you can see in fig. 3-19C. This wiring is good for single and double slips. You can also build slip switches with two more sets of points in place of the central frogs. They are still wired the same way.

Overhead and third-rail wiring. If you model electrically powered prototypes, whether street and interurban trolley cars or heavy electric locomotives, you may find it more satisfying to power them through an overhead wire. Figure 3-20A shows

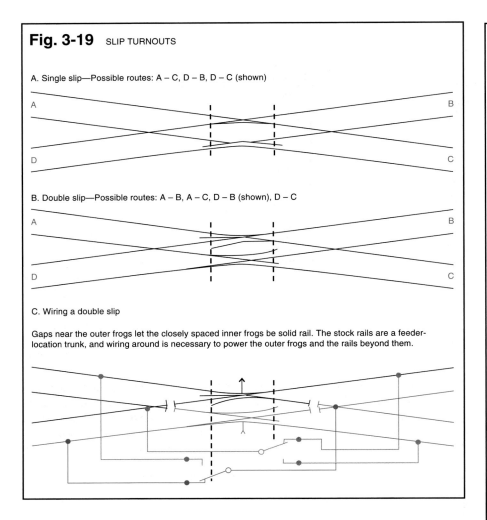

Fig. 3-19 SLIP TURNOUTS

A. Single slip—Possible routes: A – C, D – B, D – C (shown)

A   B

D   C

B. Double slip—Possible routes: A – B, A – C, D – B (shown), D – C

A   B

D   C

C. Wiring a double slip

Gaps near the outer frogs let the closely spaced inner frogs be solid rail. The stock rails are a feeder-location trunk, and wiring around is necessary to power the outer frogs and the rails beyond them.

how to arrange this kind of circuit for a pure electric railroad. The rails don't have to be insulated from each other, so you won't need to follow the two-rail wiring rules or do anything special for turning tracks. The same is true if you use a third-rail, inside or outside, in place of an overhead wire.

If you want to combine electric and "steam-road" railroading, the combination circuit of fig. 3-20B allows electrics and steam or diesel engines on the same track to be powered and controlled independently. This feature is especially useful if you want to set up an electric helper or switching district. Chapter 5 will explain how the "common return" works.

One restriction applies to this arrangement: The electrics can't be turned, since that would put their insulated wheels on the wrong side. Because most electric locomotives are double-ended this isn't much of a problem.

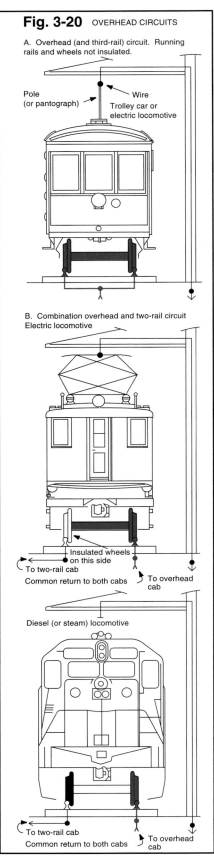

Fig. 3-20 OVERHEAD CIRCUITS

A. Overhead (and third-rail) circuit. Running rails and wheels not insulated.

Pole (or pantograph)   Wire

Trolley car or electric locomotive

B. Combination overhead and two-rail circuit
Electric locomotive

Insulated wheels on this side
To two-rail cab
Common return to both cabs
To overhead cab

Diesel (or steam) locomotive

To two-rail cab
Common return to both cabs
To overhead cab

Turning trains and engines around

C H A P T E R F O U R

From what we've learned about two-rail wiring it should come as no surprise that turning a train or engine to run in the opposite direction is a potential problem. Any track arrangement that can turn a train end for end and send it back the way it came must also turn rails of opposite polarity back on themselves and create a short circuit. This remains true whether you use all-live or power-routing turnouts; only model railroads using another conductor—overhead wire or third-rail—do not have to deal with this problem.

Some model railroaders are so leery of reversing track problems that they avoid them altogether, but that's just submitting to frustration instead of getting the better of it. Reversing tracks are handy to have on your model railroad—and they present only potential problems. A few gaps or insulated rail joiners and simple switch wiring make them easy to handle. The most basic reversing track is the reverse loop, or balloon track as it's more often called on the prototype. That's where we'll start solving the reversing track problem.

Reverse Loops

Loop a single track back into itself through a switch and you can turn a train around in one motion, fig. 4-1A, a useful trick on a model railroad. Figure 4-1B looks at what happens to the rails as conductors in this situation, and shows why there's a problem.

Figure 4-2 shows two ways to eliminate short circuits on reverse loops. Both require a pair of gaps at each end of the reversing section, the section of track that we isolate to let us control the turning movement. Because it's isolated the reversing section will

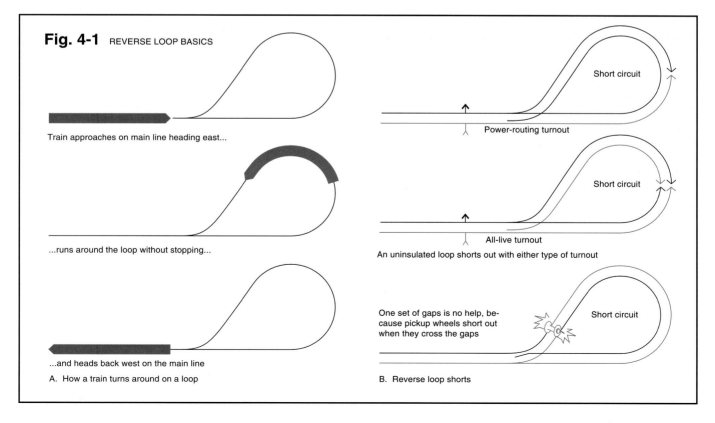

Fig. 4-1 REVERSE LOOP BASICS

Train approaches on main line heading east...

...runs around the loop without stopping...

...and heads back west on the main line

A. How a train turns around on a loop

Short circuit

Power-routing turnout

Short circuit

All-live turnout

An uninsulated loop shorts out with either type of turnout

One set of gaps is no help, because pickup wheels short out when they cross the gaps

Short circuit

B. Reverse loop shorts

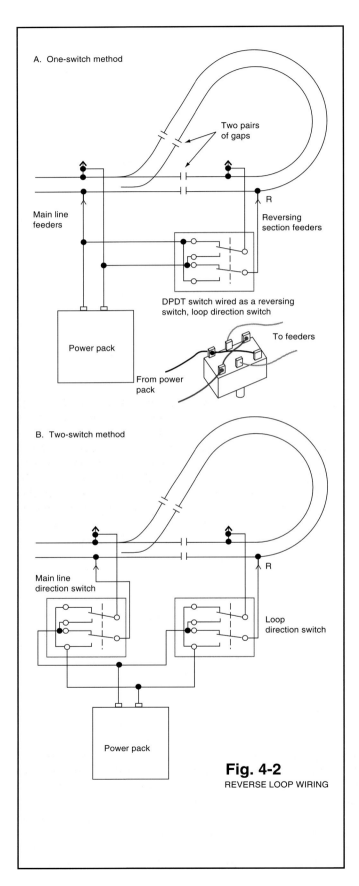

A. One-switch method

Two pairs of gaps

Main line feeders

Reversing section feeders

R

DPDT switch wired as a reversing switch, loop direction switch

To feeders

Power pack

From power pack

B. Two-switch method

Main line direction switch

Loop direction switch

R

Power pack

Fig. 4-2
REVERSE LOOP WIRING

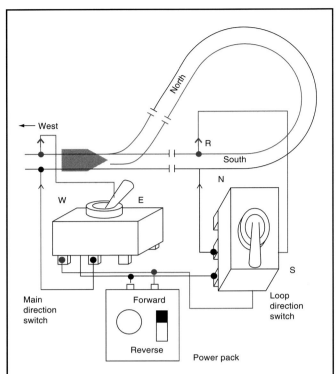

West

North

R

South

N

W

E

S

Main direction switch

Forward

Reverse

Loop direction switch

Power pack

A. Train approaches with main direction switch set for eastward travel. Loop direction switch must be set for the side of the loop that the train will enter—south in this case.

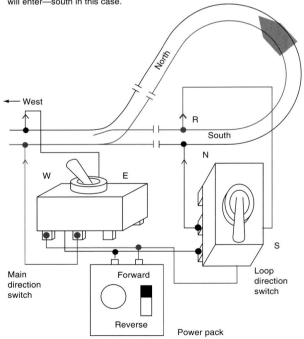

West

North

R

South

N

W

E

S

Main direction switch

Forward

Reverse

Loop direction switch

Power pack

B. Once train has entered loop, turnout and main direction switch are both thrown to let it exit and return west. The loop direction switch can be left alone once set for the train's entrance, and the power pack reversing switch remains set for forward travel throughout.

Fig. 4-3 RUNNING THE LOOP

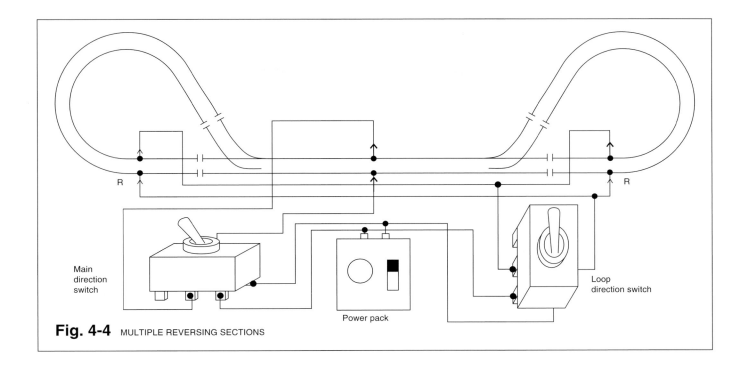

Fig. 4-4 MULTIPLE REVERSING SECTIONS

need its own set of feeders. Make sure the reversing section is at least as long as the train, engine, or self-propelled car it will be used to turn.

Besides the gaps and feeders you need one or two auxiliary reversing switches to control track polarity, in addition to the one already included in the power pack. Figure 4-2A shows the simplest wiring, with one auxiliary DPDT reversing switch, the "loop direction switch," controlling the polarity of the reversing section in the loop. Although this method is simple, it is more complex to operate. First you must set the loop direction switch to match the mainline polarity. This enables the train to enter the loop. Once the train is fully within the loop's reversing section, you must throw the reversing switch on the power pack to let the train continue in the other direction when it leaves the loop.

The catch is that the loop direction switch isn't independent of the power pack's reversing switch; therefore, polarity from the pack must also be changed while the train is in the loop. That means you have to stop the train while you throw both switches, or, if you are feeling both brave and dexter-

ous, throw both switches simultaneously and hope the train will not buck or jerk enough to derail.

Why bother with the one-switch method then? Because it has its uses. If the reverse loop on your railroad is an end-of-the-line storage track where you want trains to stop and stay, it may not be a handicap. Also, the one-switch method has advantages with some types of walkaround cabs. The loop direction switch can be built into the layout near the loop, eliminating the need to add auxiliary switches to the hand-held cabs, or extra wires to their cable tethers.

Finally, with many types of command control (Chapter 8) a locomotive's direction is independent of track polarity. This lets you wire a loop with the one-switch method, and throw the loop direction switch while the train moves around the loop without stopping. The cab reversing switch in these systems controls an electronic signal rather than track polarity, so it won't have to be changed at all.

Two-Switch Wiring

For simplicity and flexibility of operation, however, you may be hap-

pier with the two-switch method, fig. 4-2B—another example of how complexity of wiring sometimes translates into ease of control. Here there's a second auxiliary reversing switch, the "mainline direction switch." This lets you change the polarity of the main line independently of the reversing section, so the train can roll steadily around the loop and out again without stopping.

Figure 4-3 shows how the two-switch method works. For convenience it's helpful to label the auxiliary reversing switches for directions on the main line and around the loop as I've shown. The power pack switch is used only to make the engine go forward or back and isn't involved in running the loop.

What if your railroad has more than one loop? You still need only two auxiliary switches, as fig. 4-4 shows. Wire all the mainline feeders to the main direction switch, and all the reversing section feeders to the loop direction switch.

A simple way to set up two-switch reversing section control is to use the Atlas Twin, fig. 4-5. This little box contains a pair of reversing switches set

Fig. 4-5. ATLAS TWIN. The Twin is a ready-to-use reversing-section control unit incorporating two DPDT switches. The terminals on its left side connect to the power pack; the lugs on its right side connect to additional Twins, one for each reversing section to be controlled.

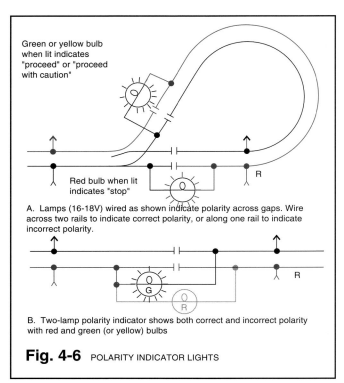

Green or yellow bulb when lit indicates "proceed" or "proceed with caution"

Red bulb when lit indicates "stop"

A. Lamps (16-18V) wired as shown indicate polarity across gaps. Wire across two rails to indicate correct polarity, or along one rail to indicate incorrect polarity.

B. Two-lamp polarity indicator shows both correct and incorrect polarity with red and green (or yellow) bulbs

Fig. 4-6 POLARITY INDICATOR LIGHTS

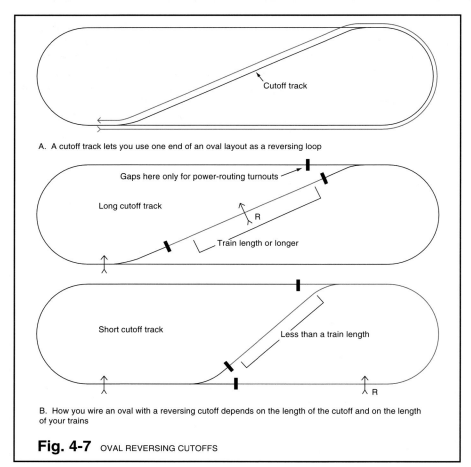

A. A cutoff track lets you use one end of an oval layout as a reversing loop

Gaps here only for power-routing turnouts
Long cutoff track
R
Train length or longer

Short cutoff track
Less than a train length
R

B. How you wire an oval with a reversing cutoff depends on the length of the cutoff and on the length of your trains

Fig. 4-7 OVAL REVERSING CUTOFFS

up so you only have to connect six wires—a pair from the power pack and a pair each to the main and reversing section feeders. It comes with instructions for reverse loop wiring.

Polarity Indicators

One of the most annoying aspects about reverse loops is that if you forget to set the auxiliary reverse switches correctly the train will hit opposite polarity when it crosses the gaps, short out, and stop. This is even more likely to happen if you have several reversing sections connected to one loop direction switch.

Figure 4-6 shows how to wire polarity indicator lights that tell when you need to throw an auxiliary reversing switch. These indicators can be either panel lamps or trackside signals, whichever is more convenient.

Reversing Cutoffs

Another problem with reverse loops is that they don't always look like the neat balloon tracks I've been using as illustrations. In fact, if you're

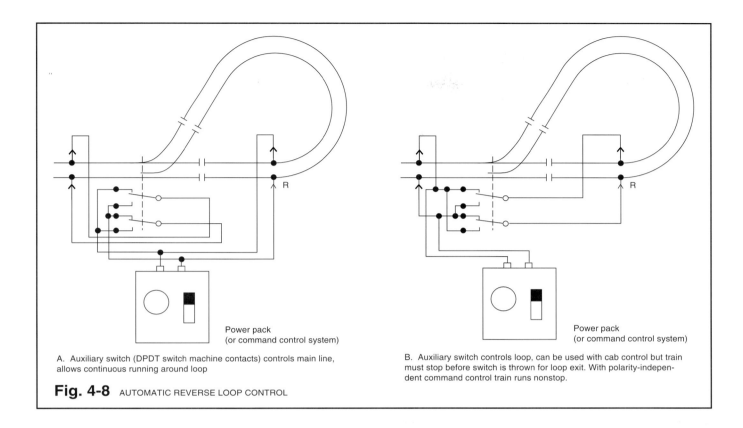

A. Auxiliary switch (DPDT switch machine contacts) controls main line, allows continuous running around loop

B. Auxiliary switch controls loop, can be used with cab control but train must stop before switch is thrown for loop exit. With polarity-independent command control train runs nonstop.

Power pack
(or command control system)

Power pack
(or command control system)

Fig. 4-8 AUTOMATIC REVERSE LOOP CONTROL

a new model railroader with a small layout, the first reverse loop you'll probably encounter is a cutoff across the middle of an oval, fig. 4-7A.

There are two ways to gap and wire this kind of reversing track, depending on both the length of the cutoff and the length of your trains, fig. 4-7B. In both cases the two-switch method, fig. 4-2B, will be more convenient, but it's a necessity with the short cutoff because the reversing section is also half of the main line.

Semi-Automatic Control

By now you may be wishing for a way to run a train through a reverse loop without throwing auxiliary switches. Figure 4-8 shows a couple of simple ways to execute this using the auxiliary contacts on a switch machine powering the loop turnout. You have to throw the turnout at least once, so you can let the switch machine take care of the track polarity.

The wiring shown in fig. 4-8A allows the train to run continuously around the loop. You let the train enter the

loop whichever way the turnout is set, and throw the turnout for the train's exit while the train is in the loop reversing section. One warning: Because this switches the polarity everywhere else but in the loop, this isn't a good way to wire a railroad if more than one train will operate at a time.

The wiring in fig. 4-8B is essentially the same as the one-switch method of fig. 4-2A, but you'll substitute the switch machine contacts for an auxiliary switch. You'll have to stop the train in the loop reversing section before throwing the turnout, but this method can be used on a multi-train

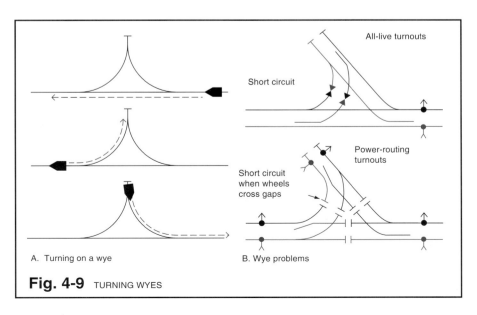

A. Turning on a wye

All-live turnouts

Short circuit

Power-routing turnouts

Short circuit when wheels cross gaps

B. Wye problems

Fig. 4-9 TURNING WYES

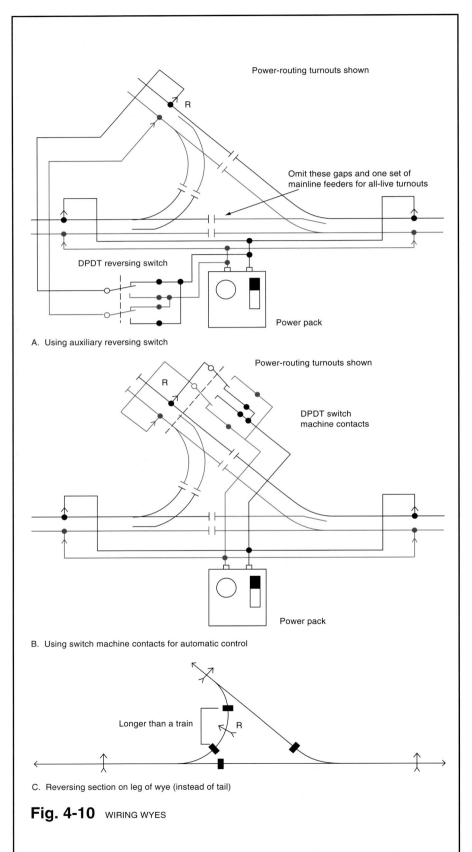

Power-routing turnouts shown

R

Omit these gaps and one set of
mainline feeders for all-live turnouts

DPDT reversing switch

Power pack

A. Using auxiliary reversing switch

Power-routing turnouts shown

R

DPDT switch
machine contacts

Power pack

B. Using switch machine contacts for automatic control

Longer than a train

R

C. Reversing section on leg of wye (instead of tail)

Fig. 4-10 WIRING WYES

layout wired for cab control (see Chapter 5).

Either of these wiring schemes could be used for multiple train operation with polarity-independent command control systems, and either would allow nonstop operation around the loop in that case.

Wyes

A wye is a triangular track arrangement with turnouts at all three corners. A train or locomotive turns on a wye by backing up, and then going ahead around the sides of the triangle, fig. 4-9A, in much the same way as when you turn your car around on a narrow street. Wyes shouldn't be confused with wye turnouts, which are track switches with equally curved diverging legs instead of one straight and one curved.

Figure 4-9B shows how problems arise in wyes. Notice that even with the turnouts isolated from each other by gaps, as required for two-rail wiring with power-routing turnouts, shorts still occur when wheels cross the gaps on one leg of the wye.

Figure 4-10 shows three ways to wire wyes. The first, fig. 4-10A using an auxiliary reversing switch, works best at junctions where the wye is an approach to a branch line and only occasionally used to turn engines or trains.

If the wye's main purpose is turning, the automatic method using auxiliary switch machine contacts, fig. 4-10B, is the simplest to operate. You won't even have to touch the power pack direction switch after running into the reversing section, since throwing the turnout also reverses the engine (except with polarity-independent command control).

If you'd prefer nonstop running use the two-auxiliary-switch method, fig. 4-2B again, with the "loop direction switch" controlling the reversing section on the wye. The same auxiliary reversing switch can control both loops and wyes if your railroad has them, just as the other auxiliary switch controls all the mainline feeders.

Also, if your junction wye is large

enough you could make one of its legs a train-length reversing section, as in fig. 4-10C. If you put this reversing section on the least-used side of the wye you won't have to bother with reversing switches for the most frequent movements.

One final point is that the polarity indicators shown in fig. 4-6 work just as well for wyes as they do for loops.

Turntables

A turntable is the most obvious kind of turning track, a rotating bridge that swings an engine or car end-for-end. The problem here is to have the rails on the turntable bridge match the polarity of the lead rails so a locomotive can run on or off the table. The solution depends somewhat on how current reaches the turntable rails.

Figure 4-11A shows one method. One turntable rail is supplied through the table's center shaft by means of a wiper below the layout, while the other takes current from the pit rail through the bogie wheels that support the bridge. If the bogies are not functional, wipers can be concealed under the bridge to ride on the pit rail. This method requires an auxiliary reversing switch. And you have to throw the switch whenever you give the table half a turn.

A better method is to make the turntable serve as its own auxiliary reverse switch, fig. 4-11B. Here each table rail is supplied by the bogie (or wiper) at one end of the bridge, and the ring rail is split in two places so it can serve both sides of the track circuit. When the bridge swings past the gaps in the ring rail the polarity of the table rails automatically changes to match that of the leads.

Make sure to locate the gaps in the ring rail so the bridge pickups, wheels or wipers, are clear of them when the table rails are aligned with any lead track. In other words, the bridge shouldn't short across the gaps when it's lined up for a track.

Of course the bridge will short across the gaps when it swings past them, but this isn't a problem because

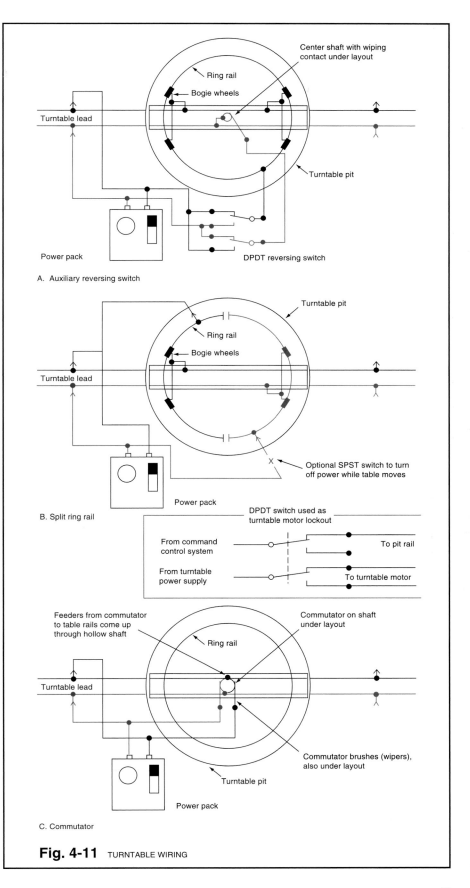

A. Auxiliary reversing switch

B. Split ring rail

C. Commutator

Fig. 4-11 TURNTABLE WIRING

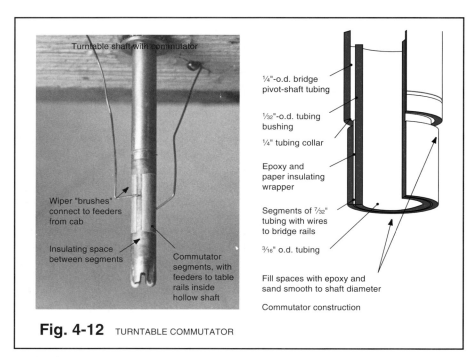

Turntable shaft with commutator

Wiper "brushes" connect to feeders from cab

Insulating space between segments

Commutator segments, with feeders to table rails inside hollow shaft

¼"-o.d. bridge pivot-shaft tubing

¹⁄₃₂"-o.d. tubing bushing

¼" tubing collar

Epoxy and paper insulating wrapper

Segments of ⁷⁄₃₂" tubing with wires to bridge rails

³⁄₁₆" o.d. tubing

Fill spaces with epoxy and sand smooth to shaft diameter

Commutator construction

Fig. 4-12 TURNTABLE COMMUTATOR

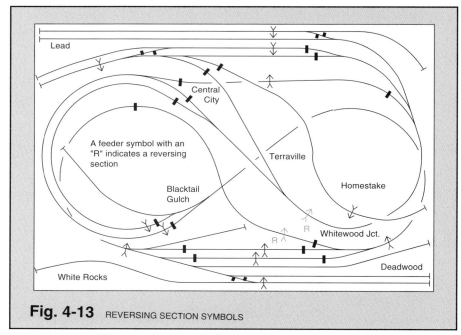

Lead

Central City

A feeder symbol with an "R" indicates a reversing section

Terraville

Blacktail Gulch

Homestake

R

R

Whitewood Jct.

Deadwood

White Rocks

Fig. 4-13 REVERSING SECTION SYMBOLS

the throttle will be turned off while you're turning a locomotive. If you use command control with constant power on the track, you may want to use the optional single-pole, single-throw (SPST) switch shown in fig. 4-11B to turn off power to the pit rail while you turn the table. If your turntable is motorized, you could make this a DPDT switch as shown in the inset, wiring it to lock out power to the turntable motor while the ring rail is energized, and vice versa. Sometimes, especially with smaller, old-fashioned turntable prototypes, powering the table track through the pit rail isn't convenient. A commutator, fig. 4-11C, will do the job with the same ad-

vantages as the split-ring-rail method.

You'll remember from our discussion of motors that a commutator is a rotating polarity switch, which is just what's needed for a turntable. The commutator can be made as either a drum or a disk attached to the turntable shaft, fig. 4-12, with two poles and two insulating slots.

As with ring rail gaps, the positions of the commutator slots, turntable bridge, and brush wipers must not allow the wipers to short across the slots when the table is aligned for any track. The turntable shaft must be hollow, so the commutator can be wired to the table rails.

The optional switches I explained for split-ring-rail wiring can also be used with a commutator, but since you'll have to make your own commutator and brushes you might as well make them "non-shorting." That means you make the slots wider than the wipers, so a wiper breaks contact with one commutator pole before it makes contact with the other.

Finding Turning Tracks

As we saw in the case of the reversing cutoff, turning tracks don't always look like the simple diagrams found in wiring books. There are several ways to find turning tracks before your train stops dead at a short circuit, and you can follow my examples in analyzing your own track plan. I'll cover reverse loops and wyes and take for granted that most of us know a turntable when we see one.

The first and most obvious signpost to look for is a reversing section symbol on a published track plan. This consists of a feeder symbol with a letter "R," fig. 4-13, just as I've used in the other diagrams in this chapter. On such a plan the designer has determined where the turning tracks are—correctly, let's hope—and all you need to do is connect the main and reversing section feeders as shown in fig. 4-4.

Not all plans include wiring symbols, though, so further analysis is often needed to find turning tracks.

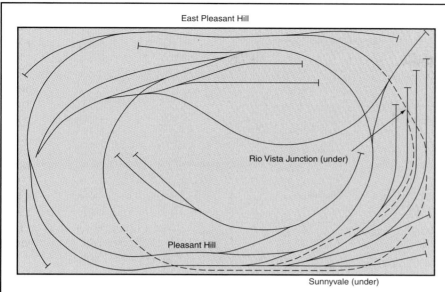

Fig. 4-14 CAN YOU FIND THE TURNING WYE ON THE PLEASANT HILL & SUNNYVALE RR?

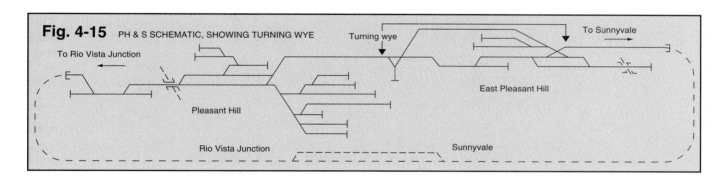

Fig. 4-15 PH & S SCHEMATIC, SHOWING TURNING WYE

shows that on this out-and-back plan the main line is mostly one big reversing loop. A reversing section belongs somewhere between the two legs of the junction turnout, and the stretch of main line I've indicated would be the best place to put it, especially if the railroad is built with the optional cutoff for continuous running.

Figure 4-16B shows the continuous route and demonstrates it doesn't involve a change of direction. This was worth checking because that cutoff looks suspiciously like a reversing cutoff. Sometimes you just want to reassure yourself that you haven't overlooked a turning track.

And let's not overlook the MB&C's other turning track, another scissors

Figure 4-14 is Don Mitchell's Pleasant Hill & Sunnyvale originally published in MODEL RAILROADER. A turning wye is woven into the top half of this plan in a less-than-conspicuous manner, but look at fig. 4-15.

When the track plan is unwrapped into a straight line the turning wye stands out clearly, even though it is a "scissors" wye with two of its legs crossing at grade. You still have some choice as to where to put the reversing section, although I'd use the simplest tail of the wye, the one at the upper right. To control this wye automatically as in fig. 4-10B, use contacts on the switch machine powering the turnout on that tail track.

If no schematic comes with the plan you can obtain the same results

by drawing your own. I'll explain how in Chapter 11.

The Arrow Method

Figure 4-16 illustrates another way to locate turning tracks. It uses John Armstrong's Murphy Bed & Credenza RR. Here you'd make photocopies of the plan, which by the way is perfectly legal as long as they're for your own use, and mark them with colored pens along the routes a train could take.

In fig. 4-16A I've started in the stub terminal on the "L" and marked arrows around the main line. I take the left-hand route the first time through the junction turnout at the bottom right corner. Notice that when I come back to that turnout the arrows are facing in the other direction. This

wye formed by the switching lead, the yard itself, and an alternate connection to the main line. Tracing a trip around all three legs, fig. 4-16C, shows where it's hiding. Here again I'd choose the simplest tail—the switching lead—as the reversing section, and control it automatically with the same switch machine that powers its turnout.

East and West

Figure 4-17 depicts the final method. Here you first mark all the gaps and feeders on your track plan, including both those needed for two-rail wiring and those for control blocks (explained in the next three chapters). Then, taking the arrowhead feeder as pointing north, label the ends of each insulated section "E" for

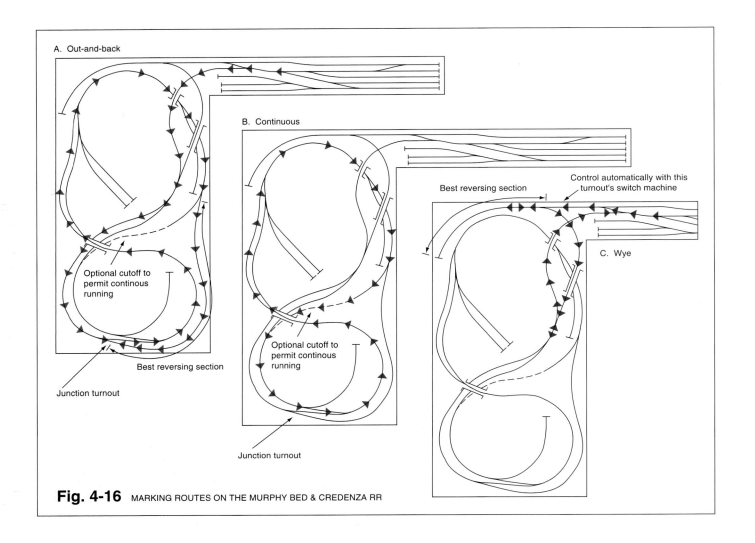

Fig. 4-16 MARKING ROUTES ON THE MURPHY BED & CREDENZA RR

Labels within figure:

A. Out-and-back

Optional cutoff to permit continous running

Best reversing section

Junction turnout

B. Continuous

Optional cutoff to permit continous running

Junction turnout

Best reversing section

Control automatically with this turnout's switch machine

C. Wye

---

east and "W" for west, fig. 4-17A. Don't worry about the prototypical operating direction of your railroad. North, south, east, and west are just convenient names for analyzing the wiring.

When you encounter a gap symbol with the same two directions on each side, two "Es" or two "Ws," you need a reversing section on one side of that gap. Add an "R" to one of the two feeder symbols, choosing the one that best fits the operating pattern of the railroad's main line.

Figure 4-17B shows plan 42 from *101 Track Plans* (Kalmbach) analyzed in this way. If the insulated section between Sanaxis Junction and Helena Mills were used for the reversing section, you'd have to make sure the auxiliary direction switches were set correctly just to let a train circle the

continuous main line. The cutoff track between Sanaxis Junction and Seaside is a better choice for the reversing section because the direction switches have to be set for it only when you wanted to turn a train.

The Dogbone

We'll finish our look at turning tracks with the "dogbone" or "waterwings" layout, fig. 4-18. This popular track schematic is a continuous loop or oval with its long sides pinched together to look like a double-track main line. The dogbone illustrates an important principle I've already made use of several times in this chapter: When the location of the reversing sections is optional the way you want to run your railroad should govern where you put them.

Look at fig. 4-18A to see how the situation arises. This is one of the plans from Ed Vondrak's "Walk- in track plan ideas in 6 x 13 feet," an article that first appeared in MODEL RAILROADER. Sending a train through the circled crossovers reverses its direction around the mainline loop. These crossovers have the same effect as reversing cutoffs across an oval, and they're less than a train-length long.

If you were building this layout and decided that most of the time you wanted to run trains continuously on the main line, the best location for reversing sections would be as in fig. 4-18B. You'd only have to set the auxiliary direction switches once to let a train make unlimited orbits in a given direction. Each trip through a crossover, though, whether to reverse a train or just for switching, would involve the auxiliary switches.

You might decide you're more interested in switching the yard and industrial sidings than in just watching trains run. In that case you'd be better off with reversing sections as shown in fig. 4-18C. You'd have to throw auxiliary switches twice for each trip around the main line, but you could switch through the crossovers and make runaround moves and not have to worry about track polarity.

Perhaps you'd want to do it both ways. You could—at the cost of some complexity in wiring. Wire the dogbone as in fig. 4-18D, with reversing sections all along one side. With this arrangement you gain maximum operational flexibility. Just remember, the way to enjoy model railroading is to run trains the way you want to, not the way the wiring lets you.

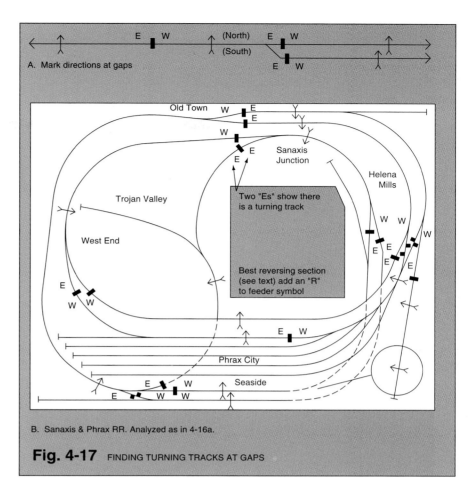

A. Mark directions at gaps

B. Sanaxis & Phrax RR. Analyzed as in 4-16a.

Fig. 4-17 FINDING TURNING TRACKS AT GAPS

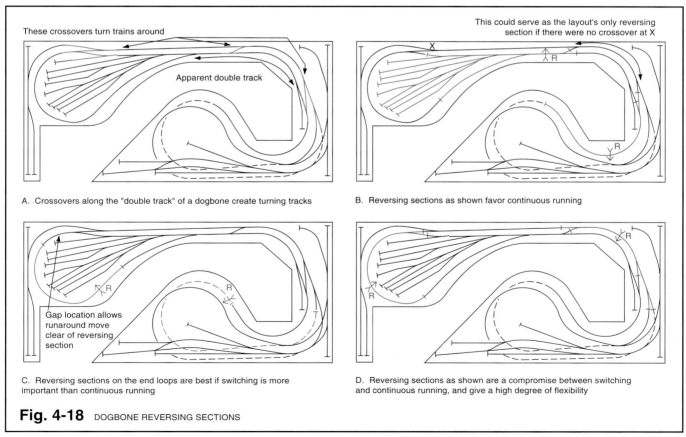

A. Crossovers along the "double track" of a dogbone create turning tracks

B. Reversing sections as shown favor continuous running

C. Reversing sections on the end loops are best if switching is more important than continuous running

D. Reversing sections as shown are a compromise between switching and continuous running, and give a high degree of flexibility

Fig. 4-18 DOGBONE REVERSING SECTIONS

Controlling two trains at once: cab control

CHAPTER FIVE

Power packs don't control trains or engines directly; they simply control the electrical polarity and voltage potential of the rails. This is indirect control because a locomotive's motor, connected to the rails, responds to changes in polarity and voltage. Any number of locomotives placed on track fed by a single power pack can only respond together to the polarity and voltage delivered by that pack—to the limit of its current capacity of course.

Adding a power pack, even a twin-throttle pack, doesn't give us independent control of more than one train or engine at a time. In fact, feeding the same track with two packs will lead to a short circuit if one reversing switch is thrown so that the packs' polarities don't match.

So how can we control two or more trains independently? I'll show you two methods. The first involves dividing your railroad into electrically isolated sections called blocks, and wiring these blocks to power packs (cabs) through electrical selector switches. This method is called cab control. This and the next two chapters will explain it in detail. The other method is command control, which does allow you to control trains directly instead of controlling the track. I'll cover command control in Chapter 8.

Basic Cab Control

Figure 5-1 shows the essential elements of the cab control system. These include:

Two cabs. I'll be using the term "cab" to refer to a set of controls for one train, a common model railroad practice. The two cabs here could be two power packs, the two throttles of a twin power pack, or something exotic like two sound systems.

Double-pole, double-throw (DPDT) selector switches. This is the same switch used for reversing but wired differently to serve as a cab selector.

Track divided into blocks. Sections of track with gaps or insulated joiners at each end, and a separate set of feeder wires for each block.

By throwing selector switches one way or the other either cab can be connected to any block. To run a train over the railroad you begin by setting the selector for the block the train is in to the cab you want to use. Then as you go, you set the selector for the next block that your train will enter for your cab.

Meanwhile another engineer can be following the same procedure with the other cab. Be sure not to let both trains enter the same block, or to assume control of both trains on one cab by throwing a block selector switch at the wrong time. With practice and coordination each of you will eventually be running a train independently on the same railroad.

The system is flexible, too. If you're in a relaxed mood and want to run just one train, set all the block selectors for one cab. You could also set a train running on the main line with one cab, then use the other cab to switch a yard or industrial complex wired as a separate block.

If you want to operate with a guest who isn't familiar with your railroad, set all the blocks except the one occupied by your train for the guest's cab. As you run your train, throw selectors for your cab as you need them, but set them back for the guest's cab as your train

Fig. 5-1. ELEMENTS OF CAB CONTROL. Here's cab control reduced to the basics: The insulated section of track, called a "block," is connected to a switch, and the switch is also connected to two power packs. You use the switch to select one pack or the other to run the locomotive in that block.

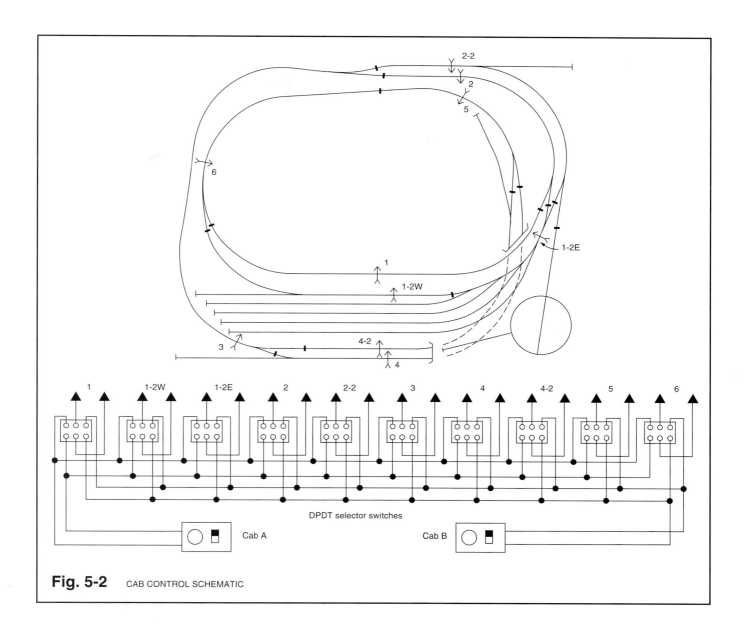

Fig. 5-2 CAB CONTROL SCHEMATIC

leaves each block. Then your visitor will be able to enjoy running his train without having to learn your control system.

If your railroad's main line is a double-track oval you might prefer operating without all the gaps and selector wiring and instead with just one cab connected to each track. With cab control wiring you can set the block selectors to run the double oval that way. You'll also be able to run a train through a crossover from one oval to the other under control of one cab, while the other cab controls another train.

Cab Control Example

Figure 5-2 uses the Sanaxis & Phrax again, the same track plan as in fig. 4-17, but without its reversing cutoff, to show a cab control wiring schematic for ten blocks. I've simplified the schematic by showing the DPDT selector switches simply as boxes with terminals.

The essential points are that wires from each cab connect to the pairs of terminals at either end of each switch, and that wires from the center terminals of each switch go to the feeders of the block that switch controls.

Note the arrow head ("north" rail)

and arrow tail ("south" rail) symbols on the feeder wires. They show how the feeder connections must be consistent for all blocks so trains won't hit reversed polarity and short out when they cross block boundaries.

Even simplified, fig. 5-2 may seem overwhelming. Figure 5-3, therefore, shows pictorially and schematically how a single block should be wired. The cab control wiring for the whole S&P RR is no more than the wiring for one block selector multiplied by ten. For any size model railroad it's that simple, adding selectors one at a time until all the blocks are connected.

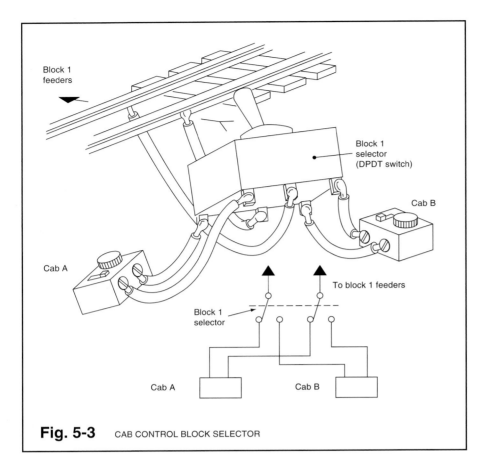

Block 1 feeders

Block 1 selector (DPDT switch)

Cab B

Cab A

To block 1 feeders

Block 1 selector

Cab A   Cab B

Fig. 5-3   CAB CONTROL BLOCK SELECTOR

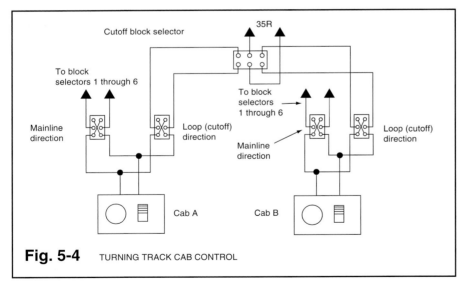

Cutoff block selector

35R

To block selectors 1 through 6

To block selectors 1 through 6

Mainline direction

Loop (cutoff) direction

Mainline direction

Loop (cutoff) direction

Cab A   Cab B

Fig. 5-4   TURNING TRACK CAB CONTROL

Turning Track Blocks

Block selectors for turning tracks can be like those for ordinary blocks, but they must be connected through auxiliary reversing switches as described in the last chapter. If you use the one-switch method for wiring a turning track only the turning track selector is affected, but with the two-switch method all block selectors must be connected through either the main line or reversing track auxiliary direction switches, fig. 5-4.

For what difference this makes to the overall wiring scheme, see fig. 5-5, the S&P RR with its reversing cutoff restored. The ten block selectors of fig. 5-2 aren't shown here. They'd be the same except they'd be connected to the mainline direction switches instead of directly to the cabs. Only one block selector needs to be added, for the one block (35) of the cutoff. It's connected to each cab's loop direction switch.

The S&P has just the one turning track block, assuming that the turntable uses one of the automatic reversing schemes shown in the last chapter. Even if it had more blocks, it still wouldn't need more auxiliary reversing switches. Any number of turning track blocks could be connected to the cabs' reversing track direction switches, just as any number of ordinary blocks could be powered through the mainline direction switches.

Common-Rail Wiring

An important variation on basic cab control block wiring is "common rail." In this arrangement one rail is common to all blocks, or electrically continuous throughout the railroad. The other rail, which I'll call the control rail, has gaps at block boundaries and a single controlled feeder for each block. Figure 5-6 shows how this works.

Note that controlling one rail is all that's needed to control the trains, because only a complete circuit through both rails will let a locomotive respond to a cab. Similarly, the cabs can share one common connection without a short, because no complete circuit, short or otherwise, lies between them.

Common-rail wiring offers several advantages, most obviously the simplification that comes from having fewer gaps and less wire. Common rail also lets you use simpler, less expensive selectors: single-pole, double-throw (SPDT) switches instead of DPDTs.

Alternately you could still use DPDTs, but with only one side of each switch needed for selector wiring, the other side could be used for the block-in-use indicator lights that I'll explain in the next chapter. Without common rail you would probably want to use 3-pole, double-throw (3PDT) selector switches to add these indicators, and as a rule the more poles and positions a switch has the more expensive it is.

Look at fig. 5-7 to see what difference common rail makes in layout wiring. This is the S&P without the cutoff again, and we'll assume for the moment that it's built with all-live turnouts. You can see that the selector switch wiring is simpler. A feeder still goes to the control rail of every block, but the only gaps are in the control rail.

The common rail is continuous everywhere on the layout and has only a single feeder. Practically, you'd want several common feeders on any size layout to eliminate the chance of trains slowing down because of voltage drop when they traveled too far from a single common feeder. On the S&P you might feed the common rail at one or two more points, but even so the wiring would be simple because all the common feeders would connect to a single wire, wire "C" at the far right end of the fig. 5-7 schematic.

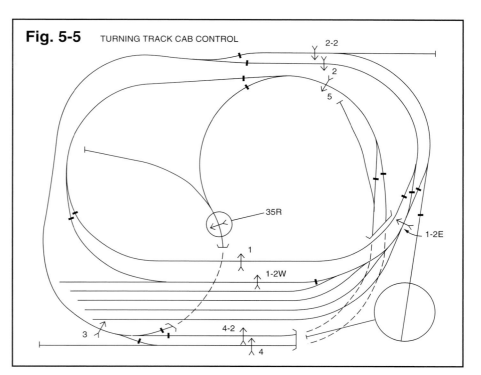

Fig. 5-5   TURNING TRACK CAB CONTROL

Common Rail with Power-Routing Turnouts

That's how common-rail wiring works with all-live turnouts, but suppose you want to use power-routing turnouts. Figure 5-8 shows what the S&P's wiring would be like in that case. I haven't included the cabs and selector switches in this figure because they would be exactly like

those in fig. 5-7. The differences all show up on the track plan, in the form of more gaps and more common-rail feeders.

The additional gaps are needed for two reasons. The first is two-rail wiring: With power-routing turnouts you have to put gaps wherever they're needed to prevent short circuits, common rail or not. That's why the S&P in

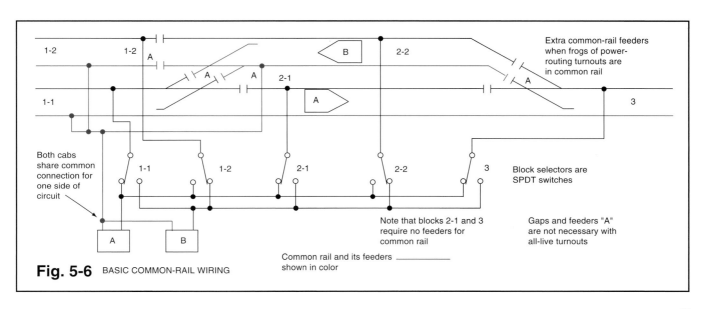

Fig. 5-6   BASIC COMMON-RAIL WIRING

Extra common-rail feeders when frogs of power-routing turnouts are in common rail

Both cabs share common connection for one side of circuit

Block selectors are SPDT switches

Note that blocks 2-1 and 3 require no feeders for common rail

Gaps and feeders "A" are not necessary with all-live turnouts

Common rail and its feeders shown in color

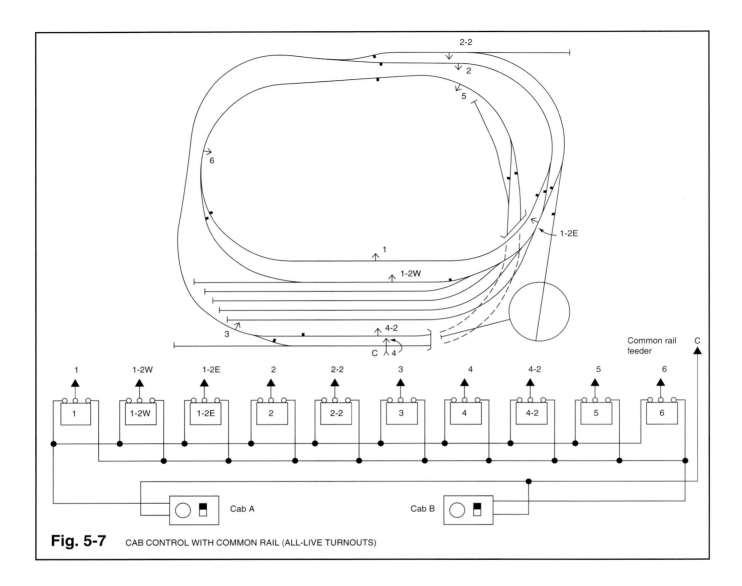

Fig. 5-7   CAB CONTROL WITH COMMON RAIL (ALL-LIVE TURNOUTS)

fig. 5-8 is back to rule 1 (remember our two-rail wiring rules from Chapter 3?): gaps in both rails at the crossovers at the right end of the Phrax City yard, at the left end of Seaside, and on the siding at West End.

The other reason is operating flexibility on the passing tracks. You want trains to be able to enter sidings, or main tracks between siding turnouts, even when the turnout at the opposite end is set for another train to take the other track. That's not possible if the common rail is being fed through the point and frog of that opposite turnout. This is why in fig. 5-8 I've put a pair of gaps in the main line at Old Town, but only a single control-rail gap in the siding.

You may find this easier to understand with isolated examples, so look at fig. 5-9. The governing rule is that the common rail can be continuous through the stock rail of a power-routing turnout, but not through a point and frog. In 5-9D, gap X and feeder Y are required by our second rule of two-rail wiring, so the lower spur turnout won't be fed from its frog.

But suppose we'd started with feeder Y instead of the common feeder at the left end of the diagram. We'd still want to add gap X and that leftmost common feeder. Otherwise throwing the turnout for the lower spur would put the whole railroad to the left of it out of common feed and so out of business.

Common Bus

Turning back to fig. 5-8, you can see with power-routing turnouts it takes eight common feeders instead of just one to get the common side of the circuit around the additional gaps. Some of these could be replaced with jumpers as in fig. 5-9D, but even without that common-rail wiring is still simpler than the wiring in fig. 5-2. That's because all the common feeders can connect to a single wire running back into wire C in fig. 5-7.

Remember that the electrical term for a single wire carrying a number of connections is "bus," so you could connect all the common-rail feeders to common bus running back to your cab control panel. Such a bus would have to be a heavier wire than the control or common feeders, since it would carry the current of all blocks at once. I'll examine wire sizes more closely in Chapter 10.

In fact, some modelers like to gap the common rail every place they gap the control rail, locating gaps and feeders just as in fig. 5-2. This makes the common rail common only by virtue of its feeder connections to a common bus.

One advantage of this common-rail variation is that the blocks can be completely isolated—though it may take a wire cutter or soldering iron to do the job—which often helps with troubleshooting. Another is some signaling systems require that every signaled block have its own pair of feeders, even if one of them is connected to a common bus. Finally, it makes it easier to be sure the track has all the gaps it needs by ensuring that any error is on the side of excess.

Power Packs and Common Rail

The most overlooked restriction on common-rail wiring is that each cab must have its own independent power supply. That means separate power packs for each cab, or multi-cab packs designed for common rail, with independent transformers.

Most older multi-cab packs share one power supply among their two or three throttles, causing short circuits with common-rail layout wiring. Some modern multi-cab packs are designed for use with common-rail wiring, but make sure the manufacturer specifies this before making a purchase.

Also, remember that an add-on throttle shares the same power supply as the original pack, and so can't be used with common rail. You can use any hand-held transistor or SCR throttle with common rail, so long as you provide it with its own independent power supply.

Turning Tracks with Common-Rail Wiring

Turning tracks can't have a common rail, since you have to be able

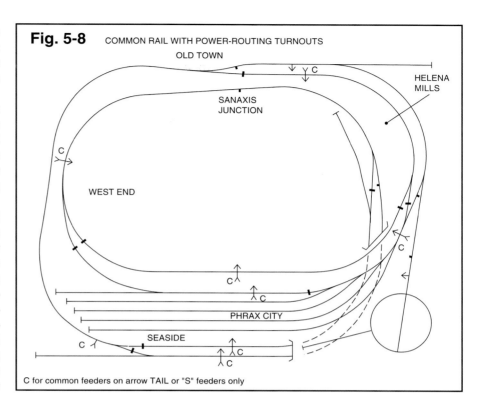

Fig. 5-8   COMMON RAIL WITH POWER-ROUTING TURNOUTS

OLD TOWN

HELENA MILLS

SANAXIS JUNCTION

WEST END

PHRAX CITY

SEASIDE

C for common feeders on arrow TAIL or "S" feeders only

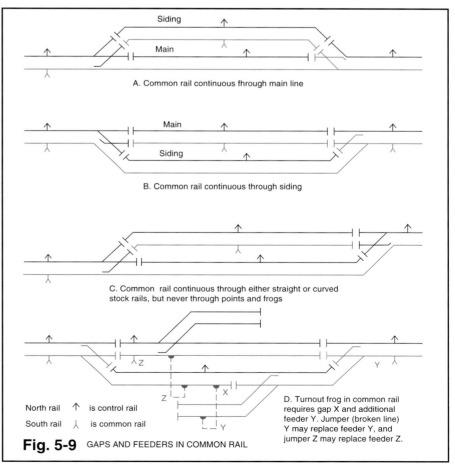

Siding

Main

A. Common rail continuous fhrough main line

Main

Siding

B. Common rail continuous through siding

C. Common rail continuous through either straight or curved stock rails, but never through points and frogs

North rail ↑ is control rail
South rail ⅄ is common rail

D. Turnout frog in common rail requires gap X and additional feeder Y. Jumper (broken line) Y may replace feeder Y, and jumper Z may replace feeder Z.

Fig. 5-9   GAPS AND FEEDERS IN COMMON RAIL

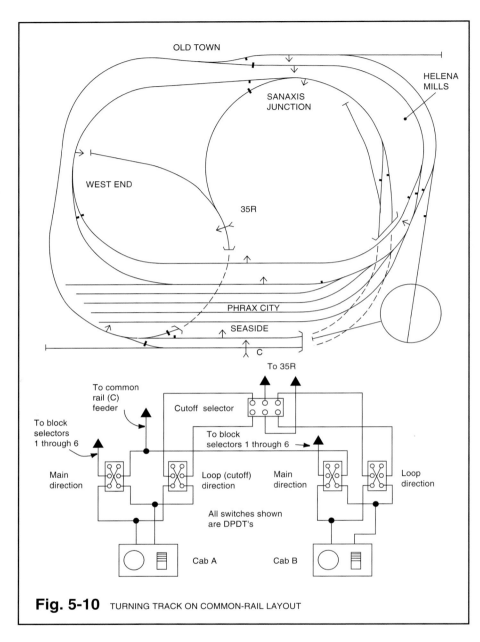

Fig. 5-10 TURNING TRACK ON COMMON-RAIL LAYOUT

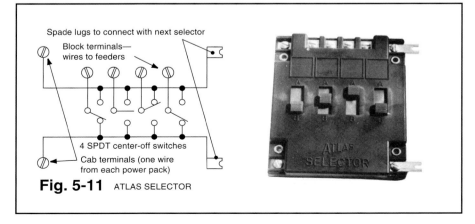

Fig. 5-11 ATLAS SELECTOR

to switch polarity between rails. That doesn't mean you can't have turning tracks on a model railroad wired with a common rail, just that the common rail can't extend into the reversing sections. Figure 5-10 shows how this works.

With its reversing cutoff restored once more, notice that the S&P track plan shows gaps in both rails at both ends of the turning track, and that the S rail (arrow tail) feeder for block 35R is not marked with a C for connection to a common bus. The other gaps and feeders are set up for all-live turn-outs, but they could also be arranged as shown in fig. 5-8 for power-routing turnouts. Regardless of the turnout type, the turning track gaps and feeders would still be the same.

The wiring diagram omits the non-turning-track block selectors. Notice also that the auxiliary reversing switches are set up pretty much as in fig. 5-5. Differences exist, however, and they're important. Only one wire from each main direction switch goes to selector switches 1 through 6, which would be SPDT switches wired as in fig. 5-7. The other poles of the main direction switches are connected together, and to the common-rail (C) feeders.

Notice that the loop direction and selector switches are isolated from the common rail connections. This wiring for the reversing cutoff works just like the two-switch examples we saw in Chapter 4; it's compatible with but not a part of the common-rail scheme.

You may have noticed I've again ignored the turntable on the S&P track plan. That's because if you wire it with one of the automatic reversing schemes in Chapter 4, you won't have to think of it as a turning track. One side of an automatic-reverse turntable circuit can connect to the common bus, just as if it were an ordinary track. I've also been ignoring the engine-house track and turntable lead—I'll get to those situations in Chapter 7.

Wyes and reverse loops on common-rail layouts, however, have to be treated just like the reversing cutoff on the S&P.

Atlas Selectors and Controllers

Atlas Model Railroad Co., the same company that makes Snap-Track and Custom Line turnouts, also sells handy components that can make common-rail cab control wiring fast and simple. The Atlas Selector is a package of four SPDT slide switches, with lugs and terminals that let you gang as many units as needed to get a switch for each block on your railroad. Figure 5-11 shows what an Atlas Selector looks like, along with a schematic of its innards.

Figure 5-12 shows how Selectors could be used to control the no-cutoff version of the S&P. Since the layout has ten blocks it takes three Selectors, leaving two switches as spares. I'm showing only the control wiring here; the layout wiring could be the same as either fig. 5-7, for all-live turnouts, or fig. 5-8, for power-routing turnouts.

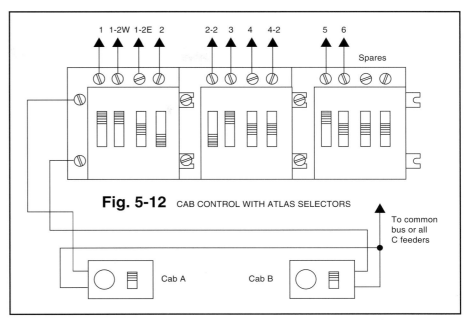

Fig. 5-12 CAB CONTROL WITH ATLAS SELECTORS

The Atlas Controller is a package of four DPDT center-off switches for controlling turning track blocks on a common-rail layout. One of the four switches, at left center on the Controller, fig. 5-13, is the selector for the reversing block. The other three are set up as reversing switches, with the two at top and bottom left controlling mainline direction for the two cabs, and the one on the right controlling the reversing loop direction.

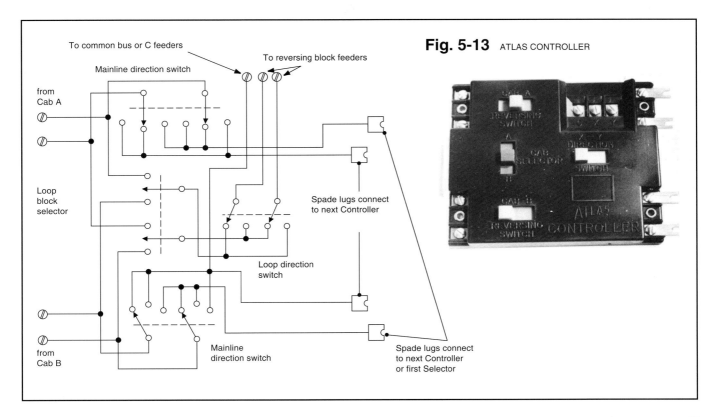

Fig. 5-13 ATLAS CONTROLLER

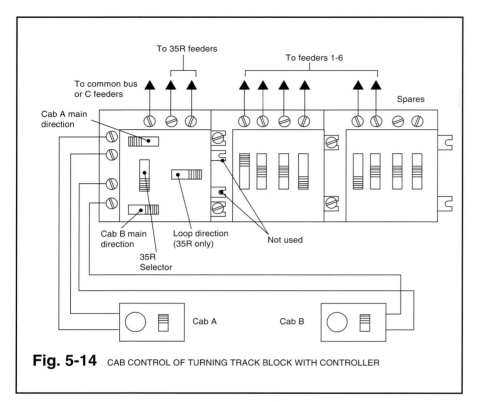

Fig. 5-14 CAB CONTROL OF TURNING TRACK BLOCK WITH CONTROLLER

Labels in figure 5-14:
- To 35R feeders
- To feeders 1-6
- To common bus or C feeders
- Spares
- Cab A main direction
- Cab B main direction
- Loop direction (35R only)
- 35R Selector
- Not used
- Cab A
- Cab B

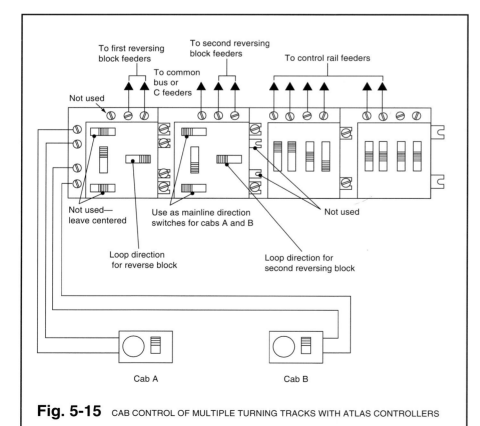

Fig. 5-15 CAB CONTROL OF MULTIPLE TURNING TRACKS WITH ATLAS CONTROLLERS

Labels in figure 5-15:
- To first reversing block feeders
- To second reversing block feeders
- To control rail feeders
- To common bus or C feeders
- Not used
- Not used—leave centered
- Use as mainline direction switches for cabs A and B
- Not used
- Loop direction for reverse block
- Loop direction for second reversing block
- Cab A
- Cab B

An Atlas Controller gives you two-switch reversing control of a reversing loop from either cab, but it's not exactly like the two-switch arrangement shown in Chapter 4. Instead of employing a loop direction switch for each cab, it uses one for each loop block. This doesn't make any difference in the way you operate the loop (or cutoff, or other turning track); it would be more complicated if you were wiring it yourself, but you don't have to worry about that because Atlas takes care of that job.

Turning once more to the good old S&P, fig. 5-14 shows an Atlas Controller combined with Atlas Selectors to control the reversing-cutoff version of that layout. Note that two wires each from the cabs connect to the Controller, and that the common-rail wire comes out of the Controller.

With this wiring you'd use the reversing switch on the cab to set forward or reverse for your locomotive, and the main direction switch for that cab on the Controller to set your train's direction around the main line.

To turn your train on the cutoff you'd use the Controller's selector switch to connect block 35R to your cab, and its loop direction switch to set direction through the cutoff. While the train was in the cutoff you'd throw the main direction switch, and the train would be able to leave the cutoff and continue in the opposite direction around the main.

If you have more than one turning track, add a Controller for each one, fig. 5-15. The Atlas Controller and Selector are modules in a system which can be extended to cover as many blocks and turning tracks as you want to have. Note that the common wire connects to the rightmost Controller, and that you use only that unit's mainline direction switches. The corresponding switches on any other Controllers must be centered and left alone.

Multiple cabs and cab control refinements

CHAPTER SIX

You can achieve lots of action on even a fair-sized model railroad with two cabs, but it's also easy to think of ways to use additional cabs. Even if two mainline trains running at once are enough for your layout, you might want to have a yard engine or a branchline train operating at the same time. More cabs let more people run your railroad with you, and model railroading is even more fun when you can enjoy it with friends.

In this chapter I'll start with a simple way to add more cabs to the two-cab wiring introduced in the last chapter, then proceed to other ways to wire multiple cabs. I'll show you how to set up cab control wiring for walkaround

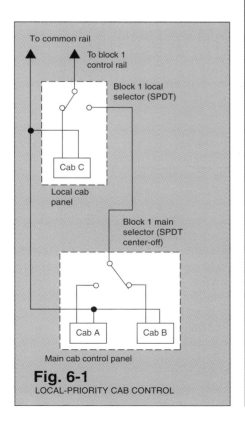

Fig. 6-1
LOCAL-PRIORITY CAB CONTROL

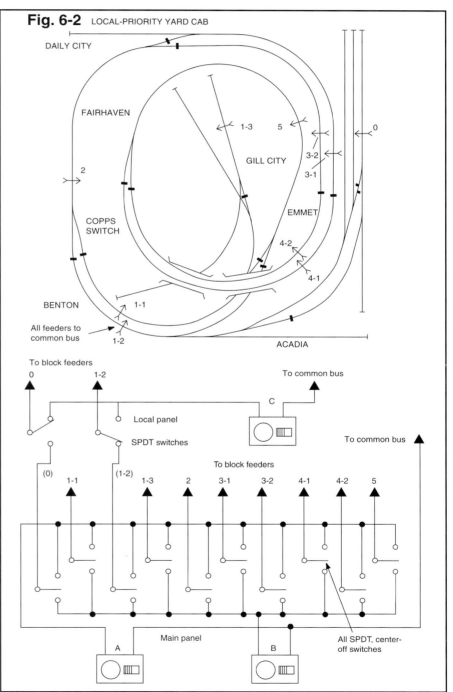

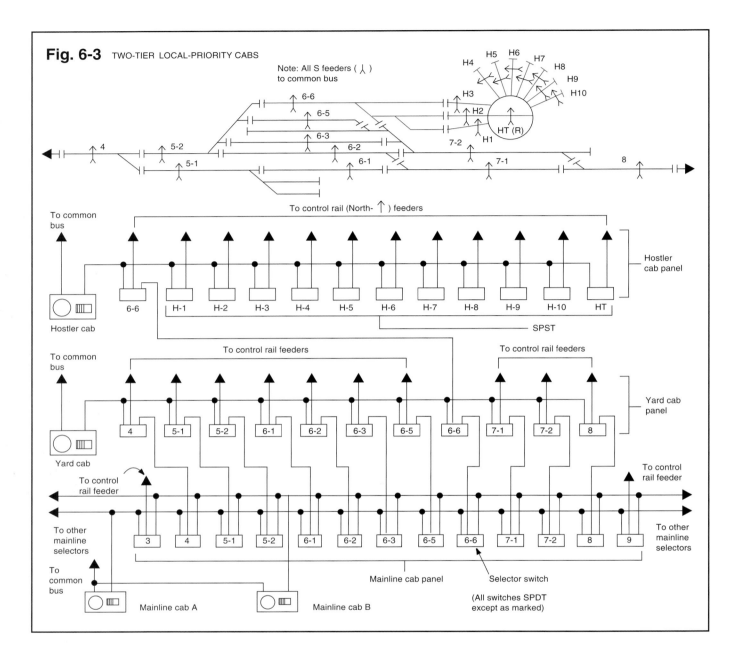

Fig. 6-3 TWO-TIER LOCAL-PRIORITY CABS

control. This eliminates the need to stay at a fixed control panel while you run a train across your model countryside. Finally, I'll mention advanced cab control systems that are beyond the scope of this book, but that you might want to know about.

For simplicity, the wiring schemes shown in this chapter and the next use a modified common rail for simplicity. On the track plans gaps are indicated for both rails, but I'll assume the south rail (the one with the arrow-tail feeder symbol) is the

common one and the south feeders connect to a common bus. The control wiring diagrams show single-pole selector switches and the cabs connected to the common bus.

In most cases the same wiring can be used without common rail by substituting selector switches with additional poles. You could use DPDT switches where I've shown SPDTs.

Local-Priority Cab Control

One of the simplest ways to include more than two cabs is the

"local-priority" system shown in fig. 6-1. It's easy to understand because it uses the same selector switches you'd use for two-cab wiring. And it's easy to use because, like two-cab wiring with double-throw switches, you connect only one cab at a time to a given block.

I call this the local-priority system because the local cab has first choice on using any of the blocks for which it has selectors. It can lock the main cabs out of its blocks, or take its blocks away from the main cabs. In fig. 6-1, note how cabs A and B have access to block 1 only when local cab C is not using it.

I think of the priority cab as a "local" cab because this wiring is so useful when you want a cab to control only part of a railroad. Whether it's just for running a yard switcher, or for industrial switching at some busy town along the main line, the handy local-priority cab needs selectors for only the few blocks in its territory.

Look at fig. 6-2, the Central Missouri RR, plan 38 from *101 Track Plans* (Kalmbach). Suppose you had this railroad wired for cab control with two cabs, but wanted to add a third cab to run a switch engine at Acadia. The figure shows how to do this with a local-priority cab. The local cab needs only two block selectors, including one for the Benton passing track that the switcher would use as a yard lead.

The logic of the priority or lockout feature in this wiring is that the yard or other local engineer has complete control of his operating area. The man on the spot can decide when to give mainline cabs and trains access to "his" blocks.

Figure 6-2 is a simple example, but nothing precludes you from using more local-priority cabs. With a large layout you still might want to start with a two-cab arrangement as in the last chapter. Then you could add local-priority cabs as operating situations—and interested operators—appeared to require them.

Also, a local-priority cab doesn't have to be just "local"—it could include selector switches for every block on your layout. That local cab should be manned by your railroad's sharpest operator, who'd release blocks he wasn't using for the other cabs. Otherwise, the priority cab could lock up the whole system.

Levels of Priority

Another variation would be to arrange local-priority cabs in tiers. Suppose you had a busy yard and wanted this arrangement: one engi-

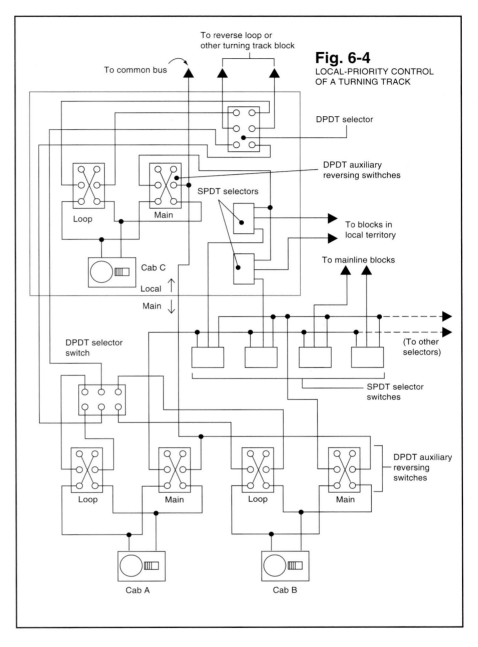

Fig. 6-4
LOCAL-PRIORITY CONTROL OF A TURNING TRACK

neer to act as a full-time hostler to move engines around the roundhouse; one full-time yard engineer to operate the yard; and two mainline engineers to run trains in and out of the yard and occasionally move engines to and from the roundhouse.

Figure 6-3 shows how to handle this—with local-priority cabs for the hostler and the yard engineer. The yard is a schematic version of Alkalai Flats from John Armstrong's article "Division points" in the November

1952 MODEL RAILROADER Magazine. For purposes of this illustration, imagine that the main line extends both ways from Alkalai Flats, under control of mainline cabs A and B. The gaps and feeders here are from the plan in that 1952 article; we'll examine the important subject of how to divide a yard into blocks in the next chapter.

As a rule, the highest control priority in this sort of wiring goes to the cab handling what would be the lowliest running job on the real railroad—

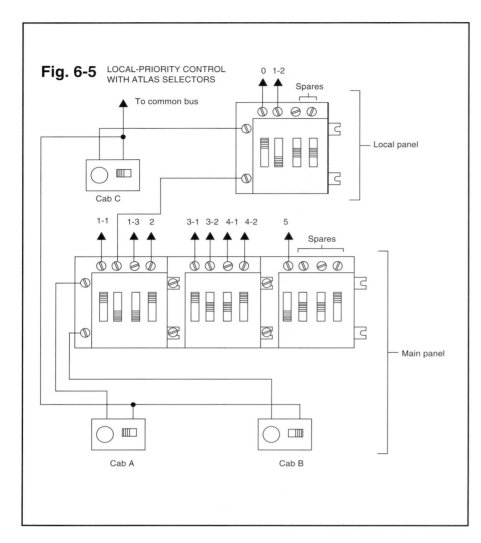

Fig. 6-5 LOCAL-PRIORITY CONTROL WITH ATLAS SELECTORS

0 1-2
Spares

To common bus

Local panel

Cab C

1-1 1-3 2   3-1 3-2 4-1 4-2   5   Spares

Main panel

Cab A   Cab B

the hostler at Alkalai Flats. The hostler cab must be able to use block 6-6 to move engines on the roundhouse leads, the left ends of the three tracks leading to the turntable. All the other cabs can select block 6-6 as well but will be connected only when the hostler has released that block.

Note that blocks H-1 through H-10 and HT, the tracks leading directly to the turntable and the turntable itself, can be used only by the hostler cab. They are controlled with single-pole, single-throw (SPST) "on-off" switches, so several engines may be left standing around the turntable.

Other cabs may run engines to and from the roundhouse lead tracks, but we'll assume it's the hostler's job to turn them and run them in and out of the house. Another assumption, made for the sake of simplicity, is that the turntable uses an automatic reversing scheme so we don't have to consider it as a turning track.

The next highest priority level is the yard cab, which can control every track in the yard except the tracks around the turntable. It can also select the mainline blocks at each end of the yard, so the switcher can make runaround moves on the main and use it as a lead for dragging out

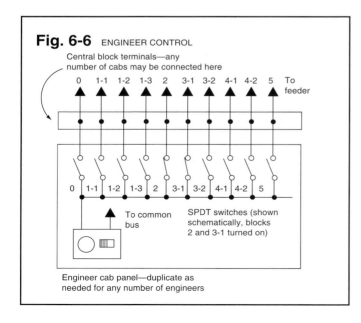

Fig. 6-6 ENGINEER CONTROL

Central block terminals—any number of cabs may be connected here

0 1-1 1-2 1-3 2 3-1 3-2 4-1 4-2 5 To feeder

0 1-1 1-2 1-3 2 3-1 3-2 4-1 4-2 5

To common bus

SPDT switches (shown schematically, blocks 2 and 3-1 turned on)

Engineer cab panel—duplicate as needed for any number of engineers

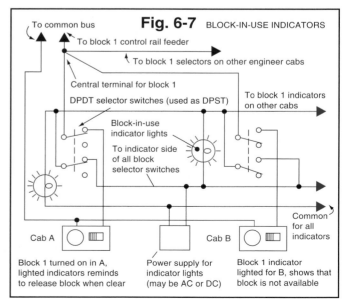

To common bus

Fig. 6-7 BLOCK-IN-USE INDICATORS

To block 1 control rail feeder

To block 1 selectors on other engineer cabs

Central terminal for block 1

DPDT selector switches (used as DPST)

To block 1 indicators on other cabs

Block-in-use indicator lights

To indicator side of all block selector switches

Cab A   Cab B

Common for all indicators

Block 1 turned on in A, lighted indicators reminds to release block when clear

Power supply for indicator lights (may be AC or DC)

Block 1 indicator lighted for B, shows that block is not available long cuts of cars. The hostler cab can lock the yard cab out of block 6-6, but the yard cab has first choice on all of its other blocks.

Still following the priority rule, all the yard cab's blocks are available for selection by the mainline cabs, but these cabs have the least claim on them. The mainline cabs can run trains through and into the yard, but only after the yard cab releases the blocks. They can even run engines to and from the roundhouse leads when the hostler cab releases block 6-6.

By the way, to achieve smooth and realistic operation the mainline cabs must be able to run trains in and out of yards. On a real railroad the mainline or road crews start and end their work in terminals. It's no great trick to wire your layout so you can imitate real railroads, and it's less trouble than passing control from one cab to another at the yard limit.

In any case, after you've digested fig. 6-3 you should be able to see other opportunities for using local-priority cabs in multiple tiers. If a turning track is in the local cab's territory, simply wire it using DPDT selector switches on both the mainline and local control panels, fig. 6-4.

Local Priority with Atlas Components

You can also achieve something similar with Atlas components. Figure 6-5 shows three-cab wiring for the Central Missouri with Atlas Selectors. This isn't as flexible as the wiring in fig. 6-2, because both the yard blocks are selected by a single switch on one of the mainline Atlas Selectors.

Because of this restriction Atlas Selectors aren't so convenient if the local cab is to control several blocks, at least not for the local cab itself. With Selectors on the mainline panel and individual switches on the local panel, you could duplicate exactly the wiring of fig. 6-2.

The design of Atlas Controllers doesn't make them useful for local-priority control except in restrictive cases, as when all the local cab's

Fig. 6-8. Two-pole, 6-position rotary switches (DP6T or 2P6pos), left, or single-pole, 12-position rotary switches (SP12T or 1P12pos), right, make good multi-position selectors; other configurations work, too. For block selectors choose non-shorting switches arranged so the moving poles break contact at one position before making contact with the next. Mount these switches like toggles through holes drilled in control panels. Control knobs must be purchased separately.

blocks are on the tail of a wye (a turning track situation).

Engineer Control

Engineer control is a variation of cab control in which each engineer uses an individual cab panel with block selectors for all blocks, or at least all blocks required for his normal operating duties. The selectors are simply on-off switches, SPST or DPST, and each cab's selectors are wired to the track blocks through the same set of feeders used by the other cabs, usually with centralized wiring terminals. Figure 6-6 shows an engineer-control cab for the Central Missouri RR.

The two advantages of engineer control wiring for multiple cabs are: You can use simple selectors to build as many cabs as you need for the number of operators you want; and you can add more whenever you need them without disturbing existing wiring.

In engineer control the engineer turns on selectors as needed to run his train through one block after another. He must remember to turn selectors off as his train leaves each block to avoid the problems that

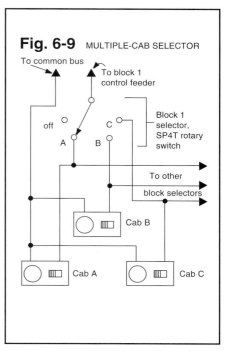

occur when more than one cab is connected to the same block. This is the biggest disadvantage of engineer control.

With the dual-cab and local-priority systems we've examined, the selector switches lock out conflicting cab assignments so you can't have two cabs connected to the same block. As long as each engineer keeps his train within the limits of blocks connected to his own cab, he can't cause electrical problems for other operators.

Engineer control gives up lockout capability to gain simplicity and flexibility in wiring, but it requires more care and cooperation from the operators. If one engineer forgets to turn off a block and another turns it on, at the least they'll have control problems, such as a stopped train starting to move on power from another train's cab. If the cab's reversing switches are set for opposite directions, a short circuit will occur on both cabs.

This potential for trouble doesn't mean engineer cabs aren't useful, but you ought to be aware of these pitfalls when choosing and using this control scheme. One simple way to help engineers avoid trouble is to

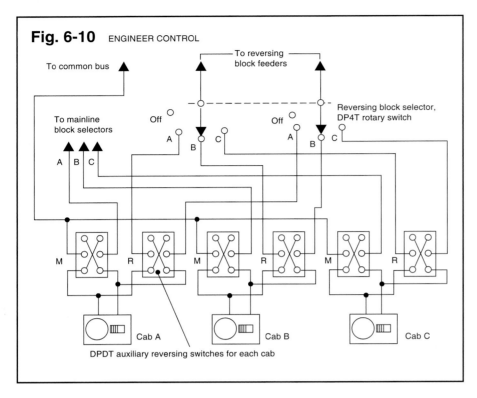

Fig. 6-10 ENGINEER CONTROL

To common bus

To reversing block feeders

Reversing block selector, DP4T rotary switch

To mainline block selectors

Off

Off

A B C

A B C A B C

M R M R M R

Cab A Cab B Cab C

DPDT auxiliary reversing switches for each cab

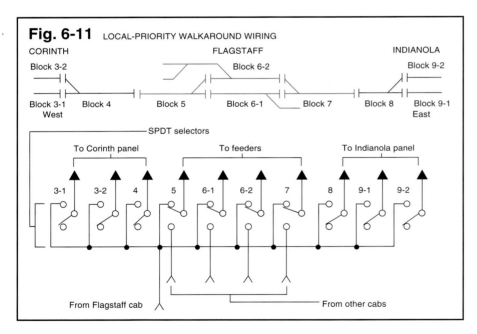

Fig. 6-11 LOCAL-PRIORITY WALKAROUND WIRING

CORINTH FLAGSTAFF INDIANOLA

Block 3-2 Block 6-2 Block 9-2

Block 3-1 Block 4 Block 5 Block 6-1 Block 7 Block 8 Block 9-1
West East

SPDT selectors

To Corinth panel To feeders To Indianola panel

3-1 3-2 4 5 6-1 6-2 7 8 9-1 9-2

From Flagstaff cab From other cabs

2. When you stop your train, as at a station or on a siding for a meet, leave the block selector on so another engineer won't inadvertently take control of your train.

3. Turn off the selector as your train leaves a block, so other engineers can use it.

Block-in-use indicators can help in other kinds of selector wiring as well, and can be added to any of the block wiring schemes in this book by using selector switches with extra poles (ruling out Atlas components, unfortunately). I'm illustrating how to wire the indicators here because engineer control needs them more than other systems.

Multiple-Cab Selectors

All the cab control systems we've discussed are limited by selector switches with at most two "on" positions. Another way to arrange multiple-cab wiring is to use selectors with more positions. One common type of multi-position switch is shown in fig. 6-8. The rotary switch makes connections to one of several positions arranged in an arc or circle. You could also use interlocked push buttons, which resemble the station selectors in car radios.

The two are almost the same for our purposes. My circuit diagrams will show a rotary arrangement, but the circuits for interlocked buttons are identical. In theory the rotary switch can cause conflicting connections, since when its contact moves from, say, the cab B position to cab D, it momentarily sweeps over the terminal for cab C. In practice this never seems to cause much trouble on a model railroad as long as you don't stop the switch in the intermediate position. Still, if you want to avoid that possibility, the interlocked push button has the advantage of not moving across intermediate positions when you change its setting.

Figure 6-9 shows how to wire a three-cab selector for a single block. The selector is a single-pole, four-throw (SP4T) rotary switch. For more

wire block-in-use indicator lights on the cab panels, fig. 6-7.

The block-in-use indicator is a light wired to an extra pole on the selector switch and interconnected with the matching lights on every other engineer panel. It shows when a block is turned on, and with that information the engineers can follow three simple rules to avoid conflicts:

1. Don't turn on a selector if its block-in-use indicator is lit, and don't run your train into a block you haven't turned on.

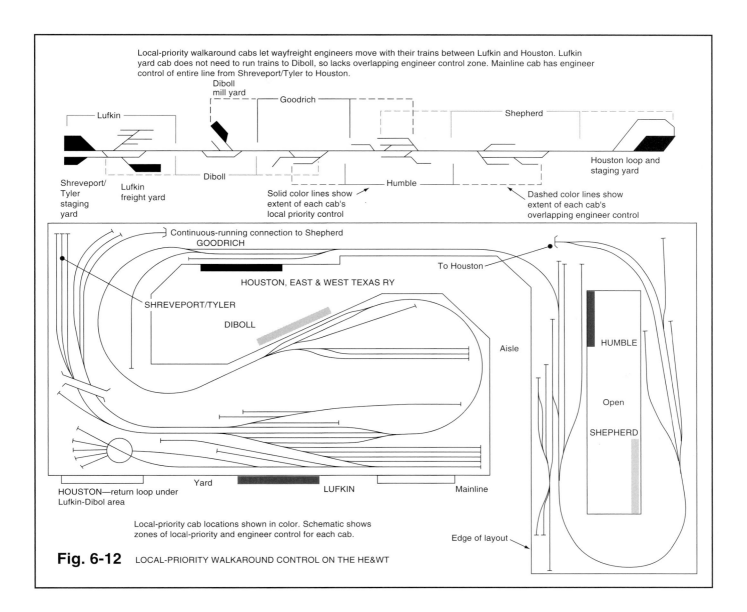

Local-priority walkaround cabs let wayfreight engineers move with their trains between Lufkin and Houston. Lufkin yard cab does not need to run trains to Diboll, so lacks overlapping engineer control zone. Mainline cab has engineer control of entire line from Shreveport/Tyler to Houston.

Lufkin

Diboll mill yard

Goodrich

Shepherd

Houston loop and staging yard

Shreveport/ Tyler staging yard

Lufkin freight yard

Diboll

Humble

Solid color lines show extent of each cab's local priority control

Dashed color lines show extent of each cab's overlapping engineer control

Continuous-running connection to Shepherd

GOODRICH

To Houston

HOUSTON, EAST & WEST TEXAS RY

SHREVEPORT/TYLER

DIBOLL

Aisle

HUMBLE

Open

SHEPHERD

HOUSTON—return loop under Lufkin-Dibol area

Yard

LUFKIN

Mainline

Edge of layout

Local-priority cab locations shown in color. Schematic shows zones of local-priority and engineer control for each cab.

Fig. 6-12   LOCAL-PRIORITY WALKAROUND CONTROL ON THE HE&WT

cabs obtain a switch with as many throw positions as you need, plus one. Using a switch with one more position than you have cabs lets you reserve one position not connected to any cab for turning the block off. This is a handy equivalent to a center-off position on a double-throw toggle.

As with the other selectors we've seen, wiring for a complete railroad is achieved by repeating the procedures in fig. 6-9 for every block. For turning track blocks use double-pole, four-throw (DP4T) switches wired through auxiliary reverse switches, fig. 6-10.

Multiple-cab selectors introduce another question: Who will operate the selectors? With engineer control each engineer can have his own selector panel, and with typical dual-cab control panels using double-throw selectors the two engineers can easily share the selectors. Convenience and comfort suffer, however, when three or more engineers share a selector panel.

What's the best way to overcome this problem? One way is to decentralize the selectors, which I'll explain shortly as a method of walkaround control. The other ways involve allowing operators other than the engineers to handle the selectors. If one operator works the selectors for the whole railroad, we call that "dispatcher control." If two or more operators each handle selectors for a part of the railroad, that's "tower control."

Dispatcher control and tower control can serve useful purposes on large model railroads with plenty of cabs and blocks, and you'll usually find them on club layouts and large home systems. They require some way of keeping the selector operators informed about the train's location and current operator. Most simply this might involve locating the dispatcher's panel where that operator could overlook the whole railroad. More elaborate arrangements

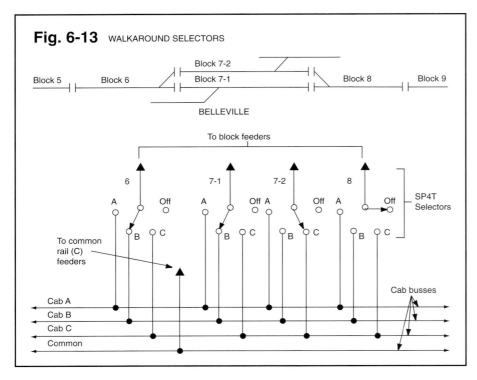

Fig. 6-13 WALKAROUND SELECTORS

would use a telephone intercom system between dispatcher or towermen and engineers, and also a block-occupancy detection system to turn on panel lights to show where trains are on the railroad.

Although dispatcher and tower control have their place, I don't like either method because they require operators who don't run trains. That can be acceptable and even enjoyable if the operators can perform prototypical jobs, like those of a real centralized traffic control (CTC) dispatcher or interlocking towerman. On the real railroad, however, those jobs don't involve setting block selectors.

It's a matter of taste but I like to keep unprototypical operating functions to a minimum and not ask any operator to carry out a job that's entirely or even mostly unrealistic. Requiring the engineer to throw block selectors isn't prototypical either, of course, but the engineer's compensation is that he gets to run the train.

Walkaround Control

All the control systems we've looked at assume the engineers will stay at a block selector panel while they run trains on the layout. Walkaround systems, on the other hand, assume the engineers will move with the trains. To make that work, we have to put the block controls within easy reach of the engineers, which means the block controls can't remain on the same central panel.

If you find the advantages of walkaround control obvious, you might want to skip this paragraph and the next two. If you wonder why this control is worth the bother, however, read on and I'll tell you why I like it.

Walkaround control lets you enjoy your modeling work up close and in action. When your superdetailed locomotive crosses your scratchbuilt bridge or passes through your hand-carved rock cut, you're there to see it instead of at the control panel across the room. If you like model railroad operation, walking around with your train gives you a stronger impression of travel and transportation than if you sit still while the train moves. You'll find switching the local freight easier and more enjoyable when you're right there to see what needs

to be accomplished, and as you work your way from town to town you'll feel some of the same out-on-the-line isolation that forces real train crews to be self-reliant.

Finally, model railroads designed to use walkaround control are better looking and easier to enjoy. Of necessity they include aisleways that provide a good look at every part of the system. And because it's easier to follow the trains if they follow the aisles, layouts with walkaround control usually feature simple main lines that progress from place to place in an understandable manner.

I'll show you several simple ways to wire a layout for walkaround cab control.

Local-Priority Walkaround

Engineers can use the same local-priority wiring we examined earlier to follow their trains at least from town to town. Figure 6-11 shows a schematic view of part of a model railroad with local-priority walkaround cabs and of the cab panel at the town of Flagstaff. Every other town, like Corinth and Indianola in this example, would have a similar panel. The Flagstaff cab has priority control of the four blocks shown in color and engineer control of the other blocks to the east and west.

The engineer of the eastbound way freight could use the Corinth cab to run his train into Flagstaff, then walk to that town and use the Flagstaff cab to work the local industry spurs. If a through train had to pass, the way freight would move into the clear on siding block 6-2, and the engineer would release blocks 5, 6-1, and 7 for use by the other cab.

When finished switching Flagstaff, the way freight engineer could run his train to the next town east from the Flagstaff panel, and then walk to the Indianola cab panel to handle his switching there. He could also walk to Indianola first and run his train from Flagstaff with the Indianola cab. In either case, before leaving the Flagstaff cab he would switch off all the

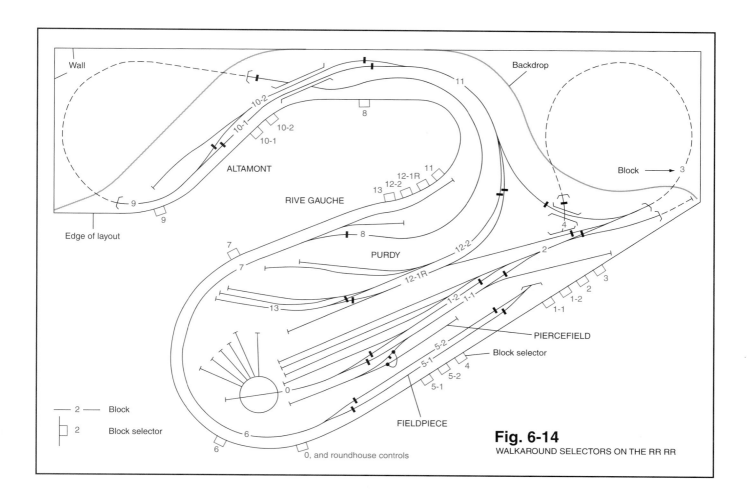

Fig. 6-14
WALKAROUND SELECTORS ON THE RR RR

selectors on that panel, to free the priority-controlled blocks for other cabs and to avoid conflicts in the engineer-controlled blocks.

Because of the overlapping controls, local-priority walkaround wiring doesn't provide lockout protection against cab conflicts. In fig. 6-11, for example, both the Flagstaff cab and the cab two towns to the east could select block 9-2 at Indianola at the same time. For this reason, adding block-in-use indicator lights to any local-priority walkaround system is a good idea.

Note in fig. 6-11 that, just as in local-priority wiring, the feeders for the local blocks—5, 6-1, 6-2, and 7 at Flagstaff—connect exclusively through the local panel's priority selectors. The "from other cabs" inputs would include connections from selectors for blocks 5, 6-1, and 6-2 on the Corinth panel; from selectors for blocks 6-1,

6-2, and 7 on the Indianola panel; and from selectors for all four on any mainline cab panels. The "to Corinth" and "to Indianola" connections from Flagstaff would go to similar "from other cabs" input locations in each of those panels.

Local-Priority Walkaround on the HE&WT

Figure 6-12 shows the local-priority walkaround control arrangements on Cyril Durrenberger's HO scale Houston, East & West Texas RR, featured in the December 1979 MODEL RAILROADER. Each of the town cabs is a local-priority cab for the blocks within and to each side of a town. Except for the Lufkin cab, each town cab has engineer control of the blocks leading into the next town in either direction, so trains can run from town to town without stopping until they reach the next station or siding.

The Lufkin cab serves as the yard cab for Lufkin yard. It isn't used to run trains between Lufkin and Diboll, so it doesn't have engineer-control selectors for the Diboll blocks. The Lufkin engineer occasionally runs trains to and from the staging yard representing the HE&WT's eastern connections via Shreveport, Louisiana, and Tyler, Texas; therefore, the Lufkin cab has engineer control of the staging yard blocks.

At the other end of the line, the Shepherd cab has engineer control of blocks all the way around the hidden Houston reverse loop, where storage tracks represent the west end of the HE&WT. For through trains, the mainline cab has engineer control of all blocks from the Shreveport Tyler staging yard through the Houston loop. With this system you could just as easily employ a dual-cab panel for the through trains, or several

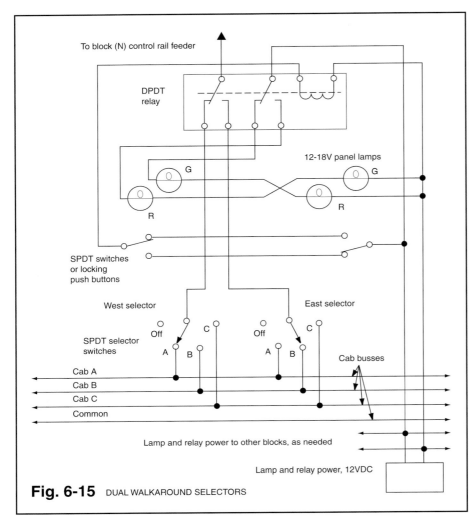

To block (N) control rail feeder

DPDT relay

12-18V panel lamps

G

G

R

R

SPDT switches or locking push buttons

West selector

East selector

SPDT selector switches

Off

C

Off

C

A   B

A   B

Cab busses

Cab A

Cab B

Cab C

Common

Lamp and relay power to other blocks, as needed

Lamp and relay power, 12VDC

Fig. 6-15 DUAL WALKAROUND SELECTORS

Walkaround Selectors

Even with local-priority walkaround control we're still talking about fixed cab panels. The engineers can't exactly walk with their trains but must move "by bounds" from town to town. If you seek more freedom, you'll want to eliminate most or all control panels. Figure 6-13 shows a way to decentralize cab control, spreading it over the entire model railroad.

The schematic at the top of fig. 6-13 shows part of a model railroad; below that you see multiple-cab selectors for four of its blocks. I've shown single-pole, four-throw (SP4T) rotary

mainline engineer cabs. HE&WT's traffic is mostly local, however, so one mainline cab is enough for Cyril.

switches, but switches with more or fewer positions will also work. The unused fourth position on each switch provides an "off" position; switches with more positions would allow for adding more cabs in the future.

The selectors in this scheme would be located along the front edge of the layout, each somewhere along the length of the block it controls, rather than in discrete control panels. As you walked along with your running train, you could set each selector for your own cab as you came to it.

Busses serve as the cab connections for each cab—remember, a "bus" is a heavy wire used to make similar connections at many locations. A common bus also connects the "C" or common feeders. At a convenient

point each cab has one output wire connected to its own bus and the other to the common bus.

As in other control schemes we've considered, the cabs themselves don't make any difference to the selector wiring. They should be walkaround throttles of some type, to take advantage of the decentralized selectors. You could use push-button throttles with multiple control stations, or you might choose hand-held throttles with multiple plug stations for the cable tethers, perhaps with a memory feature to keep the trains running while you unplugged the cable to move to a new location. The ultimate choice might be some wireless throttle that wouldn't have to be plugged into the layout. In relation to the selector wiring these walkaround throttles are all the same. Moreover, you could have any combination of throttle types connected to the cab busses.

Walkaround Selectors on the Racquette River RR

Figure 6-14 shows how walkaround selectors might be arranged on a medium-size railroad, the HO scale Racquette River RR by Leonard Blumenschine. You can see how the walkaround selectors would enable you to start a train out of the small yard at Purdy and follow it along the aisle to the tunnel at Altamont.

Next you'd take a step or two back to the right to meet the train at the lower tunnel portal, and follow it again through Rive Gauche and Fieldpiece. At the right end of Fieldpiece you'd wait until the train ducked out of sight, because it would loop around and return to you through the upper tunnel portal to enter the Piercefield yard.

I've shown individual selectors for the yards at Purdy and Piercefield, with a selector and other controls for the Piercefield roundhouse, block 0. These controls would connect any roundhouse or lead track to the cab selected by the block 0 selector. If operation became busier, either yard or both could use local-priority cab

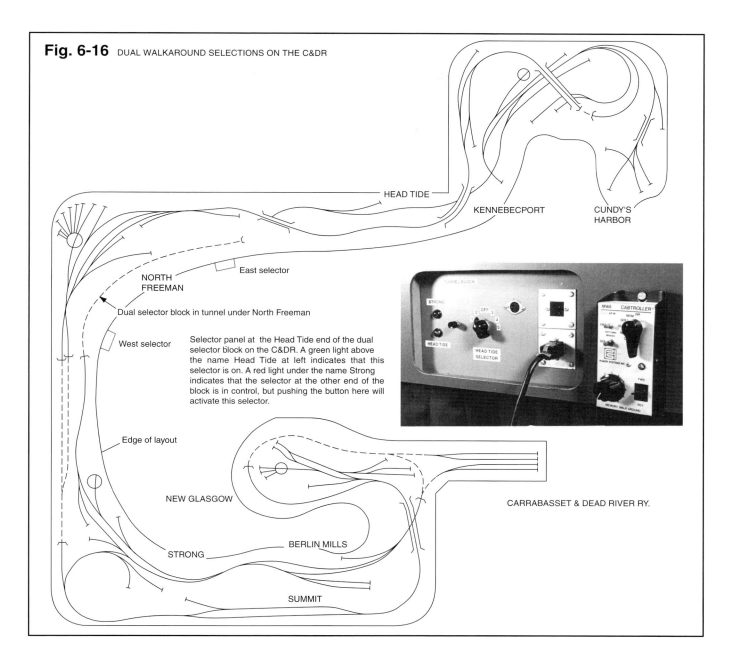

Fig. 6-16 DUAL WALKAROUND SELECTIONS ON THE C&DR

HEAD TIDE

KENNEBECPORT

CUNDY'S HARBOR

East selector

NORTH FREEMAN

Dual selector block in tunnel under North Freeman

West selector

Selector panel at the Head Tide end of the dual selector block on the C&DR. A green light above the name Head Tide at left indicates that this selector is on. A red light under the name Strong indicates that the selector at the other end of the block is in control, but pushing the button here will activate this selector.

Edge of layout

NEW GLASGOW

CARRABASSET & DEAD RIVER RY.

STRONG

BERLIN MILLS

SUMMIT

panels, perhaps with tethered, handheld cabs to give the yardmasters a little walkaround freedom.

Dual Walkaround Selectors

Compromises are usually necessary when locating walkaround selectors. Unless a block is short, the ideal place for the selector is the end your train is coming from. That way you can stay close to your train and set the selector for your cab just before the train enters the block. Although selectors at the east end of every

block would be convenient for the engineers of westbound trains, they would be in the least convenient location for running eastbound. The ordinary compromise: Put the selectors near the middle of each block. This is equally inconvenient for engineers coming from either direction. A selector at each end of a block would be nice, especially for a long block or in a place where the engineers would have to double back frequently along a narrow aisle. The wiring in fig. 6-15 accomplishes exactly that. When

your train approaches the dual-selector block, you set the near selector for your cab, then push the button to turn on that selector.

The optional indicator lights make it easy for an engineer to decide whether to throw the switch. A green light means "this selector is already turned on," while a red light means "throw the switch to turn on this selector." The diagram shows double-throw switches because they make it easier to see how the dual selectors work, but the easiest controls to use

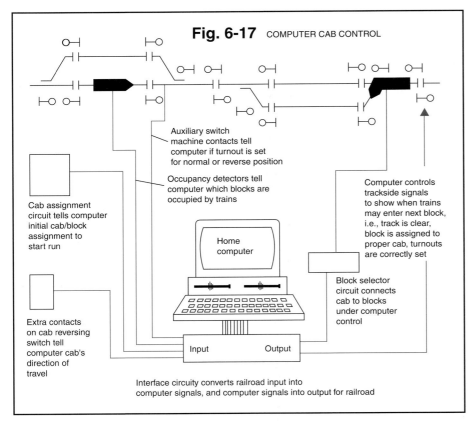

Fig. 6-17 COMPUTER CAB CONTROL

Cab assignment circuit tells computer initial cab/block assignment to start run

Extra contacts on cab reversing switch tell computer cab's direction of travel

Auxiliary switch machine contacts tell computer if turnout is set for normal or reverse position

Occupancy detectors tell computer which blocks are occupied by trains

Home computer

Input   Output

Computer controls trackside signals to show when trains may enter next block, i.e., track is clear, block is assigned to proper cab, turnouts are correctly set

Block selector circuit connects cab to blocks under computer control

Interface circuity converts railroad input into computer signals, and computer signals into output for railroad

are double-throw locking push buttons. With this arrangement a red light simply means "push the button." Figure 6-16 shows a pushbutton-controlled dual walkaround selector on Bob Hayden's HOn2½ Carrabasset & Dead River Ry.

The C&DR track plan shows how the dual selectors conveniently control the long block between Head Tide and Strong. Bob uses ordinary single walkaround selectors for his other blocks. You could use dual walkaround selectors for every block on a model railroad, but they aren't always necessary. Looking again at the Racquette River RR in fig. 6-14, you can see dual selectors might be a good idea for block 6 around the end of the layout's peninsula, but a block that loops back on itself like block 3 is more easily controlled with a single selector.

Advanced Cab Control

I'll close this chapter by briefly explaining three cab control systems

beyond the scope of this book. The first is route cab control. This is a way of simplifying engineer cab control by using a single rotary selector to turn blocks on ahead of a train and to turn them off behind it. The "route" part of the name comes from the route levers that let the rotary selector control passing sidings and other alternate routes.

The complexity of your route cab control system depends on you, with such sophisticated possibilities as cab signals showing track conditions down the line and near-automatic turnout control for the route the engineer selects. Its central limitation is that the engineer remains fixed in one place: at the route cab panel. Once you have the nearly automatic route cab, however, only a slight increase in complexity will produce a totally automatic route cab. Instead of the rotary selector use a solenoid stepper switch as the main control, employing the same block detection

that operates the cab signals to automatically advance the stepper. This gives you progressive cab control.

Progressive cab control can be the basis of a walkaround system, because after you set the cab to start a train from a given point, it can keep a walkaround throttle connected to the train wherever the engineer goes. A signal system is also necessary, however, to inform the engineer if he is in danger of running his train into a block beyond the progressive cab's control—if this happens the train will be out of control until the cab is reset.

The job of the progressive cab is threefold: It "reads" the track conditions ahead of a train, advances the selector to keep the throttle connected to the train as it moves, and sets signals to let the engineer know whether to stop or run his train. Multiply these functions by the number of cabs and you face many simultaneous decisions to keep the railroad running, a job perfectly suited for a microcomputer—the typical home computer.

Figure 6-17 shows, in block diagram, how a computer cab control system can work. An operator, either an engineer or the dispatcher, "initializes" a cab by telling the computer that a train in a given block is to proceed in a given direction, and the computer—as long as the engineer follows signal indications—keeps the cab connected to the train. For a description of one computer cab control system, see Lorell Joiner's article in the April 1983 issue of MODEL RAILROADER Magazine. Bruce Chubb's series of MR articles, "The C/MRI: A computer/model railroad interface," and book, *Build Your Own Universal Computer Interface* (Tab Books), explains how to connect a computer to a model railroad for cab control and other purposes. See the February through August 1985 issues of MR for installments describing the basic C/MRI system, and the October through December 1985 issues for computer cab control with the C/MRI.

Locating blocks

C H A P T E R   S E V E N

If you use cab control, how you locate your blocks is as important as the selector system you choose. The length of blocks and location of block boundaries have a lot to do with making a model railroad easy and fun to operate. The "right" block locations depend upon your track plan and how you want your railroad to operate, so only you can choose the best way to accomplish this.

This chapter will explain what to consider when choosing block locations and show you several workable approaches. Don't worry about getting it right the first time. Once finished, you'll always find unexpected ways to operate your railroad. Besides, rearranging block boundaries is fairly easy.

Most block location decisions force you to choose between simplicity and flexibility. In general, the fewer blocks you have the simpler, because you'll need less wiring and have fewer selectors to throw. Fewer blocks, however, give you less operating flexibility. Fewer blocks limit the number of independent trains and engines you can run, and the ones you can run will get in each others' way more often, at least electrically.

If, like me, you enjoy operating trains in prototypical fashion, you'll probably choose flexibility at the expense of simplicity. On the other hand, if you just want to turn 'em on and watch 'em run, you'll find my approach to block location needlessly complicated. I'll illustrate how to give your railroad the most in operating flexibility, and leave it up to you to take whatever simpler approach you see fit.

Locating Blocks on Track Plans

In barest principle, you can "block" your layout—divide it into control blocks—by marking off segments of main line at least as long as the normal-length train you expect to run. This principle, however, becomes a little too bare when your railroad includes yards, sidings, and other fun elements. As I'll explain shortly, the length of the track is not the only factor determining block locations. Still, thinking in terms of train length helps to clarify the principles, because one way of defining a block is to say it's

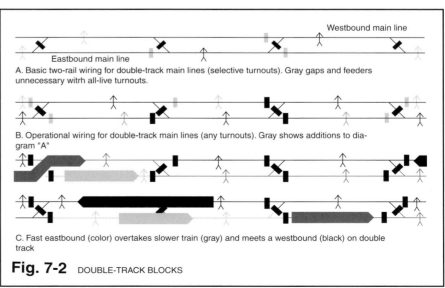

A. Basic two-rail wiring for a passing track (selective turnouts)

B. Operational wiring for a passing track (any turnouts). Color show additions to diagram "A"

C. Two trains meet at passing track

Block and train controlled by cab. A: cab. B:

Fig. 7-1   PASSING TRACK BLOCKS

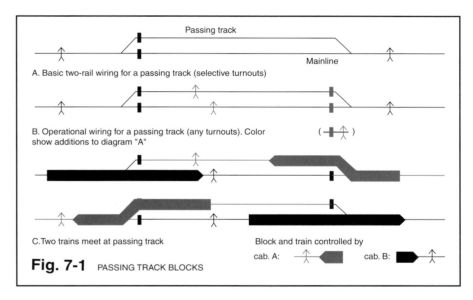

A. Basic two-rail wiring for double-track main lines (selective turnouts). Gray gaps and feeders unnecessary witrh all-live turnouts.

B. Operational wiring for double-track main lines (any turnouts). Gray shows additions to diagram "A"

C. Fast eastbound (color) overtakes slower train (gray) and meets a westbound (black) on double track

Fig. 7-2   DOUBLE-TRACK BLOCKS

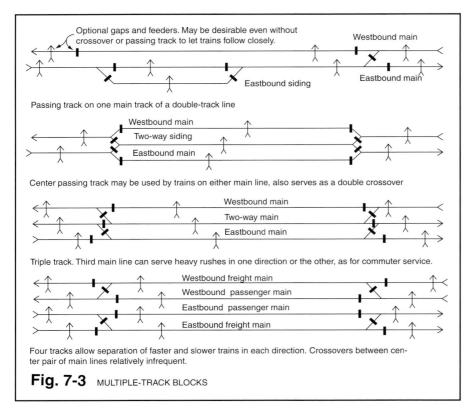

Optional gaps and feeders. May be desirable even without crossover or passing track to let trains follow closely.

Westbound main

Eastbound siding

Eastbound main

Passing track on one main track of a double-track line

Westbound main

Two-way siding

Eastbound main

Center passing track may be used by trains on either main line, also serves as a double crossover

Westbound main

Two-way main

Eastbound main

Triple track. Third main line can serve heavy rushes in one direction or the other, as for commuter service.

Westbound freight main

Westbound passenger main

Eastbound passenger main

Eastbound freight main

Four tracks allow separation of faster and slower trains in each direction. Crossovers between center pair of main lines relatively infrequent.

Fig. 7-3 MULTIPLE-TRACK BLOCKS

an electrical control section that can be occupied by only one independent train at a time. Under these terms having blocks shorter than a normal train makes little sense, but I must add two qualifications. One is that normal train length varies from railroad to railroad, depending mostly on the lengths of yard tracks and sidings. The second is that situations can emerge, which I'll explain, where it's helpful to have blocks shorter than a train.

I like to start by marking a track plan for those gaps required for two-rail wiring (see Chapter 3). Then I analyze the plan's operational features—passing sidings, yards, and so forth—and add gaps to define blocks that will allow the best and most flexible use of those features.

The process could go the other way: Put in operating blocks, then check if all two-rail requirements are satisfied. In most cases the blocks you want for operational reasons will provide the gaps you need for two-rail insulation, but check to make sure.

Remember that the turnouts you use make a difference. We've seen, in Chapter 3, that all-live turnouts need fewer gaps for two-rail insulation, but the converse is true for operational purposes. The turnouts you use will

determine how to block your layout.

You saw what's needed for two-rail insulation in Chapter 3, so here I'll start by reviewing a few basic operating situations. Then we'll examine how they apply to a whole track plan.

Passing Tracks

A passing track is a double-ended siding in predominantly single-track territory, long enough to hold a train clear of the main line while another train passes. Figure 7-1A is a schematic drawing of a passing siding with just the gaps and feeders needed to isolate the frog-to-frog turnouts. It shows selective turnouts; all-live turnouts would need none of the gaps and only one set of feeders in any location.

In fig. 7-1B I've added gaps and feeders to make separate blocks of both the main track and the passing track between the turnouts. This is the essential operational wiring for a passing track with either selective or all-live turnouts.

The meeting of two trains (a "meet") in fig. 7-1C shows the flexibility of the wiring. The trains can enter or leave opposite ends of the two tracks simultaneously, just as they can on a real railroad where no power blocks are involved. Other, more complex maneuvers are possible, such as three-train meets and double saw-bys.

Note that having a siding long enough to hold a train—or trains short enough to fit the siding—automatically gives us train-length blocks between the siding turnouts. In cases like this the design of the railroad determines block length.

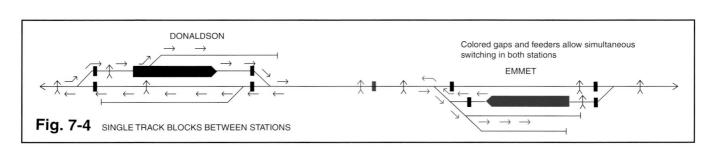

DONALDSON

Colored gaps and feeders allow simultaneous switching in both stations

EMMET

Fig. 7-4 SINGLE TRACK BLOCKS BETWEEN STATIONS

Double Track

Double track means two parallel main lines, usually with one designated for traffic in each direction. Crossovers are typically located at intervals to let trains move from one main line to the other. The minimum double-track wiring in fig. 7-2A permits eastbound and westbound trains to run without interference.

The gaps and feeders in color are unnecessary with all-live turnouts. The gaps in the crossovers between the two lines are unnecessary too, and you can get by with just one set of feeders—but why have double track unless you can run at least two trains independently?

The operational wiring in fig. 7-2B increases flexibility in two ways. For one it lets trains follow each other more closely on either track, allowing you to run more trains on the line simultaneously—"increased track capacity," they'd say on the prototype.

Even more fun is the capability of using the crossovers to run trains "against the current of traffic," or opposed to the normal direction assigned a given track, for the fancy maneuver shown in fig. 7-2C. If your terminals can generate enough trains to keep a main line this busy, double track can pose as many enjoyable operating challenges as single track.

Figure 7-3 shows blocking for other multiple-track situations I won't discuss in detail. Note that the idea behind both single track with passing sidings and multiple-track situations is to provide independent blocks on all tracks between passing-track turnouts or crossovers.

Again, the track features determine block length. For most double- or multiple-track operating maneuvers you'll want crossovers at least a train-length apart, keeping in mind that these features help define a railroad's train length.

Single-Track Switching

The block locations we've seen involve running trains, but blocks should also be located for conve-

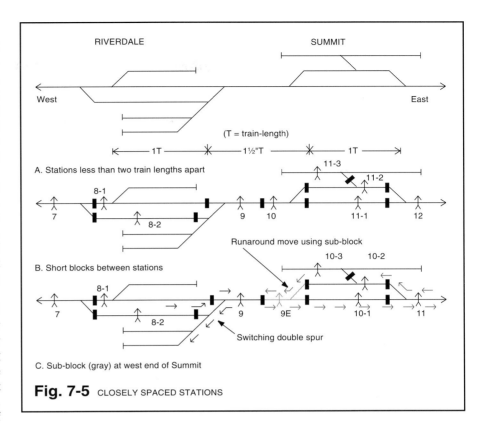

Fig. 7-5 CLOSELY SPACED STATIONS

nience when trains stop to switch. Consider fig. 7-4: An eastbound way freight at Donaldson and a westbound way freight at Emmett both need to use parts of the main line between those stations to perform their switching. With at least two blocks between the stations, the two trains can work independently without electrical interference.

Here we have choices to make about block length. We'd like the stations on a model railroad located as far apart as possible, but often they have to be close together if we want to include many of them. If stations are less than two train-lengths apart, how do we let trains share the main line in between for switching?

Figure 7-5 provides a couple of answers. In fig. 7-5A, Riverdale and Summit are only 1½ train-lengths apart. The diagram in fig. 7-5B takes the most obvious way out and puts a block boundary halfway between the stations. This is convenient for the local trains, but if your train is just

passing through you now have to worry about an extra block selector.

It's often a good idea to make things as easy as possible for the through-train engineers, even at the expense of additional complexity for the local crews—who probably wouldn't be running the way freights if they didn't enjoy a little complication. In fig. 7-5C a short and specialized local-priority block, which I'll call a sub-block, keeps operation simple for the through trains while accommodating the way freights too.

When the switch for sub-block 9E is in its normal "off" position, the sub-block is just a part of block 9. When you run a train between Riverdale and Summit you select only one block, block 9, to travel from station to station. When a way freight switching at Summit needs to run around its train, however, the engineer can switch the sub-block "on" and use it as a separate block. Meanwhile, another train switching at Riverdale can use block 9 without interference.

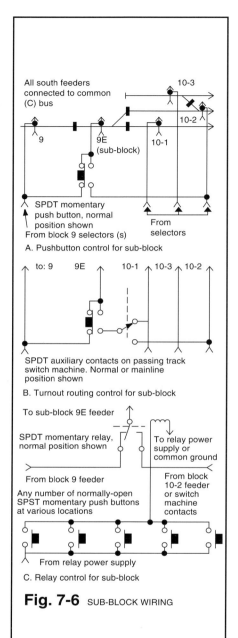

A. Pushbutton control for sub-block

All south feeders connected to common (C) bus

10-3
10-2
10-1
9
9E (sub-block)

SPDT momentary push button, normal position shown
From block 9 selectors (s)
From selectors

to: 9   9E   10-1   10-3   10-2

SPDT auxiliary contacts on passing track switch machine. Normal or mainline position shown

B. Turnout routing control for sub-block

To sub-block 9E feeder

SPDT momentary relay, normal position shown
To relay power supply or common ground

From block 9 feeder
From block 10-2 feeder or switch machine contacts

Any number of normally-open SPST momentary push buttons at various locations

From relay power supply

C. Relay control for sub-block

Fig. 7-6 SUB-BLOCK WIRING

I'll explain the wiring for the sub-block shortly, but first note that in fig. 7-5 the sub-block works better at the west end of Summit than at the east end of Riverdale. A train switching the double spur tracks at Riverdale needs to use most of block 9, so a short sub-block there wouldn't help much. On the other hand, at Summit the reason for using any of the main line between stations is to run around the train to set up moves in and out of the switch-back. Even if the sub-block is only long enough to let an engine and a couple of cars get clear west of the turnout points, it will still be helpful.

Wiring Sub-Blocks

Figure 7-6 shows how to wire the sub-block, with a couple of variations. The track schematic is a close-up of the west end of Summit station and the east end of block 9 from fig. 7-5. In fig. 7-6A sub-block 9E is wired through an SPDT (single-pole, double-throw) momentary push button. A momentary button is spring-loaded to stay in its normal position; you must push in and hold it to use the other position, and when you release it, it returns to normal. When you push the button in fig. 7-6A, sub-block 9E becomes powered by whichever cab has selected block 10-2. Release the button to normal and 9E is again powered by whichever cab has selected block 9.

I chose to connect the sub-block push button to siding block 10-2 in fig. 7-6A, because the local freight that needs to use the sub-block will probably have stopped in the siding and be

using block 10-2 anyway. If you don't want to make that assumption, or just want to allow additional flexibility in using the sub-block, use the wiring shown in fig. 7-6B. That way, when you push the button the sub-block will be powered from either mainline block 10-1 or siding block 10-2, depending on which way the siding turnout is thrown. (See Chapter 9 for a detailed explanation of switch-machine auxiliary contacts.)

I've assumed only one button operates the sub-block, located either on a local-priority cab panel or on the layout front for walkaround control. If you want to operate the sub-block from two or more control locations, use the relay wiring shown in fig. 7-6C.

Remember that a relay is a remote-controlled switch that uses an electromagnet—a solenoid coil—to move its contacts. Like the momentary push button, a momentary relay is spring-loaded to return to its normal position whenever the coil is not energized. In fig. 7-6C, pressing any button energizes the relay and operates the sub-block; releasing the button again makes the sub-block a part of block 9.

Entering and Leaving Terminals

Later in this chapter I'll discuss locating yard blocks, but for now I'd like to make a point that summarizes what we've seen of blocking for operating situations. Our goal is to locate blocks to take advantage of track patterns so that any train movement that can be made on the track will also be possible electrically. Trains tend naturally to crowd together at yards; thus, a yard offers a good illustration of this point.

In fig. 7-7 I've used a schematic version of a yard appearing in Chapter 2 of John Armstrong's book, *Track Planning for Realistic Operation*, third edition, to illustrate how to block a terminal to let several activities happen at once. In a small yard four independent trains or engines could move at once—more, even, if the turntable leads were blocked as I'll show you later in this chapter. This movement

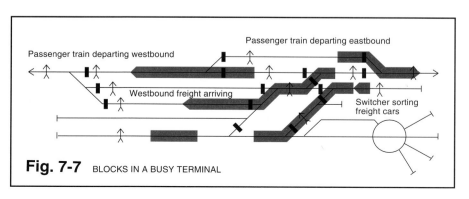

Passenger train departing eastbound
Passenger train departing westbound
Westbound freight arriving
Switcher sorting freight cars

Fig. 7-7 BLOCKS IN A BUSY TERMINAL

is fun to watch, useful in avoiding congestion, and prototypical in that the trains can perform as necessary without delays because power can't be switched to the tracks the trains must use.

Note that the yard block locations form patterns similar to those we've seen at passing tracks, on multiple tracks, and even between stations. When you grow accustomed to seeing these patterns you'll be able to block a layout almost automatically, because you'll recognize how the wiring arrangements follow track arrangements.

Blocking a Layout

In fig. 7-8 I've used Gordon Odegard's Genoa & Eastern Ry. track plan to illustrate block locations on a medium-size model railroad. For the sake of demonstration I made the assumption the G&E would be built with selective turnouts, and began by marking the gaps shown in black to accommodate two-rail insulation.

I started at Tower 4, schematically at the east end of the railroad. You can start anywhere, of course, but it helps to be systematic. From the east end I worked my way west, marking gaps between pairs of turnouts located frog-to-frog. In most cases I put the gaps closer to one turnout or the other of the pair they separate. That way they usually end up in the right places to serve as block boundaries.

The G&E doesn't have reversing tracks except for the two turntables. If it had a loop or a wye, I'd have also marked gaps to isolate it in my first pass over the plan. On the other hand I didn't worry about feeders at this stage, because their locations become obvious after the block boundaries are determined.

With the basic insulation established I worked my way around the plan again, this time marking the block-boundary gaps in color. As I did so I made assumptions about how the railroad would be operated. Because it's basically a point-to-point plan, with stub terminals and many industrial

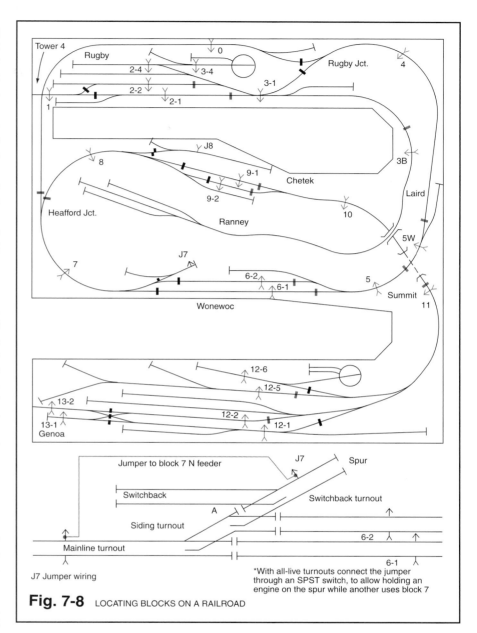

Fig. 7-8 LOCATING BLOCKS ON A RAILROAD

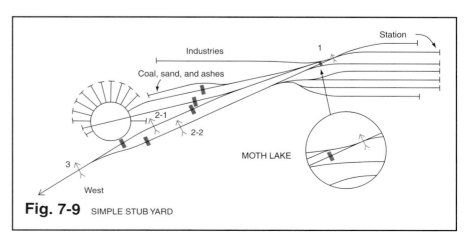

Fig. 7-9 SIMPLE STUB YARD

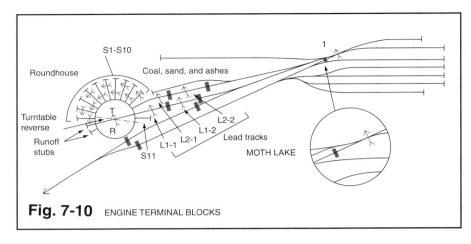

Fig. 7-10 ENGINE TERMINAL BLOCKS

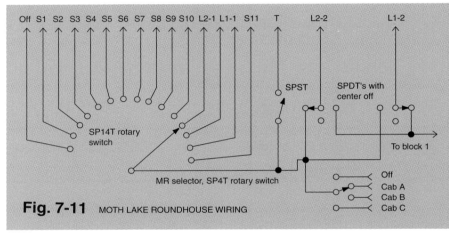

Fig. 7-11 MOTH LAKE ROUNDHOUSE WIRING

sidings, switching will be a big part of the fun. On that basis I wanted several trains and engines to switch at the same time with little interference.

Starting from Tower 4 again, follow the blocks around in numerical order to see how I've blocked the G&E. As I've said, I'll go into more detail about blocking yards later in this chapter, so I won't explain everything I've done in the yard at Rugby (or at Genoa). For the same reason I haven't shown wiring for the turntables or engine-house tracks.

Notice at Rugby, however, how block 3-1 extends up the mine branch from Ranney Switch, permitting its use as a drill track or switching lead. Past the bridge I've made the branch an independent block, so the mine run can work up at Ranney without bothering the Rugby switcher.

Returning to the main line, block 4 travels up to Laird but stops short of the spur turnout. Block 5 includes the sub-block 5W—the west end of 5—to enable a train coming from Rugby to switch the spur at Laird while another train works at Wonewoc. Wire the sub-block as shown in fig. 7-6.

At Wonewoc I've labeled the switchback J7 to indicate it would be fed by a jumper from block 7, as shown in the inset in fig. 7-8. At A I'd gap just the N rail to isolate the turnouts, so that S-rail power for J7 would be switched by the mainline and siding turnouts. That way you could hold an engine in J7 while another ran in 7. To achieve the same operation with all-live turnouts you'd need an on-off (SPST) switch in the jumper, as explained in the inset note.

Heafford Junction represents a

handy place to divide blocks 7 and 8, so two blocks lie between the towns of Wonewoc and Chetek. The continuous-run connection from Heafford Junction back to Rugby Junction isn't part of the point-to-point operating schematic; here I've labeled it block 0 (zero). Switchback J8 at Chetek is handled in the same way as J7, but with the S rail gapped and jumpered instead of the N rail.

You need two blocks between Chetek and Genoa, especially since the main line out of Genoa will have to be used as a drill track. Because no turnout lies between these towns I put the boundary of blocks 10 and 11 at a tunnel portal. A landmark like that will help operators remember where the boundary is.

At Genoa the only unusual arrangement is block 12-5. This stub track could be fed through the turnouts from block 11, but it's long and branches into a couple of spurs. Making it an independent block allows a switcher to work there while other trains come and go. By the way, if either J7 or J8 were longer and had enough spurs to let an engine get in there and switch without returning to the main line for awhile, I'd have made it an independent block with its own selector.

Blocks for Special Situations

Just about every model railroad will face situations where the general rule of one train length equals one block isn't enough. The central idea is to analyze how a given track layout would be operated, then design wiring for the way the railroad will be used.

Yard. As I pointed out earlier in this chapter, trains and engines naturally tend to crowd together at yards and roundhouses. The goal in wiring these areas is to make handling the congestion convenient and efficient. That means using a lot of independent blocks, many of which can be short since they'll mainly isolate engines and not whole trains.

To start with a simple example, fig. 7-9 shows the stub-ended Moth Lake

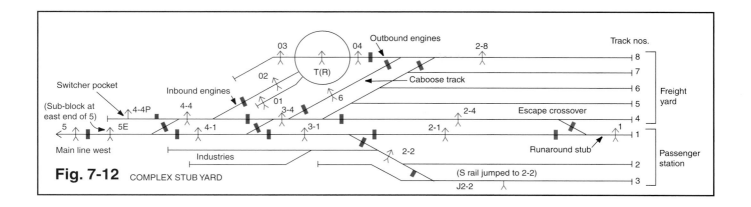

Fig. 7-12 COMPLEX STUB YARD

yard from Leonard Blumenschine's Moth Lake & Mt. Ahab RR track plan. Four blocks handle everything except the roundhouse and its lead tracks, which I'll discuss later. Block 3 is the main line extending west from Moth Lake, block 21 is a combination arrival/departure and thoroughfare track, block 2-2 is the yard lead or drill track, and block 1 is a combined escape track, station track, and industrial switching lead.

An arriving passenger train could pull in through blocks 3, 2-1, and 1, without disturbing a switcher working the yard from block 2-2. After unloading, it would back into 2-1 or 2-2 and drop its cars for the switcher to put away, then the engine would pull ahead into block 1 again to escape to the roundhouse leads.

An incoming freight could follow the same procedure if it were short enough. A longer one would pull into block 1 until its caboose was clear in 2-1. While the road engine uncoupled in 1, the switcher could come out of block 2-2 into 3, couple to the train in 2-1, then back out into 3 to break the train up on 2-2, leaving the road engine clear to back to the roundhouse leads.

An outbound passenger train could simply be spotted at the station for loading in block 1, and its engine could back out from the roundhouse, couple on, and leave town through 2-1 and 3, again leaving the switcher undisturbed in 2-2. Getting a long freight out would be more complicated. Probably

the best way would be for the switcher to build the train in the yard and extending out into the yard lead. Then it would have to stay clear on one of the block 1 spurs or a roundhouse lead, so the freight engine could leave the other roundhouse lead and join its train via 1, 2-1, and 3.

It would be handier to put a short spur at the west end of block 2-2 to serve as a switcher pocket, a place to hold the switch engine out of the way, but that's a consideration for track planning, not wiring. If you look at the original plan you'll see there just isn't room for such a pocket.

When the switcher had cars to deliver to the industries or engine service facilities, it would sort them into delivery order in the yard, then leave them in block 2-2 and run around them via 3 and 2-1 to 1. From there it could pull the cars back into block 1 and use that as a drill track to make its deliveries.

The four main blocks in Moth Lake correspond to the arrangement we've seen for passing tracks on a single-track main line. That's really the basic track plan of this yard, with some spurs and a roundhouse added so it can serve as a terminal. All I've done is recognize that track arrangement, locate the blocks accordingly, and imagine how the yard would be operated to ensure the blocks would support the operation.

Engine terminal. Let's look closely at the Moth Lake roundhouse, fig. 7-10. This is a good-sized engine ter-

minal for a model railroad, but still a simple one in plan. It provides a good example because it includes the most important basics: a turntable, a roundhouse with several stall tracks (the number is unimportant; they're all alike electrically), and two turntable leads (you can get by with one, but that's restrictive). The coal, sand, and ash spur is nice both for scenic effect and operation—it's a good "industry"—but for wiring it's just another spur off block 1.

Speaking of block 1, the main blocks we looked at earlier are all the same, but I've only identified block 1 in fig. 7-10 because it's the only one that connects to the engine terminal. Note that I've shown block 1 ending at the gaps just past the turntable lead turnouts. That's so you can move engines on the leads independently of what might be happening in block 1.

Each lead track is divided into two short blocks, and each of them is about the same length as the turntable—a good indication of how long the biggest engines on this railroad can be. We're only concerned with engines here, not trains, so we want engine-length blocks to let them bunch up. When the leads are long enough you can allow a block for an engine at each servicing and ready spot, but with shorter leads like these two blocks per track is the best we can achieve.

The turntable is a separate block too, block T. That's so you can park an engine on the table and turn it off, a

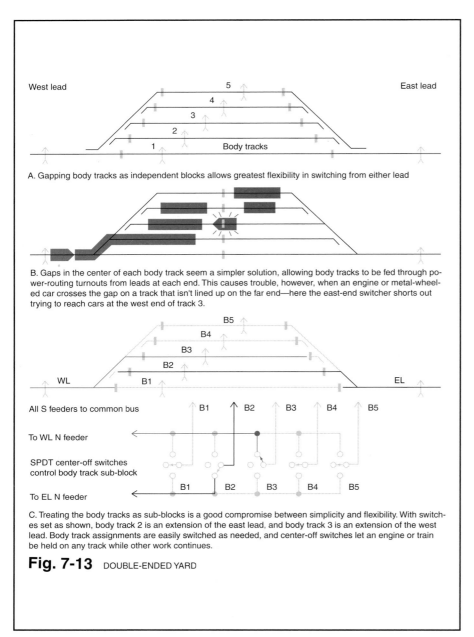

A. Gapping body tracks as independent blocks allows greatest flexibility in switching from either lead

B. Gaps in the center of each body track seem a simpler solution, allowing body tracks to be fed through power-routing turnouts from leads at each end. This causes trouble, however, when an engine or metal-wheeled car crosses the gap on a track that isn't lined up on the far end—here the east-end switcher shorts out trying to reach cars at the west end of track 3.

C. Treating the body tracks as sub-blocks is a good compromise between simplicity and flexibility. With switches set as shown, body track 2 is an extension of the east lead, and body track 3 is an extension of the west lead. Body track assignments are easily switched as needed, and center-off switches let an engine or train be held on any track while other work continues.

Fig. 7-13 DOUBLE-ENDED YARD

handy capability when you're shuffling engines on the leads.

Remember the turntable is a reversing track, as shown by the "R" next to the block T feeders. The easiest way to handle that is with one of the automatic reversing schemes we examined in Chapter 4. The dotted line labeled "turntable reverse" is the most convenient switching line: The pit-rail gaps should lie along that line, or the commutator brushes should lie on opposite sides of it, so that whenever the table crosses the line the polarity of its rails reverses.

Each stall track is also a separate block, S1 through S11. The short runoff stubs, which line up with the leads across the turntable, don't require wiring. Their only function is to catch the wheels when an excessively enthusiastic hostler overshoots the turntable.

Roundhouse wiring. That gives us 16 blocks in this engine terminal, close to the number needed for all the rest of the ML&MtA RR! They don't all need cab-selector switches, though. As fig. 7-11 shows, all of these can be grouped with one selector, which I've labeled MR for Moth Lake Roundhouse. The MR selector, which could contain fewer or more positions depending on the number of cabs, determines which cab controls the roundhouse blocks. The other four switches determine the blocks actually connected to the MR selector. I've shown a rotary switch to energize the tracks radiating from the turntable. Each of these could have its own SPST switch, like the one shown to turn the turntable (T) on or off. A rotary, however, ensures that only one of these tracks is on at a time, thus reducing your chances of running an engine into the turntable pit.

For L2-1 and L2-2 I've shown SPDT, center-off switches. These could be SPSTs as well, but the double-throw switches provide you the option of connecting the outer ends of the leads to block 1 instead of MR. That way one engineer can run an engine into or out of a lead while another hostles locomotives in the roundhouse and on the other lead.

Another way to handle the Moth Lake roundhouse would be to control it with its own local-priority hostler cab, as we saw in Chapter 6. In that case the hostler cab should be able to select block 1 and the MR block, so you could use it to shuffle engines between the leads without using the turntable.

Complex stub yard. Shown in fig. 7-12 is a more complex stub yard, taken from John Armstrong's Track Planning for Realistic Operation, third edition. Like the Moth Lake yard, it's designed to get the most operation from the available tracks by using many of them for more than one purpose. Complications increase because of the several crossovers between parallel tracks, but when you analyze the yard's operating capabilities, its added flexibility becomes apparent.

For example, an arriving passenger train would pull in on track 1. Its engine would uncouple from the train in block 2-1, and pull ahead into the runaround stub in block 1. Then the engine would back through the escape crossover to reach the inbound turntable lead via track 4, using blocks 2-4, 3-4, and 4-4.

On the other hand, when a freight arrives it enters on track 4. The engine uncouples in block 2-4, heads through the escape crossover into block 1, then backs out track 1 to reach the turntable lead. Inevitably, these multiple uses will conflict with each other from time to time—maybe the switcher won't have time to move those passenger cars from track 1 before the freight shows up—so this yard needs plenty of blocks to isolate trains from each other when operation intensifies.

Block 2-2, like 2-8, arises out of a crossover/switchback situation, and makes track 3 an independent industrial switching lead as well as a station track. The single feeder labeled J2-2 is just like the switchback jumper in fig. 7-8. It lets you power track 3 through the crossover without a separate selector or power switch, so you can hold the switcher on track 3 while a train uses block 2-2 to arrive or depart on track 2.

Block 3-4 only powers a short stretch of track 4, but it also powers freight-yard tracks 5–7 through the ladder turnouts. On the other hand, block C, the caboose track, really is short. You could wire it with an SPDT, center-off switch as a dual-control sub-block (explained below and shown in fig. 7-13C), and power it from either block 3-4 or 2-8 depending on which way the switch was thrown.

The radial tracks around the turntable (01-04) would be controlled by an SP5T rotary switch, with a separate cab selector switch as in fig. 7-11. That selector would also power the turntable, T(R), through an SPST switch to activate the table track.

In this case the drill track, block 4-4, includes a switcher pocket. I've shown it with one gap and one feeder (4-4P) to be powered from 4-4 by an SPST switch. You could just rely on throwing the crossover to kill power to the switcher, but at times you'd have both an inbound engine to get to the roundhouse lead and a passenger train departing on track 1.

Sub-block 5E would be wired as in fig. 7-6B. That way engines using the far-left crossover for runaround or escape moves could take power from blocks 4-1 and 4-4 and not interfere with trains farther out on the main line in block 5.

Also, note that the block patterns around crossovers in this yard are similar to the double—and multiple track—examples in figs. 7-2 and 7-3. Again, recognizing these patterns will give you a head start on locating blocks in these situations.

Through yard. You don't need to know much more to block a through or double-ended yard. The basic block pattern in a double-ended yard is like that of the passing siding in fig. 7-1, and for the same reason. You want

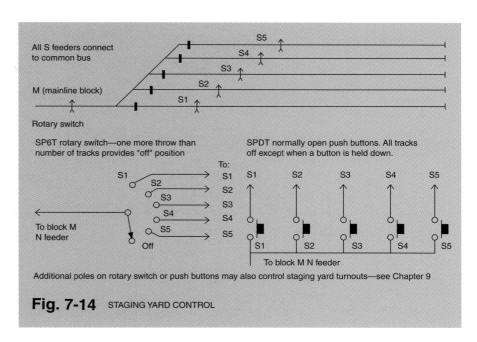

Fig. 7-14 STAGING YARD CONTROL

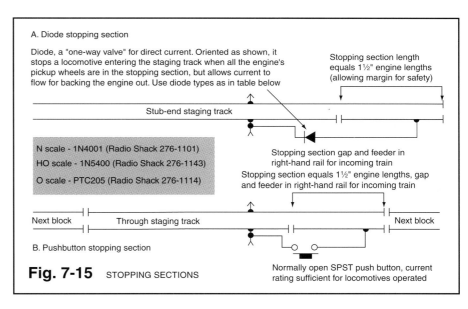

Fig. 7-15 STOPPING SECTIONS

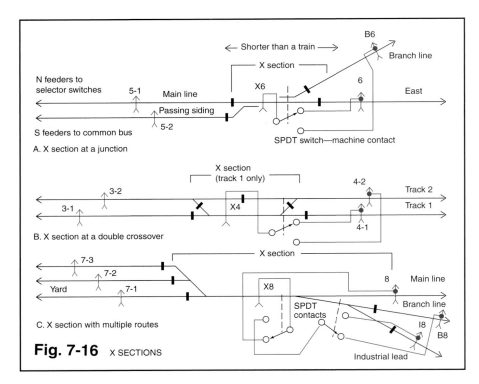

Fig. 7-16 X SECTIONS

A. X section at a junction

B. X section at a double crossover

C. X section with multiple routes

operations to proceed more or less independently at either end, as long as two engines aren't competing to use the same body track at once. Figure 7-13A shows this kind of blocking in a double-ended yard.

You might be tempted to block each double-ended track in the middle with just one set of gaps, as in fig. 7-13B. At least with selective turnouts that looks as if it's a simpler way to control this kind of yard, because each body track doesn't have to be an independent block. The problem, as the figure also shows, is that those middle gaps can give rise to short circuits whenever an engine or—even more annoyingly—a metal-wheeled car crosses them. You end up having to align the turnouts of both ladders for the same track, which spoils any chance of achieving independent switching or train movements at opposite ends of the yard.

You can limit wiring by treating double-ended yard body tracks as dual-control sub-blocks, as shown in fig. 7-13C. Throwing a body track's sub-block switch one way makes it an extension of the lead/ladder block at

one end of the yard, and throwing it the other way turns it into an extension of the opposite lead. The center-off position lets you hold an engine or a train on a body track. This sub-block wiring is particularly economical if your regular block switches can select three or more cabs.

Staging yards. Staging yards are storage tracks employed in many track plans to simulate connections or extensions of the modeled portion of an operating model railroad. If we think of the modeled area as "onstage," staging yards lie "offstage," the "wings" of our model railroad theater. Also called holding or fiddle yards, they are often hidden below a modeled scene, behind a backdrop, or even in another room.

Blocking and wiring for staging yards can be simpler than for onstage yards, because usually little or no switching is performed offstage. A couple of special requirements, however, need mention.

To start, it's best to include a switch or switches to turn off each staging yard track where a train or engine is held. That should be an

obvious requirement if you're using all-live turnouts, but even with power-routing turnouts it's best to provide a way to electrically disconnect each track over and above the selective power feed through the track switches. When you put a train away in a staging yard, you want it to stay put.

A toggle for each track could accomplish this, but two or more could be "on" at once and cause trouble. Instead, add a rotary switch including a position for each track and a separate "off" position. Another way: Control each track with a normally open push button, so that an engineer would have to hold a button down to send power to his train. Figure 7-14 illustrates both methods.

The other special requirement of staging yard wiring is that often engineers must stop trains they can't see. A special sub-block called a stopping section solves this problem. A stopping section is simply an engine-length rail not normally powered for a train entering the staging track. Even though an engineer can't see his train, stopping sections ensure that his train halts in the right place.

Figure 7-15 shows a couple of ways to wire stopping sections. The simplest is the diode method, fig. 7-15A, which is useful in stub-end staging yards where trains must back out once they have entered. A diode passes current in one direction only. Remember that the direction, or polarity, of current flow determines the direction of our locomotives' movement.

Oriented as shown, a diode makes the stopping section an open circuit—in effect "turned off"—for a train running forward to enter the staging track. When all the engine's pickup wheels enter the open-circuit section it will stop. To back the train out, however, you merely reverse the direction switch; current flowing the other way passes through the diode as if it were a solid wire, and the engine moves out in reverse.

Diode stopping sections don't help, however, in double-ended staging yards where trains or engines continue in the same direction after entering. In that case, use a normally open push button in place of a diode, as shown in fig. 7-15B. It will provide the same automatic open-circuit stop protection as the diode, and when an engineer wants to take a train out of a staging track he simply holds the button down until the engine is clear of the stopping section. The same principle applies whether the double-ended staging yard is part of a continuous track plan schematic or is wrapped around a reversing loop.

X sections. The X section, so named by Paul Mallery in a September 1958 MODEL RAILROADER article, is a kind of sub-block often useful at junctions and junctionlike situations, fig. 7-16. In fig. 7-16A, sub-block X6 should be gapped and isolated as shown for maximum flexibility in routing trains, but a separate selector switch for such a short block would be an annoyance for engineers.

Any train passing through the junction, however, will need to use either mainline block 6 or branchline block B6. That means we can use an auxiliary contact on the junction turnout's switch machine to make the X section an extension of either of those two blocks, depending on which way the turnout is thrown. (Instead of a switch machine contact, the X section could be controlled in the same way by an extra pole on the turnout's control switch, as long as it was a holding type and not a momentary switch or button.) An engineer running a train on any route through the junction need select only two blocks, instead of three.

Once you see how this works, you'll find many opportunities to use X sections to simplify your block selector requirements. Figure 7-16B shows an X section situation that can occur on multiple-track lines even without branches. Figure 7-16C shows how an X section can be controlled from multiple routes by contacts on a series of switch machines. Remember

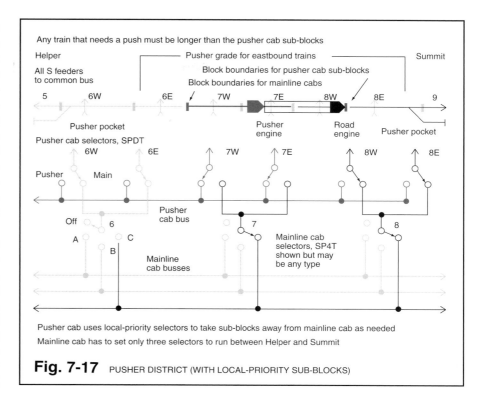

Fig. 7-17 PUSHER DISTRICT (WITH LOCAL-PRIORITY SUB-BLOCKS)

to keep things easy on yourself: If more switches lead out of one end of an X section than the other, do your control wiring on the end with the fewest switches.

Pusher districts. To close this chapter I'd like to suggest a combination of local-priority and sub-block cab control wiring I think is a good idea even though I've never seen it in use on a model railroad. Not that I'm claiming to have invented it; I'm sure somebody, somewhere already uses it.

Mountain railroading with pusher engines on the rear of heavy freight trains is fun to model, but poses problems if we duplicate it with conventional cab control. If the road engine and the pusher run at close to the same speed at a given throttle setting, you can power the train up the hill by making sure both engines remain in blocks connected to the same cab. But what if the engines don't run at the same speed, or you want to have a separate engineer to run the pusher, and maybe even want the pusher to

drop off on the fly once the train is over the summit?

You could simply include a lot of short blocks on the grade, so that the front and rear of a long train remains in different blocks. That means, however, engineers of trains that don't need help, or that are coming down the hill, must handle extra block selectors, an unnecessary annoyance and a potential cause for mistakes.

Figure 7-17 shows a pusher district wired with several short sub-blocks selected by local-priority control from the pusher cab. The pusher engineer has to select each sub-block as he pushes a train up the mountain, but the through-train engineers, even on trains with pushers, can travel over the district with less fuss.

If you attempt this, use it only with some form of walkaround control and block selection, at least for the pusher engineer. This train handling demands that the engineers stay close enough to their locomotives to see what's happening.

Command control

CHAPTER EIGHT

One of the first big advances for many beginning model railroaders is adding a second train. We'll buy that passenger train we've had our eye on, say, and get another power pack to run it. But when we go to make our purchases, the friendly clerk at the hobby shop starts telling us about blocks, cabs, selector switches, and control panels. We start wondering if we're really ready for that second train after all. It's unfortunate, but often our introduction to cab control comes as a splash of cold water on our early enthusiasm for model railroading.

Now it turns out that we can have one cab to directly control one train, a second cab to control another, and no insulated control blocks or cab control panels to get in the way of the fun. It's not as simple as buying another power pack for each engine, true, but command control is the way we always wanted to run our trains.

In Chapter 2 I defined command control as the "simultaneous independent control of multiple trains on electrically continuous tracks." Let me divide that definition into parts and show you just what it promises:

Simultaneous—our railroad will have several trains running at the same time.

Independent control—you'll run your train and I'll run mine, and neither of us will have to worry about the other, except to keep the trains from running into each other. (Real railroaders have to work at that too.)

Multiple trains—with today's newest systems, a hundred trains or more. That's capacity beyond what most of us will ever need, but such numbers also mean we can have many engines on the railroad and only the ones we want to run will be moving.

Electrically continuous tracks—all this happens on a model railroad that is essentially one big block, with power on all the rails (or at least most of them) all the time, permitting us to drive the trains wherever we want.

What Command Control Does

Another way to look at this is to compare command control with cab control in terms of just what is being controlled. Cab control is a system for switching control of sections of

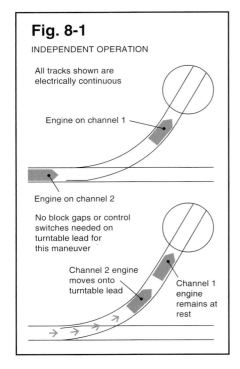

Fig. 8-1

INDEPENDENT OPERATION

All tracks shown are electrically continuous

Engine on channel 1

Engine on channel 2

No block gaps or control switches needed on turntable lead for this maneuver

Channel 2 engine moves onto turntable lead

Channel 1 engine remains at rest

Fig. 8-2. RECEIVER INSTALLATION. An example of a typical command control receiver installation, a Dynatrol model RL receiver in an Athearn HO scale GP38-2. The receiver is the printed circuit board mounted above the rear truck. Two black wires from the receiver connect to the pickup wheels through the frame and the trucks. Two gray wires from the receiver connect to the motor, which is electrically isolated from the track.

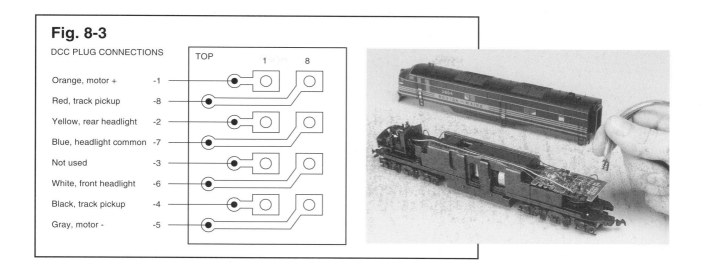

Fig. 8-3

DCC PLUG CONNECTIONS

| | TOP | 1 | 8 |

Orange, motor + -1

Red, track pickup -8

Yellow, rear headlight -2

Blue, headlight common -7

Not used -3

White, front headlight -6

Black, track pickup -4

Gray, motor - -5

track—control blocks—from one power pack or cab to another. The cabs deliver power to the blocks at their individual voltage and polarity settings, and the engines on the layout respond to whatever voltage and polarity they find on the track beneath them.

Command control controls the locomotives directly instead of controlling the track. All track is powered, and the cabs send commands to receivers in the locomotives regulating how they make use of that constant power supply.

Let's consider an example of how this enhances operation. We throw the switch to the turntable lead shown in fig. 8-1. A locomotive is already waiting there, and it's not electrically isolated from our engine on the main track. Nevertheless we can run our engine right into the lead and park it next to the other one without touching any control except our cab. I've been operating model railroads with command control for several years, but I'd been so used to the limitations of cab control that I'm still impressed by this kind of independence and flexibility in control. If you're at all interested in model railroad operation you'll immediately see the possibilities for cooperative switching, independently operated pusher engines, permissive block signaling, and more.

Command control isn't just for big

layouts, either. It's great for any model railroad where you want to run more than one train and especially nice on a small railroad where the trains are always close together. You'll never again have to flip block selectors every few seconds. Also, if you're aiming for the relaxed atmosphere of a shortline or narrow gauge railroad, command control can lend a welcome informality to your operations.

Whatever kind of railroad you have, command control makes it easier to operate with friends. It's especially helpful for first-time guests and youngsters. The best way to impress kids with model railroading is to hand them throttles and let them run your trains.

Electronics Onboard

The biggest price you have to pay for command control is that every locomotive has to carry electronic circuitry to receive and decode the command signals from its assigned cab. So far that's meant that command control users have had to install electronic gear in each engine, which involves finding room for this equipment and rewiring the locomotive, as shown in fig. 8-2. Until recently, with the advent of the National Model Railroad Association's (NMRA) Digital Command Control or DCC standard, you haven't been able to take an engine right out of the box and run it on your command control railroad.

Now a few manufacturers are offering HO locomotives with DCC decoders installed as original equipment. While the choices are still somewhat limited, we can expect to see more DCC-equipped models in the future. For most of us, however, there will still be non-equipped locomotives we already have or would like to own, and there are still good non-DCC command control systems that many model railroaders prefer to use.

Fortunately, installing onboard receivers or decoders isn't as much of a bother as it might seem at first. Fitting a decoder into most locomotives is simple, except those in N scale and the smallest HO narrow gaugers. Even most of these can yield the required space to a determined and reasonably ingenious model railroader, and command control manufacturers are working hard to develop smaller, easier-to-use receivers. Other manufacturers are offering replacement or remachined locomotive frames that allow room for command control electronics in many N scale diesels, and some HO diesels as well.

As an intermediate step between unequipped and off-the-shelf command control locomotives, the NMRA has recommended a so-called DCC socket and plug. Locomotives with these sockets are prewired for command control by the manufacturer, but come with a dummy plug with

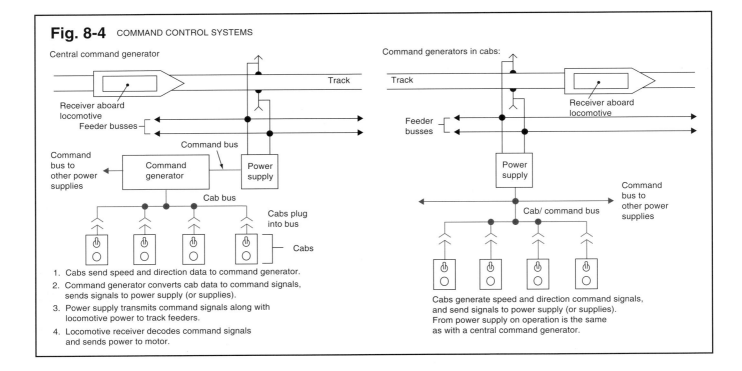

Fig. 8-4 COMMAND CONTROL SYSTEMS

Central command generator

Receiver aboard locomotive

Feeder busses

Track

Command bus to other power supplies

Command generator

Command bus

Cab bus

Power supply

Cabs plug into bus

Cabs

1. Cabs send speed and direction data to command generator.
2. Command generator converts cab data to command signals, sends signals to power supply (or supplies).
3. Power supply transmits command signals along with locomotive power to track feeders.
4. Locomotive receiver decodes command signals and sends power to motor.

Command generators in cabs:

Track

Feeder busses

Receiver aboard locomotive

Power supply

Command bus to other power supplies

Cab/ command bus

Cabs generate speed and direction command signals, and send signals to power supply (or supplies). From power supply on operation is the same as with a central command generator.

jumper connections inserted in this socket to let you take the locomotive out of the box and run it on conventional DC power. To convert to DCC or another command control system, you only have to remove the dummy plug and insert the plug wired to the DCC decoder or other command control receiver, as in fig. 8-3.

Whether the locomotive comes with a DCC plug or not, it makes a big difference that the command control installation can be completed in comfort at your workbench. Combined with the simpler railroad wiring needed for command control, this means you'll spend less time crawling around under your layout. And if you'd really rather not, some hobby shops handling command control equipment also offer installation services.

Carrier Command Control

As I mentioned in Chapter 2, more than one way exists to accomplish command control, most notably with a direct radio or infrared link from cab to locomotive. The most widely accepted form, however, is carrier command control—sometimes simplified to "carrier control"—using the rails to

carry both power and control signals. As long as we're going to run our trains on track anyway, there are many advantages to using the rails as both control and power conductors.

How Command Control Works

All command control systems share a few basic elements and functions:

• A power supply, usually incorporating overload protection for the track circuit.

• A command generator, either a central "station" with separate cabs or an individual unit in each cab.

• A decoder or receiver carried in each locomotive, set to respond only to a specific control address or channel. Refer to fig. 8-4 while I explain each of these elements in more detail.

Power supply. Command control power supplies, which are often called "power stations," generally perform three functions.

1. Providing a constant, regulated voltage as track power, with current capacity sufficient for several locomotives.

2. Providing electronic circuit protection against short circuits on the track caused by derailments or run-

ning into mis-aligned power-routing turnouts. Some power stations in systems based on the NMRA's DCC standard can also automatically reverse polarity for reversing sections.

3. Combining command signals with the track power, for transmission through the rails to receivers aboard the locomotives.

As an added benefit, the constant track voltage can power headlights, interior lights, flashers, and other special effects on locomotives and cars. It can also be used for occupancy detectors (for signal systems) like the popular Twin T and Bruce Chubb's Optimized Detector, which require a steady "bias" voltage to detect rolling stock other than moving locomotives.

A word of warning, though: Small light bulbs burning continuously at full voltage can generate enough heat to melt plastic. Protect plastic parts or models by using metal housings, lower voltages (bulbs in series), or other measures.

Command generator. The next essential feature of any command control system is the circuitry to generate the control signals transmitted through the rails. Some systems employ a central command station to generate the signals for all the control channels or addresses, with the signal for each address (or group of addresses in multiple-unit operation or double-heading) governed by the throttle and reversing switch of a separate cab. The RailCommand system from CVP Products (fig. 8-5) and most DCC systems (fig. 8-6) use central command stations.

In other systems each cab is an individual command generator that produces signals for one control address—or more only for multiple-unit operation or double-heading under control of the single cab. Power Systems Inc.'s Dynatrol (fig. 8-7) is an example of a system using individual command generators in each cab.

Whether central or individual, the command generation equipment also includes some method of assigning locomotive addresses to the cabs, to determine which cab controls which engine. Plugs, dial switches, and keypads are the most commonly used means of assigning locomotives to cabs. In some systems, including some DCC types, some simple cabs lack this assignment capability. Assignments must be made for them somewhere else in the system, by a more complex cab or at the central command station system. However the assignments are made, in general any cab can be assigned to control any locomotive.

All command control systems also include the capability of assigning at least two and most cases many more addresses to a single cab. This is called "consisting" or "m.u." capability, and allows for double-headed, multiple unit (m.u.), and hostling operations.

Wherever the commands are generated, the system wiring will include connections to carry them to the power supply for transmission through the rails, along with the track power. Usually this requires a cab bus, a cable of two or more wires that you run around your layout with sockets installed at intervals so you can plug in cabs which have short cable teth-

Fig. 8-5. RAILCOMMAND. The CVP Products RailCommand system uses a keypad and liquid crysal disply in its stationary command station to program locomotive variables. The handheld walkaround cab addresses locomotives using rotary switches and function buttons.

Fig. 8-6. SYSTEM ONE. Wangrow Electronics' System One DCC incorporates all programming controls in the keypad and LCD on its full-function memorty walkaround cab.

ers. Most command control systems provide memory walkaround capability as part of the basic package, so command control and walkaround layout designs work extremely well together. Wireless command control cabs, using radio or infrared links, are just now coming on the market.

Decoder/receiver. The link between the track power and the locomotive motor, running the engine as prescribed by the command signals sent through the rails, is the decoding and control circuitry carried aboard each locomotive. In DCC systems this is called the "decoder"; in most other systems it's known as the "receiver." Although there are some important differences between decoders and receivers, at the most basic level they perform the same functions.

The decoder or receiver is wired into the locomotive between the pickup wheels and the motor, so that track power can reach the motor only through the decoder/receiver's control circuitry. Both motor brushes must be isolated from the locomotive frame or any other direct connection to the track. Figure 8-8 shows typical basic locomotive wiring when a decoder or receiver is installed.

In non-DCC systems, the receiver is preset to respond only to commands transmitted to a specific address or "channel," determined either by digital coding or transmission frequency. Some systems may allow a receiver's address to be set by the user before it's installed in a locomotive—usually by breaking or connecting specified circuit board traces—and then that becomes the receiver's fixed address. Each receiver and thus each locomotive should have a unique address, so each engine or unit will operate independently when addressed by a cab. With older systems that offer a

Fig. 8-7. DYNATROL. Power System's Inc's. Dynatrol system uses plugs with precision resistors to select locomotive channels and control up to three locomotives from one walkaround cab in an m.u. consist.

limited number of addresses, more than one locomotive can have the same address, but all but one will have to be stored on tracks switched off from the control system for independent operation.

The most basic commands sent to the receiver are throttle and reverse switch settings, and they regulate the effective voltage and polarity of the power reaching the motor. In other words, the receiver is a remotely controlled cab aboard the locomotive, which is how command control directly controls the locomotive instead of the track.

A DCC decoder also functions as a remotely controlled cab aboard the locomotive, and in that respect is basically the same as the non-DCC receiver. However, the digital addresses of DCC decoders are set electronically rather than hard-wired, and may be changed by user commands sent through the DCC system. This feature is most significant in allowing manufacturers to sell decoder-equipped locomotives off the shelf, because DCC users can easily reprogram newly purchased locomotives with an addresses different from others already on their railroads.

Another important distinction is

that non-DCC receivers function only within their own proprietary systems. If you buy the Brand A system, it can only operate locomotives carrying Brand A receivers. But since the DCC standard is primarily a standard for the control signals sent through the rails, all DCC decoders can be expected to work with all DCC systems. If you have the Brand Y DCC system but the Brand Z DCC decoder appeals to you, the two will work together because of the compatibility of the standardized control signals.

Why might another manufacturer's decoder appeal to you? In the short time DCC has been available decoders have been offered in a wide variety of sizes and power ratings. They've also appeared with auxiliary functions such as headlights, various forms of flashers to simulate locomotive signal lights, and realistic steam and diesel sounds, all controlled from the hand-held DCC cab. In fact, one of the prime reasons for adopting the DCC standard was to encourage model railroad manufacturers to innovate within its outlines, and the manufacturers haven't hesitated to do so.

Both DCC decoders and non-DCC receivers usually deliver some form of pulse power to the locomotive

motor, and they generally provide good slow-speed control. They come in different sizes and power ratings, and both these factors are important in matching these onboard electronic units to your locomotives.

Choosing a System

The inevitable question, of course, is which system you should use. Only you can answer that, by considering which system best fits the way you want to run your railroad. Today's command control systems all work as advertised and are highly reliable, so it's a matter of choosing the combination of features and capabilities that you like best.

The best help I can offer is a list of what to look for. The following list will alert you to matters you should consider and give you a better idea of what to expect.

• System current capacity: In most basic systems, the capacity of the power supply divided by the demands of your locomotives equals the number of locomotives you can operate simultaneously. By demand I mean the peak load when a motor starts, which with some motors and drive trains can be double the continuous rating. In most systems, however, you aren't limited by the biggest available power supply, which is typically about 8 to 10 amps, and one high-powered supply isn't the best way to handle lots of engines.

In command control you add power by using gaps or insulated rail joiners to divide your railroad into two or more isolated power districts, each with its own power supply. Interconnections between supplies (the "command bus" line in fig. 8-4) carry the command signals throughout your railroad, however, and trains run from one district to another as if there were no gaps at all.

As long as the locomotives in any one district don't exceed the rating of that district's power supply, you have adequate power capacity. That gives you the flexibility to tailor a system for your own requirements and lets

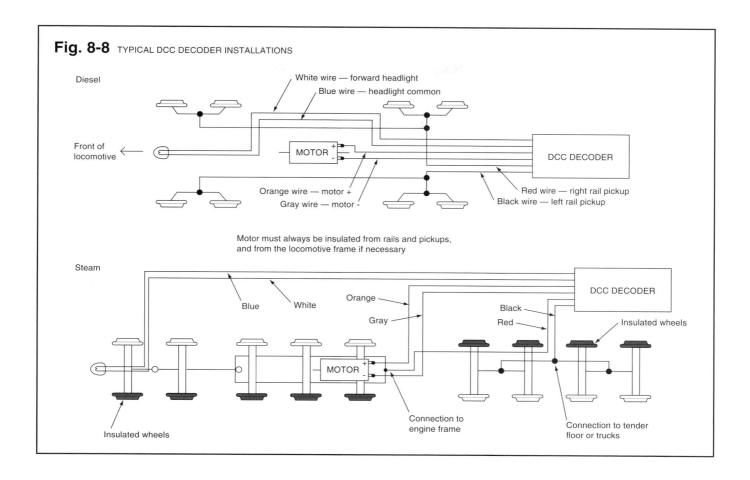

Fig. 8-8 TYPICAL DCC DECODER INSTALLATIONS

Diesel

White wire — forward headlight
Blue wire — headlight common

Front of locomotive

MOTOR

DCC DECODER

Orange wire — motor +
Gray wire — motor -

Red wire — right rail pickup
Black wire — left rail pickup

Motor must always be insulated from rails and pickups, and from the locomotive frame if necessary

Steam

Blue   White

Orange

Gray

Black

Red

DCC DECODER

Insulated wheels

MOTOR

Connection to engine frame

Connection to tender floor or trucks

Insulated wheels

you enlarge your system's power capacity as you enlarge or add trains to your railroad.

There are a couple of other advantages to building power capacity with multiple power supplies. Limiting the current that is available on a single power district is safer and better for maintenance because it prevents heavy arcing when accidental short circuits occur.

Also, remember that the circuit protection in command control systems is incorporated in the power supplies. If a whole layout is driven by a single power supply, the entire railroad will shut down if just one engineer makes a mistake. With multiple power supplies, only the district where a short circuit occurs shuts down; operators on other parts of the railroad won't even know about it.

• Decoder/receiver current capacity: As a remote-control cab aboard the locomotive, the decoder or re-

ceiver must have adequate capacity for the motor's peak current demand. In most systems you have a choice of choice of units with different capacities, and with DCC compatibility within the standard expands your choice to include decoders of any make. Current capacity is a factor of the electronic components' ability to dissipate heat, so it's related to the next item on our checklist.

• Decoder/receiver size: Since it has to fit inside the locomotive, the smaller the better, right? Well yes, but in general the smaller the unit the lower its current capacity. Look for the best compromise between small size and adequate capacity. Fortunately, the smaller locomotives have the smallest current requirements because of their smaller motors and lighter weight.

• Number of locomotive addresses: Since each locomotive must carry a decoder or receiver with a unique

address, the more addresses a system supports the more locomotives you can operate without duplication. Most modern systems support at least 100 addresses, and some many more, so this is mainly a concern for those considering older systems. As I mentioned earlier, you can have more locomotives on a layout than your system has addresses, by using electrically dead tracks to store engines with duplicated addresses, but this is obviously a limitation of operating flexibility.

• Address selection: All systems have some means of assigning or designating which cabs will control locomotives on which addresses, but you'll have many choices of methods and control types. Beyond the obvious options of dials or plugs or keypads is the number of address digits the system accepts. In some cases this is only two, but other systems support three- and some four-digit

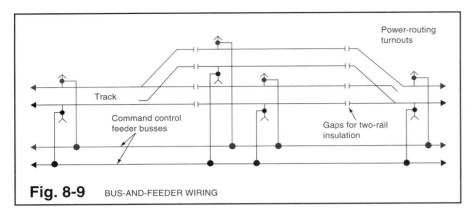

Fig. 8-9 BUS-AND-FEEDER WIRING

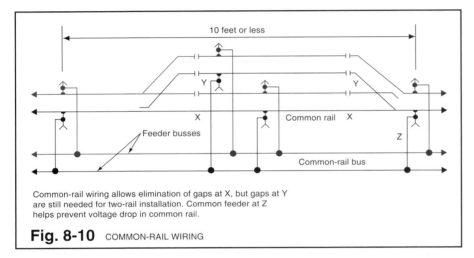

Common-rail wiring allows elimination of gaps at X, but gaps at Y
are still needed for two-rail installation. Common feeder at Z
helps prevent voltage drop in common rail.

Fig. 8-10 COMMON-RAIL WIRING

addresses. When restricted to two-digit addresses, most command control users match the address with the last two digits of a locomotive's number. At the other end of the scale, a four-digit address means you can use a locomotive's full number to assign it to a cab, which is certainly the most easily understood and most flexible approach.

• Throttles: Command control cabs come with a variety of throttle configurations, and again, how you like to run your trains should govern your purchasing decision. You'll find cabs with a range of both rotary (knob, dial, or thumbwheel) and push-button speed controls. Some makers offer only one type or the other, but several offer a choice within one system, and within such systems different types of cabs can operate together. There are also cabs with momentum and braking effects.

Direction controls offer another range of options, including switches, two push buttons (one for forward and one for reverse), a single button (changes direction every time it's pushed), and the speed control buttons (pushing the "reverse" button will slow the engine if it's moving forward, but once the engine is stopped, pushing reverse starts it moving in reverse). For both speed and direction control, your best bet is to try the cabs you think you want and make sure you're comfortable with them.

Still more options are available in function controls. These allow you to control headlights and other onboard effects, and in DCC systems to control turnouts and other layout functions through the use of stationary acces-

sory decoders. Cabs are offered with various ranges of function controls from the most basic—or none—to keypads capable of using or adjusting every one of what can be a very considerable number of features.

One word of caution regarding the limits of the Digital Command Control standard: The design of cabs and of the bus that links them to the command generator and power station is not part of the DCC standard. So cabs and busses from one maker are not necessarily interchangeable with those of another. It happens that two manufacturers—North Coast Engineering and Wangrow—do use a common system design and therefore have compatible cabs and busses. Another, Power Systems Inc., offers add-on infrared or radio wireless walkaround cabs that plug into the cab bus used by these two companies. Beyond such areas of manufacturers' agreement, however, you shouldn't expect to be able to mix and match cabs and busses from different DCC makers.

• Multiple-unit operation or "consisting": Almost all command control systems offer some capability to control two or more locomotives with different addresses from a single throttle. This replicates the multiple-unit ("m.u.") control used in real diesel and electric locomotives. The same feature also allows double-heading steam locomotives, even though real steam double-headers couldn't be driven from one throttle and had to have a crew in the cab of each engine. Systems with multiple-unit capacity allow you to specify which engines will operate together as an m.u. consist—that's why this is sometimes called "consisting"—and even to see that all units in a consist move in the same direction no matter which way they're facing.

Different systems use different methods of addressing a consist. In some the consist must be assigned its own number, while in others the consist can be addressed by the number of a designated lead unit.

• Walkaround control: You won't find a better match than command control and walkaround operation. Walking along with your train is easier and more enjoyable with no cab selectors to worry about, and the layout wiring is easier too.

All command control systems offer some form of basic memory walkaround control, meaning they'll keep your train moving while you unplug your cab's cable tether from the cab bus and plug it into another socket farther down the line. Some also offer wireless walkaround control, with either radio or infrared links. Each cab in such wireless arrangements consists of two parts, and hand-held control transmitter unit that you carry with you and a stationary receiver unit that plugs into the system's cab bus. As I mentioned earlier, one old-line command control supplier, Power Systems Inc., maker of the pre-DCC Dynatrol system, even offers wireless cabs for DCC.

• Lighting effects and sound: Headlights you can turn on and off, signal lights of the Mars or Gyralite type, and flashing beacons and ditch lights are all options you can enjoy with today's command control receivers and decoders. Since the circuits for these effects are built right into the decoder or receiver, there's no need for add-on electronics in the locomotive. Locomotive sound systems are also available, both steam and diesel, and in DCC these have so far taken the form of combination decoders and sound circuits available from aftermarket suppliers. The same onboard unit both runs the engine and generates the sound, although of course these also require a separate onboard speaker. These sound decoders typically allow you to blow the whistle, ring the bell, and control other sound effects from the function controls on the cab.

• Locomotive performance variables: The DCC systems and CVP Products RailCommand offer the capacity to adjust many factors affecting locomotive operation, including starting voltage (to reduce or eliminate a throttle's "dead band"), accel-

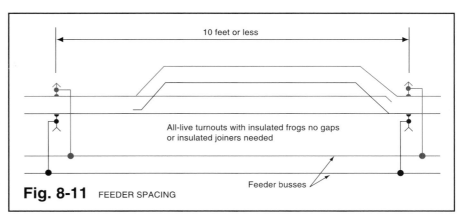

Fig. 8-11 FEEDER SPACING

eration and deceleration curves, and maximum speed.

In DCC this information is stored in each locomotive's decoder, so most adjustments must be done on the isolated programming track, although some systems allow certain variables to be programmed "on the main track." With RailCommand the variables are stored in the command station, which has a keypad and LCD display for making these settings, and no programming track is required.

Control of these locomotive variables does add greatly to the flexibility of these systems and can bring real and worthwhile improvements in locomotive performance. Adjusting these variables can allow locomotives of very different performance characteristics to work together in m.u. consists, but be wary of trying to set all your locomotives to behave exactly alike. That can lead to making your better performers match your worst, as the lowest common denominator, so the overall performance won't be as good as you'd hoped.

• Accessory control: Digital Command Control systems have the capacity to operate accessories such as switch machines and signal lights by sending signals to stationary accessory decoders mounted beneath the layout or concealed in structures. In its simplest form, these decoders are simply connected to the track and receive both power and control signals through the rails. While that

might be effective on small layouts, it's obvious that the accessories' power requirements will be a drain on the train-running power, and the rails aren't the most efficient signal carriers over long distances.

A better way to employ accessory decoders is to provide them with a power source separate from the track power, and to connect them to the track bus wires to receive command signals instead of through the track itself. This will make the accessory operation more reliable and prevent it from robbing power from the trains.

Controlling turnouts and other accessories from hand-held control cabs does eliminate the need for control panels and all their attendant wiring, but you might consider if that's really the way you want to run your railroad. An engineer in the cab of a real locomotive can turn on the headlight and blow the horn, but can't line a track switch, change a red signal to green, or turn on the light in the depot.

However, accessory decoders can be used in a realistic manner under the control of a dispatcher or tower operator, perhaps with computer assistance for realistic route, interlocking, and signal control, while providing a real saving in wiring. Instead of having to run wires all the way from a central control station to each switch motor, signal, or other device, you can place the accessory decoders near the devices they operate. They need

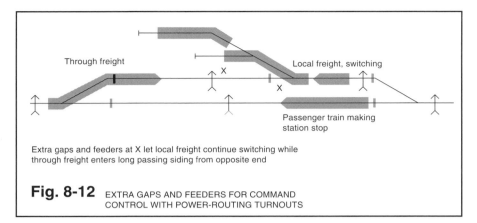

Extra gaps and feeders at X let local freight continue switching while through freight enters long passing siding from opposite end

Fig. 8-12 EXTRA GAPS AND FEEDERS FOR COMMAND CONTROL WITH POWER-ROUTING TURNOUTS

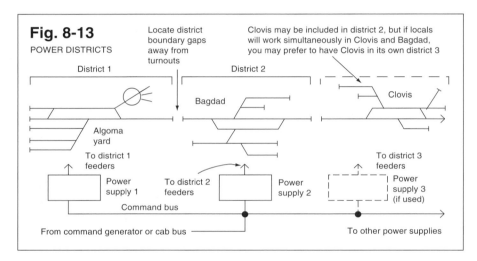

Fig. 8-13
POWER DISTRICTS

Locate district boundary gaps away from turnouts

Clovis may be included in district 2, but if locals will work simultaneously in Clovis and Bagdad, you may prefer to have Clovis in its own district 3

have only four input connections from wires running all over the layout, two from the track bus for control signals and two from an accessory power bus. The output wiring need only be long enough to reach the nearby accessories.

• Computer interfaces: Most DCC systems and the CVP Products Rail-Command system come with RS-232 connections that allow connection to a port on a personal computer. For DCC, software is available to allow cab assignments, consisting, and locomotive performance adjustments to be done from the PC's keyboard, in many cases in a more transparent and easily understood fashion than by use of a throttle keypad. (In RailCommand, these functions are performed with the command station's keypad and

LCD readout, so no separate computer is necessary.)

Digital Command Control software also allows accessory decoders to be operated from the PC, preparing the way for realistic Centralized Traffic Control dispatching or interlocking tower operation as I mentioned earlier. These applications are beyond the scope of this book, but they are capabilities you should be aware of in case they have any bearing on your decisions about command control purchase.

Command Control Wiring

Wiring a layout for command control systems is simpler than wiring it for cab control. Don't be misled, though, by promises of "two-wire" control or the elimination of most

feeders and all gaps. That's not possible except on the smallest, simplest layouts.

I'll review the general considerations for command control layout wiring. These apply to all systems, but of course you should read the manufacturers' instruction manuals for special requirements.

Two-rail wiring. Command control still uses the rails as conductors, and as the two sides of the running power circuit, so the two-rail wiring rules covered in Chapter 3 still apply. Turnouts still make a difference, and a railroad with power-routing turnouts will require almost as many gaps and feeders as for cab control. The central difference is that instead of running back to block selectors on control panels, all the feeders connect directly to the same pair of bus wires, fig. 8-9. That in itself is a big simplification in wiring, and it saves a lot of wire on larger layouts.

Turnouts. Some modelers prefer to use all-live turnouts with command control, for two reasons. These turnouts don't require gaps to maintain two-rail insulation, and they are less susceptible to back-to-back shorts involving metal wheels that aren't correctly gauged. The first of these is unquestionably true, but as I'll explain a little later there are situations in which you may want to have gaps even with command control. If that's the case, the gaps required for two-rail insulation with power-routing turnouts won't be much of a bother.

As for back-to-back shorts, when wheels and turnouts are correctly gauged such shorts won't happen. The NMRA Mark IV standards gauge includes a tab to check the space between turnout points and stock rails, as well as slots for checking wheel gauge. When these dimensions are correct, a metal wheel can't simultaneously touch turnout rails of opposite polarity, so the best answer to back-to-back shorts is to keep track and wheels in gauge.

Of course, the turnout wiring shown back in fig. 3-12, with points isolated from the frog and permanently connected to the stock rails allows even power-routing turnouts to be free from accidental back-to-back shorts. Commercial power-routing turnouts aren't available with this wiring, but they can be modified, and handlaid turnouts can be built this way.

One way or the other I've found this not to be a serious problem. You can pretty much use whatever turnouts you like with command control as long as you understand how they are wired and how to wire them in a layout.

Common rail. You can use common rail with command control. As we saw in Chapter 5, this lets you eliminate some—but not all—gaps in one rail. The common rail will require more feeders for command control. Chapter 10 examines conductor capacity in more detail, but for now, realize that rail materials don't equal copper wires for effective long-distance conduction. It's a good idea to have a feeder at least every 10 feet along the common rail, fig. 8-10.

The same premise applies to railroads with all-live turnouts. You might not need gaps to use command control on such a system, but dropping a feeder from each rail to a pair of power feeders at least every 10 feet is good practice, fig. 8-11. Some command control users and manufacturers prefer to have feeders connected to every individual length of rail, which has the advantage of not relying on rail joiners to be good conductors.

Extra gaps and feeders. Situations may arise in which you'd want to have more gaps and feeders with command control. This will most likely occur on spur tracks where, with cab control, it was convenient to isolate a locomotive by lining a turnout against it so you could run another engine. Since each locomotive can move independently in command control, you might want to provide extra gaps and feeders such as those shown in fig. 8-12, to keep all the tracks powered no matter which way the turnouts are set.

Turning tracks. Reverse loops, wyes, and turntables still need special

treatment with command control, again because we're still working with a two-rail circuit. One major simplification, however, arises from the fact that locomotive direction is governed by control signals independently of track polarity.

The significance of this fact is that with command control you can reverse the polarity of the rails underneath a moving train and it will keep moving in the same direction. That means you can use the simplest one-switch turning track wiring shown in Chapter 4, including automatic polarity switching using switch-machine auxiliary contacts as shown in figs. 4-8B and 4-10B.

Some DCC manufacturers provide another approach to automatic turning track control in their power stations or power boosters. These boosters can be set to reverse polarity automatically when a short circuit occurs at a power district gap. The reversal is instantaneous, so the short won't cause trains to stop or even hesitate By using such a booster to power only the turning track or reversing block, you get automatic turning track control with no additional wiring, although at the cost of one booster per turning track.

(Those who realize that DCC uses a form of alternating current for track power and control signals may question the use of "polarity" in the previous paragraph. Even though the true polarity of the current is reversing many times per second in each rail, bringing the two opposing rails together still causes a short circuit, just as shorts can occur in AC house wiring. Strictly speaking the DCC booster automatically reverses the phase of the current, but polarity remains a convenient shorthand term for describing what happens in two-rail model railroad wiring.)

You will have to pay attention to turning tracks when wiring your railroad, but with automatic polarity switching you can forget about them when you're running trains by command control.

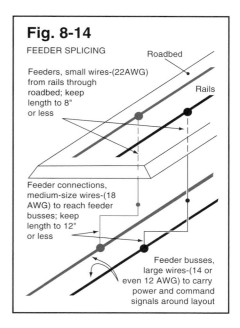

Fig. 8-14
FEEDER SPLICING

Roadbed

Rails

Feeders, small wires-(22AWG) from rails through roadbed; keep length to 8" or less

Feeder connections, medium-size wires-(18 AWG) to reach feeder busses; keep length to 12" or less

Feeder busses, large wires-(14 or even 12 AWG) to carry power and command signals around layout

Block gaps. Even with command control you may want to gap your railroad as if you're using cab control. Having a layout divided into isolated blocks can still come in handy for troubleshooting, and for occupancy detection if you ever want to install a signal system.

Also, if you have more locomotives than control channels or addresses, you may need to include blocks in your terminals where you can isolate and switch off engines with duplicate addresses. It's also a good idea to isolate each track in holding and staging yards as blocks, so you can keep waiting trains turned off when they aren't supposed to be moving.

Power districts. I said earlier that it's a good idea to divide a command control railroad into several sections, each with its own power supply. This is the best way to build up the power capacity of the total system, and the independent circuit protection in each power district keeps accidental shorts from shutting down the whole railroad, fig. 8-13.

Locate power district boundaries in stretches of plain track away from turnouts. This helps avoid accidental shorts across a boundary. Even if you use common rail everywhere else, you

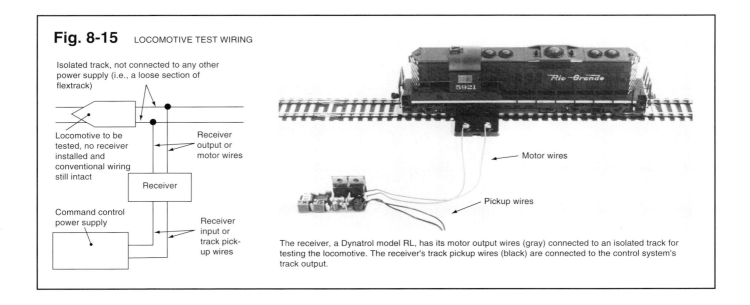

Fig. 8-15 LOCOMOTIVE TEST WIRING

Isolated track, not connected to any other power supply (i.e., a loose section of flextrack)

Locomotive to be tested, no receiver installed and conventional wiring still intact

Receiver output or motor wires

Receiver

Command control power supply

Receiver input or track pick-up wires

Motor wires

Pickup wires

The receiver, a Dynatrol model RL, has its motor output wires (gray) connected to an isolated track for testing the locomotive. The receiver's track pickup wires (black) are connected to the control system's track output.

must gap both rails at a power district boundary. When connecting the power supplies, be sure that track polarity is the same on both sides of the power district gaps.

Layout wiring. Command control wiring has to be able to carry both running power and control signals, and for several trains at once. The combination requires a solid current path with heavy-gauge wire and positive connections. If the power drain exceeds the capacity of the wiring the voltage can drop, causing distortion of control signals and erratic train performance.

Even on the smallest layouts, power busses should be at least No. 18 wire; No. 16 would be better. For bigger systems switch to No. 14 or even No. 12—this gets into house wiring sizes, but that's what it takes. Control or throttle busses, the cables carrying the control inputs back to the command generator or power supply, don't need to be as big because they carry only low currents: See the manufacturer's recommendations.

You can use light-gauge feeder wires—No. 22, for example—to drop from the rails through the roadbed. Small wire won't cause trouble over short distances, but if the feeders

have to extend more than 6 or 8 inches to reach the busses you should splice them to a larger intermediate size, as in fig. 8-14.

Track. Pay special attention to rail joints—remember, rails are conductors. Rail joiners alone are not adequate conductors for command control, and you'll need to solder them, solder bond wires around them, or solder feeder wires to every length of rail as explained in Chapter 1.

As a minimum you need feeders every 10 feet to avoid voltage drop and signal loss in the rails. Also make sure you have a positive current path through both routes of every turnout. "Wiring around" turnouts through auxiliary contacts is especially important with command control.

Command control needs clean track, too. This is always a good idea, but vital with these systems.

Locomotives. The final step in the current path to the decoder or receiver and motor is the locomotive itself. Locomotives need clean pickup wheels, and as many of them as possible.

Most motors perform well on the output of command control decoders and receivers, but you'll enjoy the best results if the motor's peak cur-

rent drain is well within the capacity of the control electronics. This argues for efficient, low-current motors, but you don't necessarily have to remotor your entire roster. Many stock motors work very well with command control, including those in the popular Athearn HO diesels.

You can see how a locomotive will perform on command control before you install the receiver or decoder in it. First put the locomotive on a track connected to a conventional power pack, and use an ammeter to test its current drain. You want to be sure that the locomotive's peak current, when it first breaks into motion and when its wheels slip, is within the capacity of the decoder or receiver you want to use.

If the current drain is okay, disconnect the power pack and connect the receiver or decoder as shown in fig. 8-15. Use a command control cab to run the locomotive, and you'll see exactly how well it will perform on the system.

Be sure your locomotives are mechanically sound and run freely with no binds before you install decoders or receivers. Then you'll be able to appreciate all the advantages of these advanced control systems.

Turnout control

CHAPTER NINE

After you get the trains running, the next most important wiring on a model railroad is for control of powered or "remote control" turnouts. Many kinds of mechanisms can power turnouts, but the most popular types fall into two general categories:

Twin-solenoid switch machines use pairs of electromagnets, solenoids, to move iron or steel armatures back and forth. The armatures move the turnout points through levers, cranks, and other forms of linkage, fig. 9-1. Twin-solenoid machines are used to power turnouts in the popular Atlas and similar sectional track lines.

Gear-driven switch motors employ geared-down electric motors to move turnout points more slowly than the snap action of solenoids, fig. 9-2. The slower action resembles real railroads' switch motors and is easier on your turnout points.

Screw- and worm-drive switch motors use "limit switches," contacts which open and stop the motor, to limit their travel. The display motors commonly adapted to model railroad use contain internal gearboxes for slow motion. Because of their low current drain and robust design, they can be allowed to simply stall under power when they've moved the turnout points as far as they will go. This has the advantage that the stalled motor always pushes the point against the stock rail. For this reason, this type of switch motor is sometimes called a "stall motor."

Switch machines and switch motors require different control wiring; I'll discuss them separately.

Switch Machine Control

The solenoid coils of twin-solenoid switch machines can only be energized momentarily. They need a burst of power just sufficient to throw the turnout, and if powered for too long they will overheat, melt their insulation, and short circuit or "burn out." Figure 9-3 shows the basic circuit for switch machine control using both momentary push buttons and spring-loaded momentary toggle switches. You push the button and quickly release it, or press the toggle to one

Fig. 9-1. TWIN-SOLENOID SWITCH MACHINE. Shown here from left to right, an Atlas machine for tabletop mounting with Atlas HO turnouts, a Peco machine for concealed mounting in the roadbed with Peco N and HO turnouts, and Rix products and N. J. International machines for concealed under-table mounting with turnouts of any make or scale.

Fig. 9-2. SWITCH MOTORS. Shown here from left to right, front row, worm-drive motors from Fulgurex and Lemaco, and a screw-drive motor from Scale Shops. In the back row, gear-drive motors from American Switch and Signal (Hankscraft display motor) and Circuitron. All are meant for concealed under-table mounting, and for use with turnouts of any make or scale.

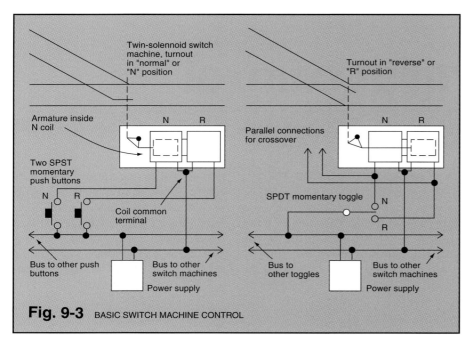

Fig. 9-3 BASIC SWITCH MACHINE CONTROL

Twin-solennoid switch machine, turnout in "normal" or "N" position

Armature inside N coil

Two SPST momentary push buttons

Coil common terminal

Bus to other push buttons

Bus to other switch machines

Power supply

Turnout in "reverse" or "R" position

Parallel connections for crossover

SPDT momentary toggle

Bus to other toggles

Bus to other switch machines

Power supply

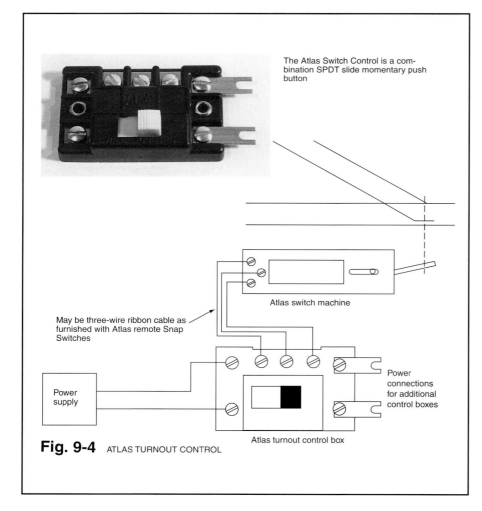

The Atlas Switch Control is a combination SPDT slide momentary push button

Atlas switch machine

May be three-wire ribbon cable as furnished with Atlas remote Snap Switches

Power supply

Power connections for additional control boxes

Atlas turnout control box

Fig. 9-4 ATLAS TURNOUT CONTROL

side and let it spring back to center.

To throw two turnouts at once, as for a crossover, wire the two machines parallel to a toggle or pair of push buttons, also in fig. 9-3. Your power supply must be adequate to throw both machines simultaneously; if the turnouts don't throw together for the normal and crossover routes, reverse the coil connections on one machine.

The Atlas turnout control box shown in fig. 9-4 employs a combination slide switch and momentary push button. You slide it to one side or the other, then push and release. Note that the Atlas circuit looks different, but that's only because the common connection for the two switch machine coils is routed through the control box instead of going directly to the power supply.

To a limited extent, the Atlas control box indicates the turnout's position by the location of its sliding button. It's not reliable because the button can slide back and forth without throwing the turnout unless pushed.

Probe-and-Stud Control

Here's another form of momentary control. In the probe-and-stud method shown in fig. 9-5, the probe is connected to the switch machine power supply, while the studs in the track diagram on the control panel are connected to the coils. You move the probe along the route you want to use, wiping it across every stud along the way, to line the turnouts for that route.

The probe-and-stud method is simple and inexpensive to install and easy to use because it's so graphic. There's no harm, by the way, in briefly energizing a coil that has already pulled in the armature—one already "thrown." When you're in doubt about a turnout's position, push the button, toggle the switch, or wipe the stud to make sure.

Parallel Controls

An advantage of twin-solenoid switch machines is that they're easy to control from multiple positions. Where turnouts may be used by

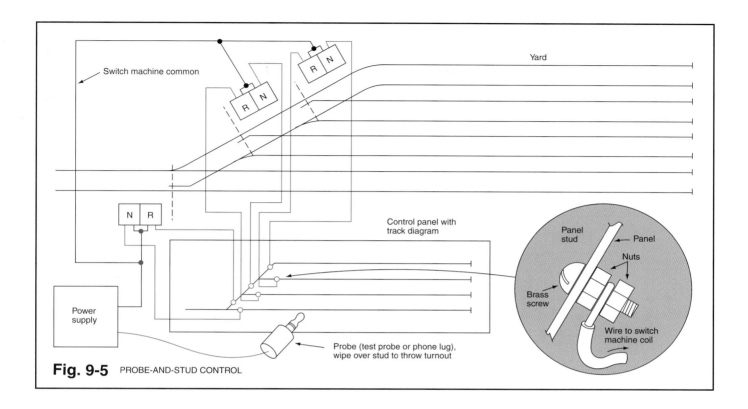

Fig. 9-5 PROBE-AND-STUD CONTROL

operators at different control panels, you can simply duplicate the turnout controls on each panel, wiring them in parallel, fig. 9-6.

Parallel controls preclude determining turnout position by control position, because a turnout may have been thrown by a control on another panel. If you want positive indications of turnout position, you can use panel lights controlled by auxiliary contacts, as I'll explain at the end of this chapter.

Automatic Route Control

Another advantage of twin-solenoid switch machines is that they are easy to wire with diodes for automatic route control, fig. 9-7. Instead of having to throw turnouts one by one to line a route for one of the yard tracks, you simply push one button. This automatically energizes all the switch machine coils needed to align that route—and no others.

The diodes make this work. Think of a diode as a one-way electrical valve, fig. 9-8. Direct current can flow through it only if the polarity is cor-

rect, positive on the diode's anode and negative on the diode's cathode; otherwise, the circuit is blocked. The diodes in fig. 9-7 keep the coils not needed from being energized by blocking false circuits through other coils.

Although twin-solenoid switch machines can operate on either AC or DC power, automatic routing with diodes requires DC power. Also, because this wiring can energize several coils at once, it's best—often necessary—to

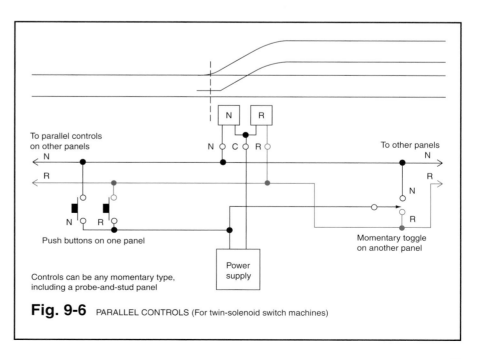

Fig. 9-6 PARALLEL CONTROLS (For twin-solenoid switch machines)

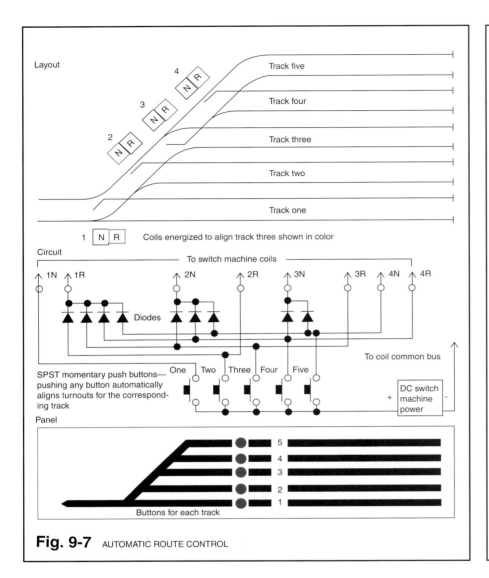

Track five

Track four

Track three

Track two

Track one

Layout

1 [N R] Coils energized to align track three shown in color

Circuit

To switch machine coils

1N 1R   2N   2R   3N   3R 4N 4R

Diodes

To coil common bus

SPST momentary push buttons—
pushing any button automatically
aligns turnouts for the corresponding track

One Two Three Four Five

DC switch
machine
power

Panel

5
4
3
2
1

Buttons for each track

Fig. 9-7 AUTOMATIC ROUTE CONTROL

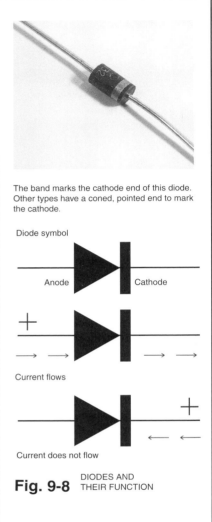

The band marks the cathode end of this diode.
Other types have a coned, pointed end to mark
the cathode.

Diode symbol

Anode   Cathode

Current flows

Current does not flow

Fig. 9-8 DIODES AND
THEIR FUNCTION

use a capacitor-discharge power supply as I'll explain later.

Figure 9-9 shows how to plan an automatic routing circuit. This is called the "diode matrix," although it's not necessary to build a matrix to wire the diodes. The matrix is a planning device; its purpose is to help you see which coils will be controlled by two or more buttons. Those are the coils that need diodes in every connection; coils controlled by only one button do not need a diode.

In fact, once you have built one or two of these circuits there's a good chance you might not need a matrix. Remember the rule, "coils controlled by two or more buttons need a diode

in every connection," and you'll probably be able to work out the circuit in your head.

Building a Route-Control Circuit

Figure 9-10 shows how to build an automatic routing circuit. The two center rows of terminal strips serve mainly to support the diodes; where diodes aren't required I've bridged them with solid, bare bus wire. The lower terminals are for wires from control buttons, and the upper ones for wires to coils. Note that all the diodes are oriented the same way, with their anodes toward the positive terminal of the power supply.

(The circuit would work exactly the same way with the supply polarity reversed, so long as all the diodes were reversed too.) Just about any inexpensive silicon diodes can be used for automatic route control, though in theory they should be rated for two to four times the current required for one switch machine coil and twice the power supply voltage. In practice most diodes can momentarily handle more current and voltage than their ratings, so these values aren't critical. Radio Shack has 3A, 50V diodes, type 1N5400, catalog No. 276-114, which will work with most twin-solenoid machines.

Switch Machine Power Supply

Often the most readily available source of switch machine power will be the AC accessory terminals on a power pack. A power pack can be an adequate supply for the small solenoids in most sectional track switch machines, though you may find that the train slows down momentarily when you throw a turnout or, especially, a crossover.

For most switch machines with larger coils, as sold separately and usually intended for mounting under a layout, a power pack usually won't be an adequate supply. If the machine just hums or buzzes when you throw it, you need more power. A separate supply is also the answer to keeping the trains moving steadily while you throw turnouts.

A good switch machine supply should have a capacity of 4–6A at 16–20V. A large transformer supplying AC at these levels is fine, and many modelers have used old toy train transformers for this purpose. Or you could employ a separate DC power supply—it may not justify the extra cost, but switch machines will be quieter when operated on DC. Remember, too, that DC is necessary for automatic routing with diodes.

Large transformers are expensive, however, as are old toy transformers, and they have another disadvantage. All that power makes it easier to damage a coil by applying power for too long, and it also causes arcing ("sparking"), which burns up button or toggle contacts.

For these reasons, the best switch machine supply is the capacitor-discharge type. A capacitor stores electrical energy, allowing a small, inexpensive power source to build up a big charge. When discharged it supplies abundant DC power, enough to throw a whole yard ladder's worth of turnouts, but only in a short burst. It can't overheat switch machine coils, and it's easier on control contacts too. It's exactly the same power supply used in electronic photo flash units to give a lot of light from small batteries.

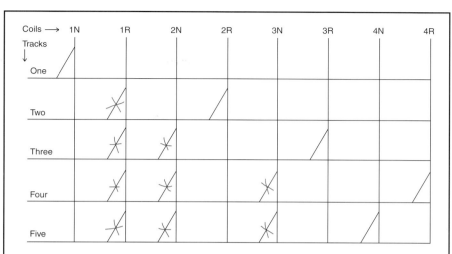

Using a matrix to plan an automatic routing circuit (example shown for yard in fig. 9-7)

Step one: Draw matrix with lines labeled for tracks and coils.

Step two: Draw diagonal connections showing which coils must be energized to align a given track.

Step three: Mark connections wherever there are two or more for one coil (two or more in a vertical column). The connections marked represent diodes needed for the automatic routing circuit.

Compare the completed planning matrix to the circuit diagram in fig. 9-7

Fig. 9-9   DIODE MATRIX (a planning device)

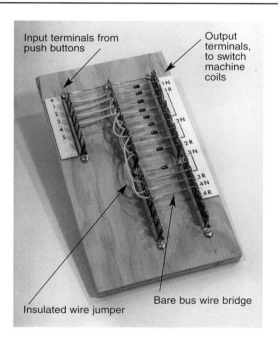

Fig. 9-10. BUILDING A ROUTE CONTROL CIRCUIT. This is the route control circuit designed in fig. 9-10, showing an easy method of construction. The first thing you do is screw solder-tag terminal strips to a small piece of plywood. Then you solder in the diodes and bridges of solid bare bus wire according to the matrix design, and finally you add the insulated jumper wires for each push-button input. This should be done one at a time. The terminals on the left connect to the push buttons, so label them for the corresponding tracks. The plus sign shows that the diodes are oriented for positive input on this side. The terminals on the right side connect to the switch machines, so label them for the normal- and reverse-position coils of the four machines. Notice that coils 1R, 2N, and 3N are represented by groups of terminals. The terminals in each group are connected with bus wire, and the coil for that group may connect to any terminal.

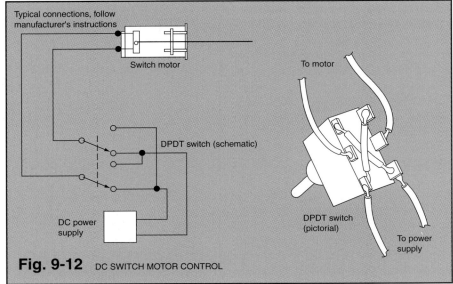

Fig. 9-12 DC SWITCH MOTOR CONTROL

Fig. 9-11. CIRCUITRON SNAPPER. The Snapper is a ready-to-use CD power supply for twin-solenoid switch machines. It must have an external low-voltage AC power supply, which can be the AC accessory terminals of a power pack or a small independent transformer.

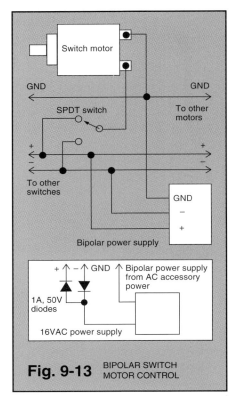

Fig. 9-13 BIPOLAR SWITCH MOTOR CONTROL

Capacitor-discharge supplies are available from several manufacturers. One well-known model is the Snapper from Circuitron, fig. 9-11; there is also the Switch-a-roo by BL Hobby Products. Each requires a separate transformer for power.

Wiring for Switch Machines

Whatever power supply you use, be sure to employ heavy-duty wiring to your switch machines. Small, sectional-track switch machines on small layouts can function with light-gauge wire. For everything else consider No. 18 wire a minimum size, and use larger wire for long runs and for common busses serving machines that throw simultaneously (as in a diode automatic routing system).

If a machine throws sluggishly or not at all, try connecting it closer to your power supply. If it works that way, your machine and supply are okay, and your problem is inadequate wiring. I'll have more to say about layout wiring in the next chapter, but if you remember that switch machines need plenty of power and big wire, you won't go far wrong.

Switch Motor Control

Switch motors operate best with holding rather than momentary con-

trols. That's because they act slower than solenoids, and a short burst from a push button usually won't be enough to achieve full travel. You can use momentary buttons and hold them until you're sure the turnout is thrown, but it's easier to use a control that will do that for you, like a toggle. The panel switch then serves as a good indicator of turnout position. A holding control is also necessary to use the holding feature of a stall motor.

The exact control you need for a switch motor depends on the power supply you use. You can drive most of these motors with an ordinary DC power supply in the range of 8–12VDC, using a DPDT switch, fig. 9-12. The switch wiring should be familiar: It's a reversing switch, here controlling the direction of a switch motor instead of a train.

Bipolar Supplies

Using simpler control switches can be enough of an advantage that some switch motor suppliers recommend employing a bipolar DC power supply. A bipolar supply includes three output terminals: positive (+), negative (–), and common or ground. As fig. 9-13 shows, an SPDT switch is sufficient for reversing the polarity flowing to the switch motor with a bipolar supply.

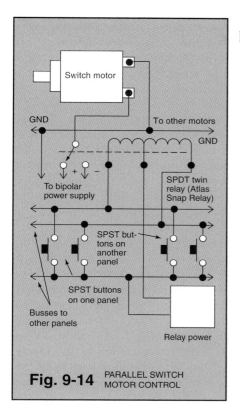

Fig. 9-14 PARALLEL SWITCH MOTOR CONTROL

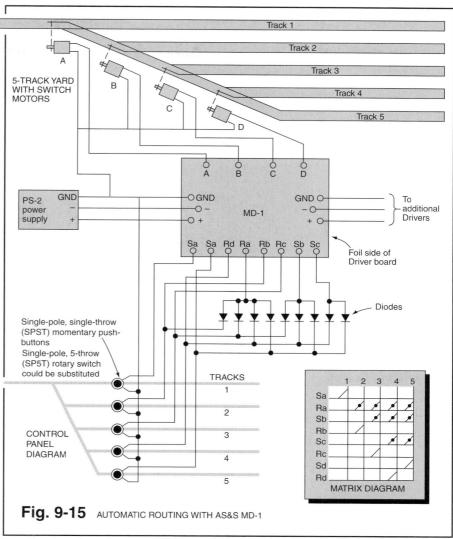

Fig. 9-15 AUTOMATIC ROUTING WITH AS&S MD-1

The American Switch & Signal Division of Electroplumbing sells a bipolar supply for its Slow Motion Switch Motors. This model PS-2 supply is rated at 12VDC, 2A, and can be used with any switch motor within that capacity.

Other Control Considerations

Switch motors don't lend themselves easily to control from different locations: If you wire parallel switches, conflicting switch settings will cause short circuits. Parallel control is possible, fig. 9-14. One SPDT (or DPDT) relay controls the switch motor, but the relay is controlled by push buttons (or other momentary controls), which can be wired in parallel on any number of control panels.

Automatic route control is also harder to accomplish with switch motors. The diode wiring that works with solenoids won't work here because of the need for polarity reversal. Electronics beyond the scope of this book are required, however.

A commercial circuit for easy auto-matic route control with diodes for low-current stall motors is available. American Switch & Signal's MD-1 Motor Driver can be used with diode wiring as shown in fig. 9-15 for route control of AS&S Slow Motion Switch Motors (or other similar motors, such as Rebco's). Each MD-1 circuit can drive up to four motors, and MD-1s may be ganged to control whatever number of motors you need.

Wiring for Switch Motors

All switch motors use little power compared to solenoid switch machines, and No. 22 wire is adequate for most layout wiring. One situation that could require more power would be several stall motors installed around a large layout. In that case you would want heavier bus wires because all the motors would be drawing power all the time. With a conventional supply, I've found that No. 18 wire works best; with a bipolar supply, use No. 18 at least for the ground bus.

Auxiliary Contacts

Most switch machines and switch motors include auxiliary contacts, in effect, relay switches that throw when the turnout is thrown. Figure 9-16 shows common auxiliary contacts. There are many good ways to use these contacts; here are three of the most common: to "wire around"

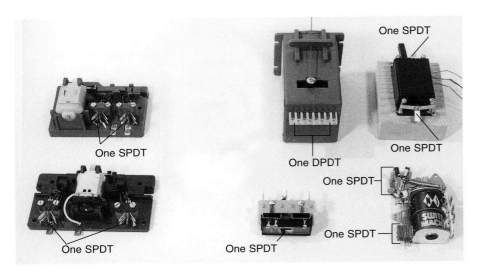

Fig. 9-16. AUXILIARY CONTACTS. Shown here are a variety of auxiliary contacts on different types of switch motors and machines. The Fulgurex and Lemaco motors both have DPDT contacts. The Peco machine does not come with auxiliary contacts, but Peco offers SPDT units that clip onto the bottom of the machine. The Circuitron Tortoise has SPDT contacts. The Rix machine comes with two sets of SPDT contacts that can be installed with the machine. The N. J. International machine has side-mounted DPDT blade contacts and an independent set of SPDT contacts on its actuating cell crank.

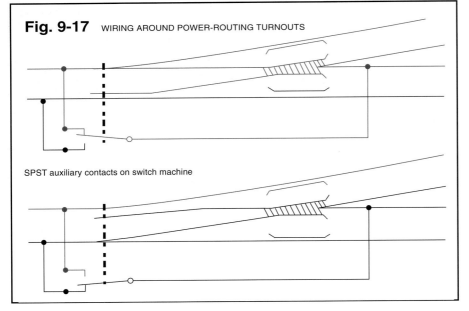

power-routing turnout points, as cutoffs to protect solenoid coils, and for position indication.

Wiring around. This is a good idea with power-routing turnouts because it bypasses the sometimes questionable contact between points and stock rails. The same method can also be used to power isolated frogs, such as the metal frogs in Atlas Custom Line Mark II turnouts. Figure 9-17 shows how to wire around a turnout using SPDT auxiliary contacts.

Similar contacts on a control switch can accomplish this too, but that requires more wiring and can lead to short circuits, especially with slower-moving switch motors. If the switch contacts close for the opposite stock rail before the turnout point opens, a short circuit occurs. This "make-before-break" contact short is especially troublesome with command control, because power always remains on the track. Switch machine or switch motor contacts won't have this problem, unless there's excessive play ("slop") in the mechanical linkage to the points.

Another potential problem affects the point linkage. Some twin-solenoid machines have SPDT contacts with the switching terminal grounded to the metal arm or crank where the linkage attaches. This can lead to a make-before-break short, but it's easy to avoid by inserting some insulation into the linkage, such as the plastic tubing on the actuator wire in fig. 9-8.

While wiring around is a good practice for all turnouts, it isn't often necessary with stall motors—good thing since these don't include auxiliary contacts. These motors push points against stock rails with strong force, enough to ensure good contact unless the rails and points are unusually dirty.

Coil cutoff. The cutoff contact wiring in fig. 9-19 protects solenoid coils from burnout by breaking the circuit to a coil when the switch machine throws in its direction. The SPDT contact breaks the ground connection for one coil and makes it for the opposite one, so even if someone is leaning on a button, the switch machine remains safe.

Note that in many twin-coil machines the common connections from the two coils are joined at a central terminal. To use coil cutoff contacts you must unsolder that connection and re-route the wires through the auxiliary contacts.

With cutoff contacts (fig. 9-19) you can control a twin-solenoid machine with a nonmomentary switch, like an SPDT toggle.

Position indication. You can employ SPDT contacts to control

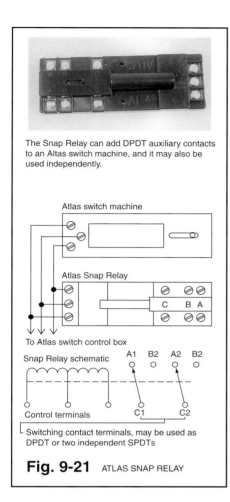

The Snap Relay can add DPDT auxiliary contacts to an Altas switch machine, and it may also be used independently.

Fig. 9-21 ATLAS SNAP RELAY

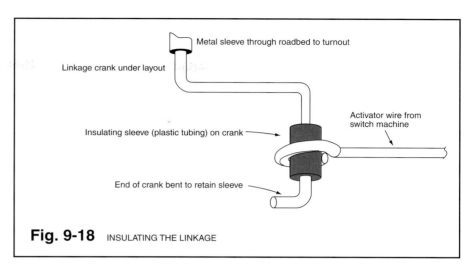

Fig. 9-18 INSULATING THE LINKAGE

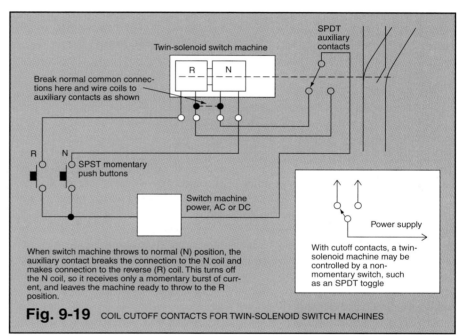

When switch machine throws to normal (N) position, the auxiliary contact breaks the connection to the N coil and makes connection to the reverse (R) coil. This turns off the N coil, so it receives only a momentary burst of current, and leaves the machine ready to throw to the R position.

With cutoff contacts, a twin-solenoid machine may be controlled by a non-momentary switch, such as an SPDT toggle

Fig. 9-19 COIL CUTOFF CONTACTS FOR TWIN-SOLENOID SWITCH MACHINES

panel or trackside signal lights showing which way turnouts are thrown, fig. 9-20. Again, extra contacts on the control switch could handle the panel lights with less wiring, but employing switch machine or switch motor contacts provides a positive indication. This is especially handy if you use parallel turnout controls on more than one panel, because the indicator lights show the actual position of the turnout "in the field."

Although the popular Atlas sectional track switch machines do not include auxiliary contacts, you can achieve the same effect by using Atlas No. 200 Snap Relay. This is a twin-coil relay you can wire in parallel with the switch machine, fig. 9-21. It provides a pair of SPDT contacts, which you can also use as a single DPDT switch. The Snap Relay can also serve as the latching relay in fig. 9-14.

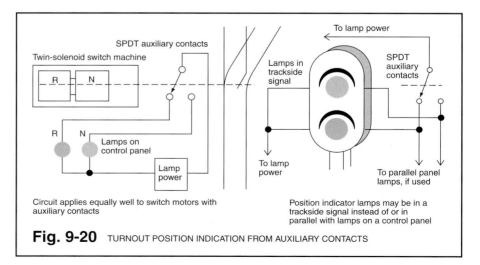

Circuit applies equally well to switch motors with auxiliary contacts

Position indicator lamps may be in a trackside signal instead of or in parallel with lamps on a control panel

Fig. 9-20 TURNOUT POSITION INDICATION FROM AUXILIARY CONTACTS

Layout wiring

CHAPTER TEN

The preceding chapters have helped you decide on the control wiring for your railroad—and given you a good idea of how to plan it. This chapter and the next will cover how to install wiring on—under!—the layout. We'll start by examining handy wiring tools, then discuss how to choose wire, systematically install wiring, connect wiring to the track, and wire accessories.

Wiring Tools and Techniques

If you're building a layout you've probably accumulated many of the tools necessary for wiring: a power drill or two, an assortment of screwdrivers, needle-nose pliers, a utility knife, and even the good old hammer. In addition, a few more-specialized tools are essential, and a couple are nice to own though not necessary.

Wire cutters and strippers. These most basic wiring tools are shown in fig. 10-1. The diagonal-cutting pliers are good for cutting wire in tight corners, and the big electrician's pliers can cut, bend, and crimp large wires.

The combination tool includes pliers, cutters, and strippers. You set the end of your insulated wire in the numbered stripping notch for its size, close the jaws, and pull the wire through to remove the insulation and expose the bare conductor. You can also close the jaws around the middle of a wire and pull the tool to expose an inch or two of the conductor for a tee splice (read on).

The automatic strippers remove insulation, too, but faster and more consistently. Again you place the insulated wire in the appropriate notch. Then squeeze the handles (the jaws will close automatically), pull the wire through a measured distance, and release it. For big wiring projects automatic strippers are worth the $15–$20 price for a good pair. They provide a mechanical advantage that makes stripping large wire and tough insulation easier, especially for tee splices.

Speaking of splices, fig. 10-2 shows some useful types. For strength and

conductivity it's important to make any splice a tight mechanical connection and to solder it to ensure this. You can twist a splice of small wires tight with your fingers, but for heavy wire use pliers. Wrap each splice with insulating tape or cover it with heat-shrinkable tubing to avoid accidental short circuits.

There's now an even quicker and easier way to make wire splices, using IDCs, insulation-displacement connectors, from the 3-M Corp.'s Scotchlok line. Also known as Scotchlok connectors or suitcase connectors, these plastic fittings hold two wires parallel while you force the connector's U-shaped, slotted metal "knife" through the wire insulation and into the metal conductors. See fig. 10-3.

The knife must be pressed flush with the body of the connector, a job requiring pliers with plenty of leverage like Channelocks. Then the suitcase lid can be folded over and snapped in place to form a strong, insulated splice.

IDCs come in several sizes to accept different gauges of wire, and they're color coded so you can easily select the right one for the wire you're using. On my own layout I'm using mostly brown No. 567s, sized for 10–12 AWG wire on the through or "run" side and 14–18 AWG wire on the single-ended or "tap" side; and red No. 558s for 18–22 AWG wire on both sides.

With IDCs you can make either end-to-end or tee splices, and they're slotted on the run side to slip over a wire that's already in place. No stripping is required for either wire, and the only cutting is to cut the tap wire to length. Whenever you have many connections to make to bus wires, as when you want to drop feeders from

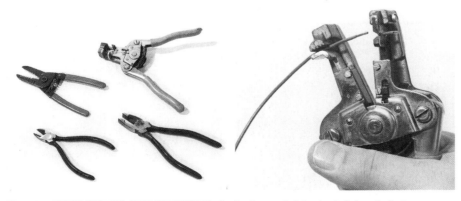

Fig. 10-1. WIRE CUTTER AND STRIPPERS. At the lower left in the left-hand photo you see a pair of diagonal-cutting pliers, and at the lower right, lineman's or electrician's pliers. At the upper left is a combination tool—pliers, cutter, and stripper—and at the upper right is an automatic wire stripper. The right-hand photo shows how the automatic stripper holds and neatly strips a wire.

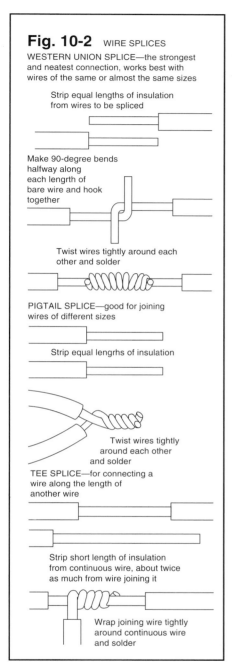

Fig. 10-2 WIRE SPLICES

WESTERN UNION SPLICE—the strongest and neatest connection, works best with wires of the same or almost the same sizes

Strip equal lengths of insulation from wires to be spliced

Make 90-degree bends halfway along each lengrth of bare wire and hook together

Twist wires tightly around each other and solder

PIGTAIL SPLICE—good for joining wires of different sizes

Strip equal lengrhs of insulation

Twist wires tightly around each other and solder

TEE SPLICE—for connecting a wire along the length of another wire

Strip short length of insulation from continuous wire, about twice as much from wire joining it

Wrap joining wire tightly around continuous wire and solder

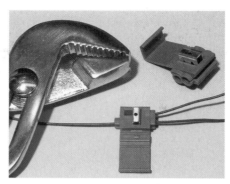

Fig. 10-3. Wires are easily joined using 3M's Scotchlok connectors (also called "suitcase connectors"). They are offered for various wire gauges. Wires are inserted, the metal wire connector is crimped down with pliers, and the lid is snapped shut.

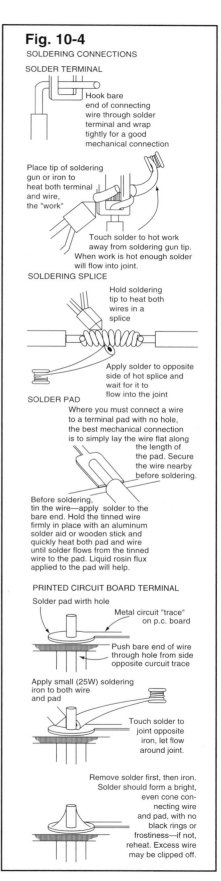

Fig. 10-4
SOLDERING CONNECTIONS

SOLDER TERMINAL

Hook bare end of connecting wire through solder terminal and wrap tightly for a good mechanical connection

Place tip of soldering gun or iron to heat both terminal and wire, the "work"

Touch solder to hot work away from soldering gun tip. When work is hot enough solder will flow into joint.

SOLDERING SPLICE

Hold soldering tip to heat both wires in a splice

Apply solder to opposite side of hot splice and wait for it to flow into the joint

SOLDER PAD

Where you must connect a wire to a terminal pad with no hole, the best mechanical connection is to simply lay the wire flat along the length of the pad. Secure the wire nearby before soldering.

Before soldering, tin the wire—apply solder to the bare end. Hold the tinned wire firmly in place with an aluminum solder aid or wooden stick and quickly heat both pad and wire until solder flows from the tinned wire to the pad. Liquid rosin flux applied to the pad will help.

PRINTED CIRCUIT BOARD TERMINAL

Solder pad wirth hole

Metal circuit "trace" on p.c. board

Push bare end of wire through hole from side opposite curcuit trace

Apply small (25W) soldering iron to both wire and pad

Touch solder to joint opposite iron, let flow around joint.

Remove solder first, then iron. Solder should form a bright, even cone connecting wire and pad, with no black rings or frostiness—if not, reheat. Excess wire may be clipped off.

every length of rail, IDCs will pay for themselves in time saved. They typically run around 25 to 30 cents apiece in small quantities in hardware stores, but they're cheaper when you buy them in bulk, and that's how you'll use them once you appreciate their speed and convenience.

Soldering gun. A fast-heating soldering gun is the most convenient tool for working under a model rail-

road and inside its control panels. I like the Weller DualHeat 100/140W model for most work, but for heavy wire (No. 14 or larger) a 200W gun would be better.

Along with the gun, use a 60/40 (60 percent tin, 40 percent lead) rosin-core solder—Kester Multicore is a popular brand. The rosin core is the "flux" that keeps the work pieces you want to join from oxidizing as you heat them. It also helps the molten solder to flow. A separate flux is sometimes helpful, and Kester makes a liquid rosin flux you can brush on where you need it.

NEVER use an acid flux, even one labeled "noncorrosive," for electrical connections. Some residual flux remains inside most joints, and current flow will cause the acid to eat away at the joint from within. Eventually you'll have a "cold joint" that won't conduct current and a difficult-to-track-down open circuit. A good rule is to assume flux not identified as rosin is unsafe for electrical soldering.

Most solder connections occur at wire splices and terminals. Figure 10-4 shows how to handle them. Soldering is a chemical process that depends upon heat to let the solder molecules bond to the work. Follow these steps to make good solder joints:

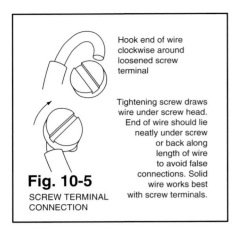

Fig. 10-5
SCREW TERMINAL CONNECTION

Hook end of wire clockwise around loosened screw terminal

Tightening screw draws wire under screw head. End of wire should lie neatly under screw or back along length of wire to avoid false connections. Solid wire works best with screw terminals.

1. Make sure the work is clean, using a file, knife, or wire brush to expose a bright metal surface if necessary, and make a good mechanical connection. If you're using a separate flux, apply a small amount now.

2. Hold the hot soldering gun to the joint so it touches both pieces to be joined.

3. Touch the solder to the work, not to the tip of the gun. When the work is hot enough to melt the solder it is at the right temperature for the chemical bond. Allow a small amount of solder to flow into the joint.

4. When the joint appears wet with solder, remove the solder, then the gun, being careful not to disturb the joint.

5. Keep the joint still until the solder cools with a bright, shiny surface. If the work moves before the solder cools, it will make a cold joint, one with a dull or frosted surface, which will not be a reliable connection.

Crimping tool. Before I explain this tool I need to say something about screw terminal connections. Figure 10-5 illustrates the right way to attach a wire to a screw terminal, like a power pack or sectional track terminal, or on a screw terminal strip. This method works well with a single solid wire of small to medium size; with multiple connections, stranded wire, or large solid wire it's not as effective. A better way is to use wire terminals, fig. 10-6.

The crimping tool in fig. 10-6 is for installing solderless wire terminals or "lugs," which can be used with either solid or stranded wire. Vaco and Xcelite are two widely distributed crimping tool brands, and Vaco makes solderless terminals in several styles. For most layout wiring I prefer uninsulated open-end terminals, also called "spade lugs"; these come in sizes to match different wire gauges.

To install a solderless terminal, strip a short length of insulation equal to the length of the terminal sleeve. Slip the terminal over the bare conductor, then crimp or squeeze the sleeve closed in two places with the crimping tool to make a tight connection.

Heat gun. This is a nonessential tool, but handy if you have lots of wire splicing to do, fig. 10-7. I've mentioned heat-shrink tubing, an insulating tubing made of plastic that shrinks when heated. You slip the tubing over a soldered splice, apply heat, and the tubing shrinks tight to insulate the joint.

If you work fast a still-warm solder joint will often start the shrinking, but usually it takes more heat to pull the tubing in tight. You can hold a match, a lighter, or a hot soldering iron near the tubing, but the heat gun is the best tool for this job. By the way, it may look and work as if it's an industrial-strength hair dryer, but it is not safe for drying your hair!

Mechanic's creeper. Again nonessential, but nice if you must spend time under a layout. This low platform on casters, fig. 10-8, can save wear and tear on your clothes, your muscles, and your temper.

Some people have added chair backs to creepers to make themselves more comfortable, but I was able to wire in real comfort when I built the Washita & Santa Fe project layout for MODEL RAILROADER. I made the W&SF benchwork high for scenic and

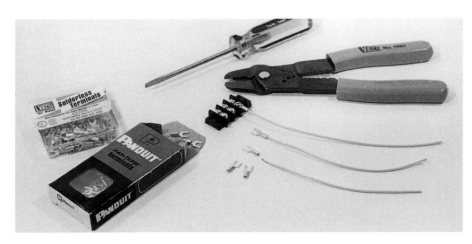

Fig. 10-6. **CRIMP-ON WIRE TERMINALS.** These "solderless" terminals, which you install by crimping them onto the stripped end of a wire, make the neatest connections to screw terminals. These terminal connections are solid and dependable, and are easy to disconnect for changes or troubleshooting.

Fig. 10-7. **HEAT GUN.** This tool uses a heating element and a blower to produce a stream of hot air that quickly and neatly tightens heat-shrink tubing around a wire splice.

viewing reasons, and with about three feet clear under the L girders I could sit in a castered swivel chair and roll in to work below the layout.

Trouble light. I call this nonessential only because I've done plenty of wiring without one, but it's dark under most layouts and a light like the one in fig. 10-9 is a help. In fact, between working in the dark and bumping and scraping my head, I'm about at the point where I'm ready to outfit myself with a hard hat and a miner's lamp!

Choosing Wire

Wire sizes are designated by American Wire Gauge (AWG) numbers, such as "No. 18" or "18-gauge." The lower the number the bigger the wire. A No. 12 solid wire, for example, is .080″ in diameter, while a No. 20 solid wire is .032″ in diameter. Stranded wire is rated in the same scale, but is larger in diameter for a given number, so that its multiple strands have the same area in cross section as the equivalent solid wire.

Wire size is important because wire itself introduces resistance into a circuit, and too great a resistance can reduce the voltage or current available to run a train or throw a turnout. A common example of this is a train that runs slower when further away from the terminal track feeders in a simple sectional track layout, fig. 10-10.

Running wires from the power pack to a second terminal solves the problem because the copper wires have less resistance—they're better conductors—than nickel silver, steel, or even brass rails. A wire's resistance is determined by both its length and diameter, among other factors. On a larger layout where feeders run many feet from a cab to a distant block, undersize wire can introduce enough resistance to cause the same slowing.

Problems can be even more pronounced with other equipment. In Chapter 9 I explained how twin-solenoid switch machines may work sluggishly or not at all if their wiring can't

Fig. 10-8. MECHANIC'S CREEPER. A creeper, a low platform on casters, is a handy and relatively comfortable way to get under a layout to work on wiring.

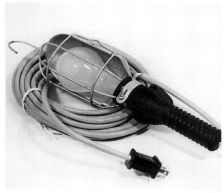

Fig. 10-9. TROUBLE LIGHT. Is it too dark under your layout? Can you really see what wires and terminals you're working on? The trouble light provides helpful illumination and an extension outlet for power tools.

carry the heavy currents they require. With command control systems, as we saw in Chapter 8, feeder wiring has to be able to supply several trains at once, and excessive resistance in the wiring can distort control signals and cause erratic operation.

Two other factors affect a wire's resistance: the metal it's made from and the voltage applied to it. Copper is one of the best conductors, and copper wire is so readily available and easy to use, especially in soldering, that it's not worth worrying

about other materials. Voltage is mostly determined by the trains and equipment we want to use; wire length is determined by the dimensions and designs of our layouts. That leaves wire size as the easiest factor for us to control.

Guide to Wire Sizes

Figure 10-11 is a conservative rule-of-thumb guide for selecting copper wire sizes for model railroad feeder circuits. Wiring for twin-solenoid switch machines should employ at

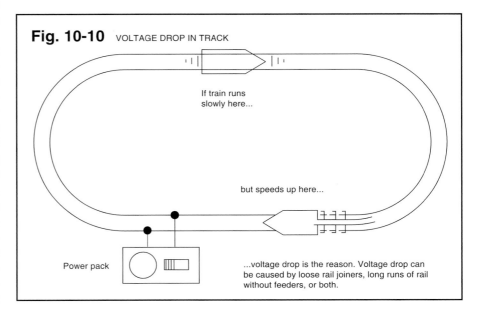

Fig. 10-10 VOLTAGE DROP IN TRACK

If train runs slowly here...

but speeds up here...

Power pack

...voltage drop is the reason. Voltage drop can be caused by loose rail joiners, long runs of rail without feeders, or both.

Fig. 10-11 WIRE SELECTION CHART

AWG wire sizes to carry:

For wire lengths (one side of circuit) up to:	1A	3A	5A	10A
6"	28	24	22	20
12"	24	22	20	18
8'	22	20	18	16
12'	20	18	16	14
20'	18	16	14	12
30'	16	14	12	10

Fig. 10-13

SAMPLE LAYOUT COLOR CODE

TRACK

Controlled block feeder:	White
Common feeder:	Black
Reverse section feeders:	Red

SWITCH MACHINES

Common or ground:	Green
Normal:	Blue
Reverse:	Yellow

ACCESSORY LIGHTING

Common or ground:	Green (can be shared)
Power:	Brown

Fig. 10-12

USING WIRE ON THE LAYOUT

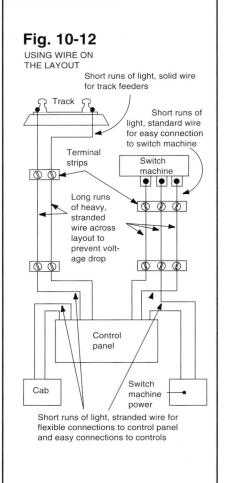

Short runs of light, solid wire for track feeders

Track

Short runs of light, standard wire for easy connection to switch machine

Terminal strips

Switch machine

Long runs of heavy, stranded wire across layout to prevent voltage drop

Control panel

Cab

Switch machine power

Short runs of light, stranded wire for flexible connections to control panel and easy connections to controls

Control panel

Terminal strip

Feeder cable

Feeders are located so that several may be connected at each "cable head" terminal strip. Cables are grouped for the most direct run to cable heads.

Fig. 10-14 CABLE RUNS ON A LAYOUT

least the same size as 3A track feeders, unless you're using a capacitor discharge supply that delivers more than 20V. In that case the 1A feeder size wire will be adequate because of the higher voltage.

For command control systems, you should assume that the feeder wiring must deliver the maximum rated current of the power supply to every part of the railroad, or at least every part of a given power supply district. For example, a pair of feeder busses extending 20 feet from a 5A supply should be No. 14 wire. This should meet or exceed most command control manufacturers' recommendations.

Connecting No. 18 or larger wires directly to rails, control switches, or switch machines/motors is difficult and impractical. It's also unnecessary, because short lengths of smaller wire won't add appreciably to the resistance of a long run of large wire.

Solid or Stranded

Besides choosing wire size, you have the option of using solid or stranded wire. Solid wire is neater at terminals and splices and enjoys the advantage of compactness since it is smaller for a given AWG number than stranded wire of the same gauge. Stranded wire is more flexible, and not likely to break if moved or rearranged.

Figure 10-12 shows a wiring system that takes advantage of the different wire gauges and both solid and stranded wire. One exception to fig. 10-12 is that with large sizes, No. 12 or higher, it's usually more convenient and inexpensive to employ solid wire in sheathed cables as used for house wiring. This stuff is so stiff and unwieldy it's unlikely to shift around enough to break accidentally.

Color Coding

A final consideration in choosing wire is color coding. Using wires with different insulation colors helps you keep track of your circuits. On any but the simplest layouts, however, it won't be practical to use different colors to identify wires to each block or switch machine. Stocking many different colors is expensive, and it will be hard to find enough colors. Besides, too many colors becomes almost as confusing as too many wires all the same color.

Using color codes to identify different circuits is, however, worthwhile. Figure 10-13 suggests a way to color code a model railroad's wire so you can easily remember what's what when you're under the layout. The colors represent suggestions; use whatever colors you have or can find, but use them consistently.

Wiring Organization

There are a couple of good reasons for keeping your wiring organized. First, most control systems require substantial wiring under the layout. If your wiring isn't neat it will continually interfere with future projects. Also, when problems arise—and none of us is perfect—they'll be easier to isolate if you can tell which wire goes where. Here are three ways to ensure sound wiring organization.

Cables. One of the most effective ways to keep wiring neat and well organized under the layout is to group wires heading the same direction into cables. Run the cables in straight lines, fig. 10-14. Generally it's best if cables follow the lines of benchwork girders or joists, to protect the cables and to keep all areas open for other work.

A simple way to make cables is to wrap a couple of turns of electrical tape around a group of wires every 12″ or 18″, fig. 10-15. Tying a cable is good for flexibility, because wires can be pulled out and others slipped in fairly easily. This also applies to some extent to the spiral cable wrap.

Figure 10-16 shows several ways to hang cables under the layout. The simple kitchen cup hooks are a favorite of mine: The hooks keep the cable in place well enough and permit easy removal and rearrangement. Heavy cables, like sheathed No. 12

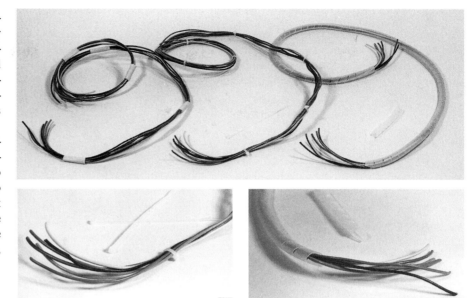

Fig. 10-15. MAKING CABLES. The top photo shows three ways to bundle loose wires into cables, from the left: masking tape, a convenient expedient; cable ties, polyethylene straps that lock when you pull them tight around the wires; and spiral wrap, an expandable polyethylene sheath. The closeups (above left and right) give you better looks at the cable ties and spiral wrap.

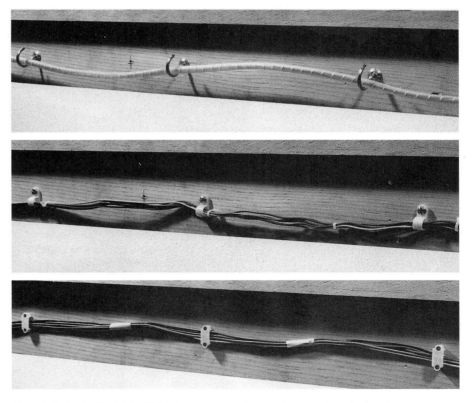

Fig. 10-16. HANGING CABLES. Three ways to hang cables under a layout (from top to bottom): with ordinary kitchen cup hooks; with plastic cable clamps screwed to the benchwork; and with plastic cable staples nailed to the benchwork.

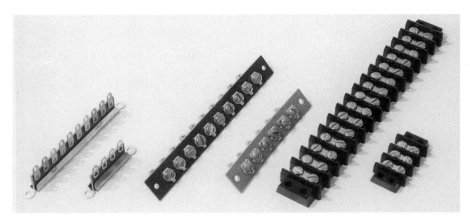

Fig. 10-17. TERMINAL STRIPS. At the left are two examples of solder-terminal strips, sometimes called tag strips. They have metal bases that can be screwed in place and metal loop solder terminals riveted to a strip of insulating material. In the center are two screw-and-solder-terminal strips. They are designed to mount on a panel or metal chassis box with the screw terminals outside and the solder terminals inside. At the right are a couple of screw-terminal strips, also called barrier strips because they have plastic walls between terminals to help prevent accidental bridge connections.

shows common types, all of which come in varying sizes with different numbers of terminals.

Terminal strips make convenient places to organize wiring, to sort out wires going from one place to another, and to identify what's what. The feeders coming from the layout to a control panel, for example, can actually terminate at a terminal strip behind the panel. There you can sort out block feeders in numerical order, say, and line them up for orderly connection to the panel controls.

A terminal strip is also a good place to change from one size wire to another, as from a heavy bus cable to small track feeders. Once terminal strips are in place, they make it easy to add or change connections.

Furthermore, terminal strips come in handy for troubleshooting, because you can use them as test points for reading voltages without stripping or disconnecting your wiring. In extreme trouble, you can easily disconnect wires at terminal strips to isolate the problem, and reconnect them once it's fixed.

Figure 10-4 shows how to make connections at solder-lug terminal strips; screw-terminal connections are shown in fig. 10-5. For greatest reliability, put cable hangers or other supports near the terminal strip, so that the terminal connections don't have to support the weight of a cable.

Often it's handy to bridge several terminals for common connections, fig. 10-18. Solid, bare bus wire is available in common AWG sizes; use it to bridge screw terminals as well as solder types. The terminal bridges, fig. 10-18 are made for this purpose and easier to use.

Record keeping. Complex wiring can ambush you. Each block or switch motor is easy to hook up, but once you've wired the whole layout it's easy to forget what you've done. If more than one person works on a layout's wiring, confusion will occur that much sooner.

The obvious solution to this problem: written records. Although

Fig. 10-18. BRIDGING TERMINALS. Sometimes you want to connect two or more terminals on a terminal strip together. Terminal bridges like these are available for barrier terminal strips, and you can bridge solder terminals with solid bare bus wire.

Fig. 10-19. LABELING TERMINALS. Take time to clearly mark your terminal connections when you install them, and you'll save yourself a lot of headaches when you trace or change circuits. Here dry-transfer (rub-on) lettering has been applied to a small strip of illustration board, and then that was glued in place next to the terminal strip.

house cable, need something more positive, and the nail-in-place cable clamp in fig. 10-16 does a good job.

It's a good idea to keep cables above the lowest edge of benchwork members—alongside an L girder, for example—so they will be out of your way when you're moving around under the layout. Don't drill holes in

the benchwork joists and thread wires through them, however, since this requires more work than is needed to run the cables. It also makes wiring and benchwork changes more difficult.

Terminal strips are insulating material with screws or solder lugs for attaching wires. Figure 10-17

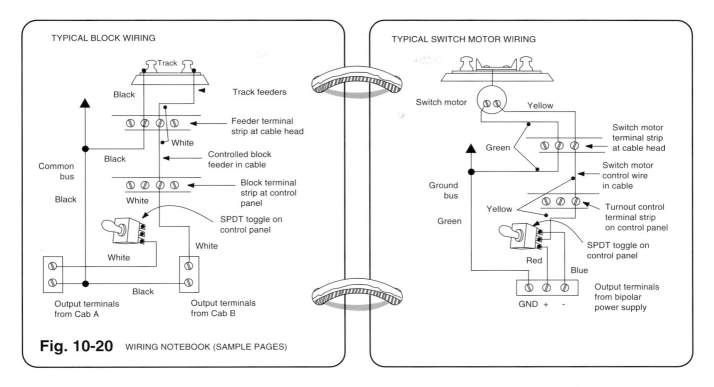

TYPICAL BLOCK WIRING

Track

Black — Track feeders

Feeder terminal strip at cable head

White

Black — Controlled block feeder in cable

Common bus

Black

White — Block terminal strip at control panel

SPDT toggle on control panel

White

White

Black

Output terminals from Cab A

Output terminals from Cab B

TYPICAL SWITCH MOTOR WIRING

Switch motor

Yellow

Green — Switch motor terminal strip at cable head

Ground bus

Switch motor control wire in cable

Yellow

Green — Turnout control terminal strip on control panel

SPDT toggle on control panel

Red

Blue

Output terminals from bipolar power supply

GND + -

Fig. 10-20 WIRING NOTEBOOK (SAMPLE PAGES)

record keeping shouldn't evolve into a project in itself, careful note-taking can reduce those episodes of confusion. Start by adopting a system of nomenclature as I'll describe in the next chapter, and record it on a track plan of your layout in a loose-leaf notebook.

Use your nomenclature to label terminal strips, fig. 10-19, and cables disconnected from their terminals. Also, label switches and buttons inside a control panel and switch machines and other devices under the layout.

For the rest of your notebook you'll only need a few pages to draw and label wiring for one typical block, one switch motor, one walkaround cab bus, and so forth, fig. 10-20. This gives you a record of how your layout is wired without drawing every wire. The records must be simpler than the layout to be useful, and if keeping them becomes too much of a chore most of us won't follow through.

Special situations, like reverse loops or automatic routing on a yard ladder, require their own pages. Even so, only a highly complicated layout would require more than a couple dozen record sheets in the binder.

Track Wiring

Here we're dealing not with theory but with the nuts and bolts of insulating and making connections to the rails. First look at the basic products for sectional track systems, fig. 10-21.

The plastic rail joiners replace metal ones to insulate rails; they can be used in one or both rails depending on whether you use common-rail wiring. The terminal track section

provides screw terminals for feeder connections; be sure you know which terminal connects to which rail. "Terminal joiners" are regular metal joiners that come with feeder wires soldered to them; they give you the flexibility to locate feeders in places where you do not want to use a standard terminal track section or to avoid having unrealistic screw terminals alongside your track.

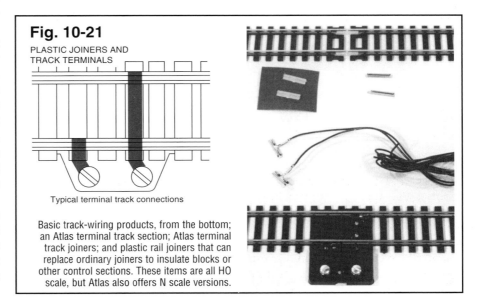

Fig. 10-21

PLASTIC JOINERS AND TRACK TERMINALS

Typical terminal track connections

Basic track-wiring products, from the bottom; an Atlas terminal track section; Atlas terminal track joiners; and plastic rail joiners that can replace ordinary joiners to insulate blocks or other control sections. These items are all HO scale, but Atlas also offers N scale versions.

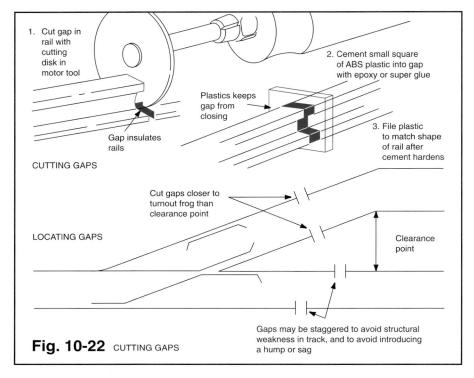

1. Cut gap in rail with cutting disk in motor tool

Gap insulates rails

CUTTING GAPS

Plastics keeps gap from closing

2. Cement small square of ABS plastic into gap with epoxy or super glue

3. File plastic to match shape of rail after cement hardens

LOCATING GAPS

Cut gaps closer to turnout frog than clearance point

Clearance point

Gaps may be staggered to avoid structural weakness in track, and to avoid introducing a hump or sag

Fig. 10-22 CUTTING GAPS

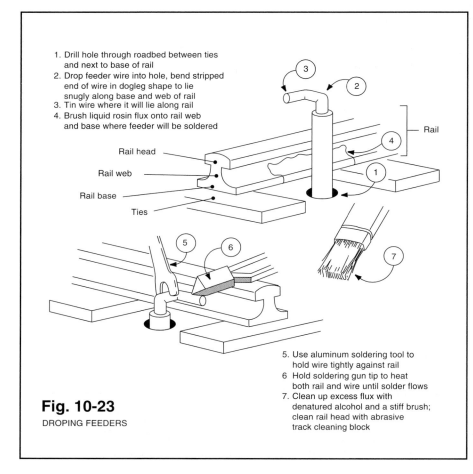

1. Drill hole through roadbed between ties and next to base of rail
2. Drop feeder wire into hole, bend stripped end of wire in dogleg shape to lie snugly along base and web of rail
3. Tin wire where it will lie along rail
4. Brush liquid rosin flux onto rail web and base where feeder will be soldered

Rail head

Rail web

Rail base

Ties

Rail

5. Use aluminum soldering tool to hold wire tightly against rail
6 Hold soldering gun tip to heat both rail and wire until solder flows
7. Clean up excess flux with denatured alcohol and a stiff brush; clean rail head with abrasive track cleaning block

Fig. 10-23
DROPING FEEDERS

Now we'll examine techniques you can employ to serve these same functions in any track.

Cutting Gaps

When you lay flextrack or hand-made track, it's simplest to make the rails continuous, then come back and cut insulating gaps where needed. That has structural advantages too, since plastic rail joiners lack the stiffness to hold rails in line on curves. I prefer to use plastic rail joiners in crossovers made with ready-to-lay turnouts. This avoids having to cut gaps after the fact in close quarters. Otherwise, I find cutting gaps after the track is laid is the best way to go.

Figure 10-22 shows how to cut and fill a gap. A motor tool is essential, since saws and rail nippers won't do the job. Wear eye protection because pieces of a broken cutting wheel fly off at high speed, and you'll likely be looking right at it.

The plastic filler keeps the gap from closing if the rails expand or "creep," move lengthwise, as they can and will do. If you use light gray acrylic-butyl-styrene or ABS plastic, such as that sold by Plastruct, the filler will be practically indistinguishable from nickel silver rail. A closed gap may cause a short circuit that's hard to trace because its source won't be easy to determine.

Figure 10-22 also conflicts with the conventional rule of putting gaps at "clearance points," where the diverging routes are far enough apart to separate safely passing rolling stock. My experience is that in the heat of operation, people often try to squeeze more cars into a siding than you figured they should. But if it's physically possible, why penalize it? Even if it's not, why have both a collision and a short circuit?

Additionally, having the gap close to the turnout frog provides a structural advantage when using flextrack. The tie strip used in turnouts is usually stiffer than that in flextrack, and, besides, it isn't made with spaces to let it flex. If you cut only the rail, the intact tie strip will help to hold the rail in line on both sides of the gap.

Dropping Feeders

An old favorite technique for making feeder connections to the track is shown in fig. 10-23. Using small-gauge, solid wire helps make the feeder unobtrusive on a finished layout scene, especially when the track is painted and weathered. "Tinning" the feeder helps with this too: With a clean rail and liquid rosin flux, you won't need additional solder and won't end up with an unsightly blob.

The rail must get hot enough to melt the solder to effect a good chemical bond. If you use a sufficiently large soldering iron or gun you can heat the rail quickly enough to avoid melting plastic ties and throwing the track out of gauge. A 140W gun is adequate with Code 100 rail.

"Just right" is what you want in a soldering tool for this work. A large soldering iron might curl up the ties as soon as you bring it near, but a worse mistake is to use an iron or gun that's too small. A small, low-wattage iron will take too long to heat the joint, and meanwhile the rail can conduct enough heat to melt or soften ties away from where you're working.

As a precaution you may wish to place a metal, three-point track gauge across the rails on each side of the feeder. The gauges act as heat sinks to protect the ties, and hold the rail in gauge if the ties should soften.

Another method, effective with hand-laid track, is shown in fig. 10-24. This makes the feeders practically invisible, though they'll also be inaccessible if a cold joint develops.

My favorite way to make "invisible" feeder connections is shown in fig. 10-25. Using 22 AWG solid wire in HO scale, the spike-head feeder can be very close in size to common track spikes, and when painted will be indistinguishable from them. The spike-head feeder will also be small enough to be used inside the rail, where the wheel flanges run, as well as outside. This means that feeders can be placed

on the side of the rail away from the normal viewing angle, so they'll be out of sight but still accessible.

Any of these hidden feeder methods is especially useful when you drop feeders from every length of rail, for the bus-and-feeder approach described in Chapter 1. You'll necessarily have a lot of feeders, and you don't want them to attract attention. The chief advantage of the bus-and-feeder method is that copper wire serves as a better conductor for a given size than brass, steel, or especially nickel silver rail. Bus-and-feeder wiring can practically eliminate voltage drop or loss of command signals, so long as the busses are large enough.

Don't use bus-and-feeder wiring as an excuse to eliminate rail joiners. Rail joiners are far from perfect as electrical connections, but their structural strength is an advantage in both the construction and reliable service of model railroad track. Besides, there are ways around their electrical faults.

Soldering or Bonding Rail Joiners

For various reasons—loose fit and oxidation to name two—rail joiners can add unnecessary resistance to your track circuit. Figure 10-26 shows two simple ways to overcome this.

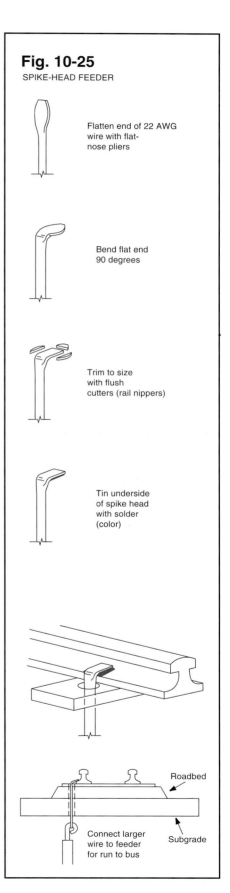

Fig. 10-24 HIDDEN FEEDERS

Rail smaller than Code 100— solder feeder under base of rail beford laying. Feeder may be soldered between ties on underside of flextrack

Code 100 and larger rail—drill wire-sized hole into base and web of rail, solder feeder into hole before laying rail

Fig. 10-25
SPIKE-HEAD FEEDER

Flatten end of 22 AWG wire with flat-nose pliers

Bend flat end 90 degrees

Trim to size with flush cutters (rail nippers)

Tin underside of spike head with solder (color)

Roadbed

Subgrade

Connect larger wire to feeder for run to bus

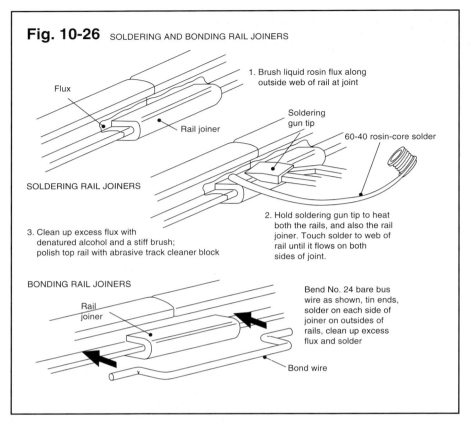

Fig. 10-26 SOLDERING AND BONDING RAIL JOINERS

Flux

Rail joiner

SOLDERING RAIL JOINERS

1. Brush liquid rosin flux along outside web of rail at joint

Soldering gun tip

60-40 rosin-core solder

3. Clean up excess flux with denatured alcohol and a stiff brush; polish top rail with abrasive track cleaner block

2. Hold soldering gun tip to heat both the rails, and also the rail joiner. Touch solder to web of rail until it flows on both sides of joint.

BONDING RAIL JOINERS

Rail joiner

Bend No. 24 bare bus wire as shown, tin ends, solder on each side of joiner on outsides of rails, clean up excess flux and solder

Bond wire

A small plug-in transformer like this one from Cir-Kit Concepts makes a convenient power supply for bulbs and other low-cost accessories

Fig. 10-27

ACCESSORY POWER AND SERIES WIRING

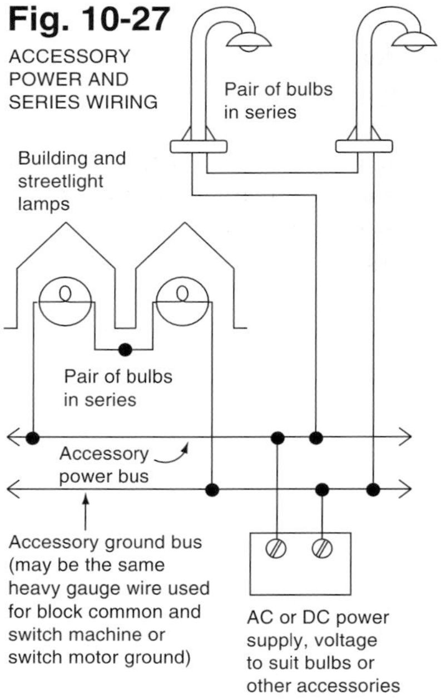

Pair of bulbs in series

Building and streetlight lamps

Pair of bulbs in series

Accessory power bus

Accessory ground bus (may be the same heavy gauge wire used for block common and switch machine or switch motor ground)

AC or DC power supply, voltage to suit bulbs or other accessories

Soldering the joiners is the easiest. Make sure to heat both rails and the joiner at once, and use liquid rosin flux to let the solder flow inside the joiner. That way you need only a small amount of solder.

Bond wires are named for their prototypical counterparts, used to ensure conductivity for signal circuits around bolted-bar ("fishplate") rail joints. Small wire is adequate because the bonds are so short, and the soldering technique is just like installing feeders. Bond wires are more work than just soldering the joints, but they do allow for expansion and contraction.

It's really more a matter of track-laying than wiring, but even if you are concerned about expansion and contraction, I'd recommend soldering joiners on curves and using bond wires or feeders to every rail on straight track. Soldered joiners make it easier to lay smooth curves, and the straightaways usually allow enough rail movement for all but the most extreme temperature and humidity changes.

Accessory Wiring

Model railroad accessories don't need wiring much different from what we've seen for train and switch machine control. It can be simple or complex depending on how much control you want.

Accessories do draw power, perhaps not much individually, about 100mA per grain-of-wheat bulb, but it all adds up. If you have more than a couple of lighted buildings or other such current users, it's worth having a separate power supply for them. Light bulbs work equally well on AC or DC, and you can power many with a small plug-in transformer, fig. 10-27.

The illustration also makes a basic point about wiring small bulbs for both interior and exterior lighting. Usually they are more than bright enough on half their rated voltage or less, and they last longer at the lower voltage. Similar bulbs wired in series divide the available voltage, an easy way to control brightness and prolong bulb life.

An AC accessory supply can share a common return bus with AC switch machine power, and even with DC switch motor and cab control wiring, fig. 10-27. Any AC supply, however, should be kept completely isolated from command control wiring.

Control panels

CHAPTER ELEVEN

Put control panels in places that make controlling your railroad easier, and design them so they don't detract from the main attraction: the trains. We will examine what influences where you put panels, then see how to design and build them.

Locating Control Panels

With a small railroad the control panel should go on the front, at the best viewing position, and near the main switching location. Of course these may vary, so you begin to get an idea of the choices you can make.

Figure 11-1 is an example of a simple layout that might be wired with a basic cab control system including two cabs sharing a common selector panel (Chapter 5). The layout is my Jefferson, Memphis & Northern. On

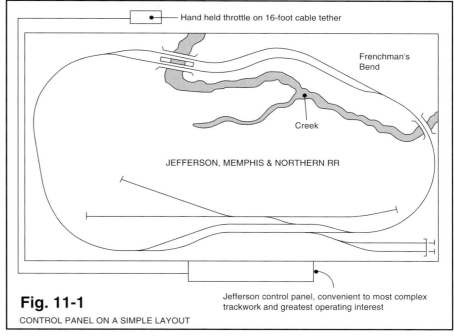

Hand held throttle on 16-foot cable tether

Frenchman's Bend

Creek

JEFFERSON, MEMPHIS & NORTHERN RR

Jefferson control panel, convenient to most complex trackwork and greatest operating interest

Fig. 11-1
CONTROL PANEL ON A SIMPLE LAYOUT

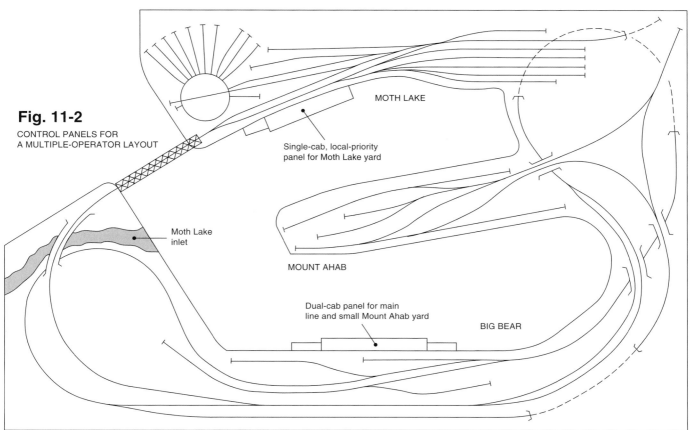

Fig. 11-2
CONTROL PANELS FOR
A MULTIPLE-OPERATOR LAYOUT

MOTH LAKE

Single-cab, local-priority
panel for Moth Lake yard

Moth Lake
inlet

MOUNT AHAB

Dual-cab panel for main
line and small Mount Ahab yard

BIG BEAR

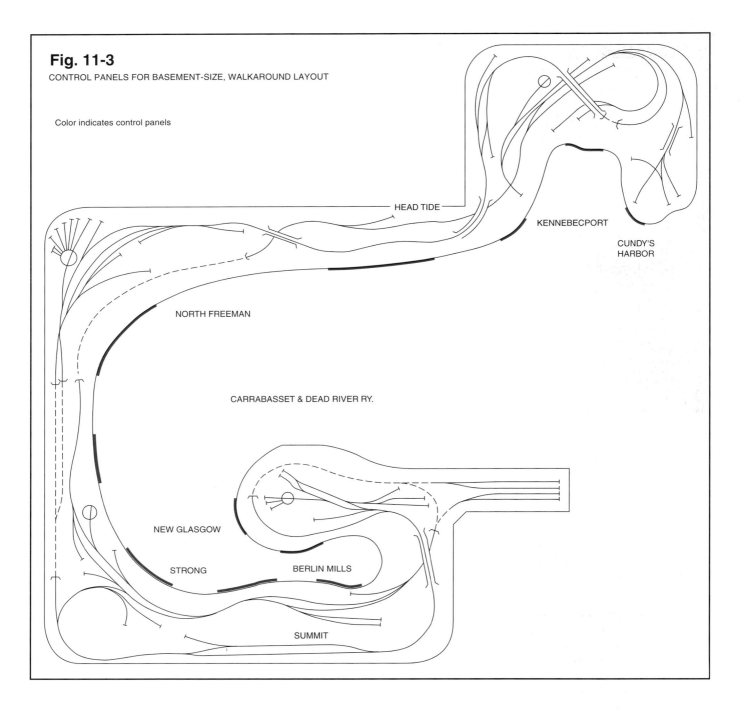

Fig. 11-3

CONTROL PANELS FOR BASEMENT-SIZE, WALKAROUND LAYOUT

Color indicates control panels

HEAD TIDE

KENNEBECPORT

CUNDY'S HARBOR

NORTH FREEMAN

CARRABASSET & DEAD RIVER RY.

NEW GLASGOW

STRONG

BERLIN MILLS

SUMMIT

the 5 x 9-foot (HO) JM&N, the best panel location is at the station in Jefferson, up front and on top of the switching. Still, you might want a tethered throttle too, so you can stay in control while watching a train snaking along the creek through Frenchman's Bend.

For larger railroads with more operators, locate multiple panels to suit the needs of each operator. The track plan in fig. 11-2 is Leonard Blumenschine's 11 x 18-foot (HO) Moth Lake & Mount Ahab. I've shown it with a dual cab panel at Big Bear, convenient for two engineers running trains on the main line. This panel could also control the small yard at Mount Ahab. The yard at Moth Lake is big enough to have its own engineer/yardmaster, so I've shown a single-cab panel there. It would be wired for local-priority control of the yard and its approach (Chapter 6 and see figs. 7-9 and 7-10).

Railroads designed for walkaround control won't have a "main panel" or single master control location. Instead they'll have several smaller panels controlling portions of the railroad. Bob Hayden's HOn2½ Carabasset & Dead River Ry. includes decentralized cab control wiring (Chapter 6). Figure

11-3 shows how he's placed the controls on local panels convenient to the blocks and turnouts they operate.

The same principle applies to command control railroads using walkaround operation, although with command control you won't need control panels except for turnout controls at places with complex trackwork. Figure 11-4 shows some examples of this on MODEL RAILROADER Magazine's HO scale Milwaukee, Racine & Troy RR.

Control panels are usually mounted on the layout edge or fascia, though all but the smallest panels should be solidly supported by the benchwork. For small table layouts there's generally no problem with the space the panel takes up, but when panels extend into confined aisleways or operating spaces they can become obstacles. Where you have a choice, locate panels in the widest parts of your aisleways, to allow for other operators to pass the one working at a panel.

The aisle space a control panel takes up depends a lot on its shape, and for convenient viewing its shape depends on the height of the layout. The higher your layout the steeper you can make the face of a panel, as shown in fig. 11-5.

A couple of methods permit you to remove panels from the aisleway altogether: recessing them into the layout or mounting them overhead (suspended from the ceiling), fig. 11-6. The recessed panel may be more complicated to build, but of the two I'd choose this one because it wouldn't need the long cables required to connect an overhead panel to the layout.

You can even build movable or portable panels to add flexibility in panel location. Figure 11-7 suggests possibilities, all of which I've seen used on model railroads. They involve more complicated carpentry and require flexible, multiconductor "umbilical" cables, so I'd want a strong reason to tackle the extra trouble.

Designing Control Panels

Most of us like a graphic track display on a control panel, so relating

Fig. 11-4. TURNOUT CONTROLS ON THE MILWAUKEE, RACINE & TROY. For walkaround operation, turnout controls may be located on the front edge of the layout next to the turnouts they control. In the left-hand photo, the switches controlling passing-siding turnouts are simply mounted in the layout fascia. In the right-hand photo, an important yard-entrance crossover rates a rotary-switch control and a small panel with position-indicator lights (LEDs).

the controls to the railroad is easier for visitors and regular operators. The most direct way to accomplish this is with a track plan schematic, fig. 11-8. With a simple layout like this one, Bill Baron's Somers Junction RR, the schematic is clear enough. The curves are represented as angles to make the schematic easier to lay out with masking tape, but note that the turnouts are shown in their correct left- or right-hand orientation. Gaps may be left in the schematic lines to indicate block boundaries.

Figure 11-9 shows a control panel schematic for the same railroad, but with the track plan "unwrapped" into a straight line. It doesn't make much difference here, but for a more complex, multi-lap track plan the straight-line schematic is easier to follow. Also, a straight-line schematic can help make a shallower panel that doesn't protrude so far from the edge of the layout. It also has a psychological advantage in representing the railroad as going from one place to another rather than as a loop.

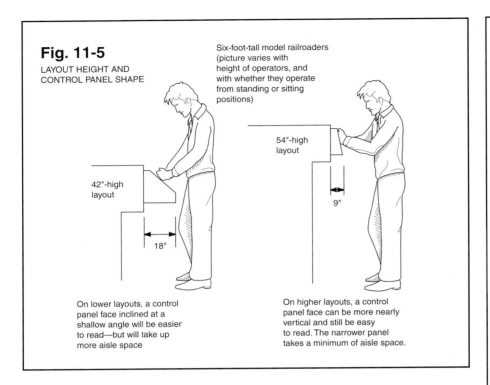

Fig. 11-5

LAYOUT HEIGHT AND
CONTROL PANEL SHAPE

Six-foot-tall model railroaders (picture varies with height of operators, and with whether they operate from standing or sitting positions)

54"-high layout

42"-high layout

9"

18"

On lower layouts, a control panel face inclined at a shallow angle will be easier to read—but will take up more aisle space

On higher layouts, a control panel face can be more nearly vertical and still be easy to read. The narrower panel takes a minimum of aisle space.

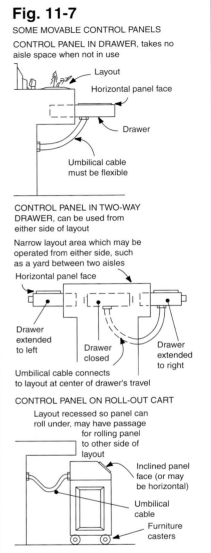

Fig. 11-7

SOME MOVABLE CONTROL PANELS

CONTROL PANEL IN DRAWER, takes no aisle space when not in use

Layout

Horizontal panel face

Drawer

Umbilical cable must be flexible

CONTROL PANEL IN TWO-WAY DRAWER, can be used from either side of layout

Narrow layout area which may be operated from either side, such as a yard between two aisles

Horizontal panel face

Drawer extended to left

Drawer closed

Drawer extended to right

Umbilical cable connects to layout at center of drawer's travel

CONTROL PANEL ON ROLL-OUT CART

Layout recessed so panel can roll under, may have passage for rolling panel to other side of layout

Inclined panel face (or may be horizontal)

Umbilical cable

Furniture casters

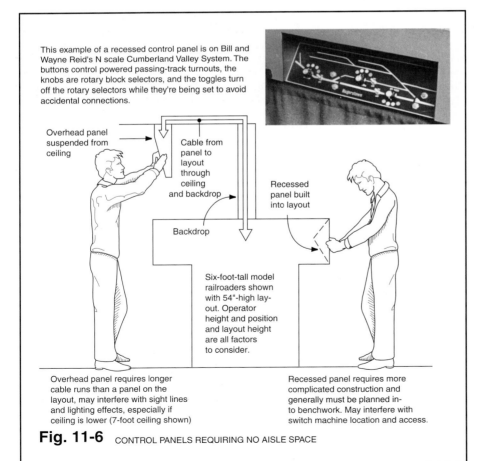

This example of a recessed control panel is on Bill and Wayne Reid's N scale Cumberland Valley System. The buttons control powered passing-track turnouts, the knobs are rotary block selectors, and the toggles turn off the rotary selectors while they're being set to avoid accidental connections.

Overhead panel suspended from ceiling

Cable from panel to layout through ceiling and backdrop

Recessed panel built into layout

Backdrop

Six-foot-tall model railroaders shown with 54"-high layout. Operator height and position and layout height are all factors to consider.

Overhead panel requires longer cable runs than a panel on the layout, may interfere with sight lines and lighting effects, especially if ceiling is lower (7-foot ceiling shown)

Recessed panel requires more complicated construction and generally must be planned into benchwork. May interfere with switch machine location and access.

Fig. 11-6   CONTROL PANELS REQUIRING NO AISLE SPACE

When a panel controls only part of the railroad it needs only a partial schematic. Figure 11-10 shows two examples, a yard panel for local-priority yard control, and a panel controlling one station and the adjacent mainline blocks in a walkaround system. In both cases the straight-line schematic is best—the rest of the track plan doesn't concern us, and with the walkaround example we want to reinforce the idea of travel from place to place.

Nomenclature

As part of the organization of your wiring, as well as the process of designing control panels, you should set up some system of nomenclature. You want this system not only for blocks and turnouts but also controls, cables, terminals, and other connections. Figure 11-11 provides suggestions. Perhaps the simplest way is found in fig. 11-11A, though when you have more than one parallel track in a given location it's not easy.

The variant in fig. 11-11B is the one I've used throughout the track plan examples in earlier chapters; it's effective for identifying parallel tracks as parallel and helping you locate their positions along the railroad. An option not shown would be to use even numbers for parallel tracks north or east of the main line and odd numbers for tracks to the south or west, i.e., if block 12-1 is the main line, block 12-2 is the north (or east) siding and 12-3 is the south (or west) siding.

Figure 11-11C shows a system I haven't seen used but which shows promise, particularly for walkaround railroads. The idea is that named blocks and tracks would be easier to relate to places on the railroad than numbers. For easy labeling of cables and terminals the names could be represented by initials, such as "SCE" for "Spanish Creek East."

In any case, these are just suggestions; if you can think of a better way, use it. What matters is that your system is easy for you to use and simple to explain to your friends and guest operators.

The Panel Face

To return to the design of the control panel face, you must remember to take the size of your switches, buttons, lamps, and other control components into account. On the panel front you need to allow room for easy manipulation of just the right control, and for labeling. Behind the panel you must allow for the bodies of the controls, and for the wiring they will need. Both considerations argue against cramming everything into the tightest arrangement.

The best way is to have samples of

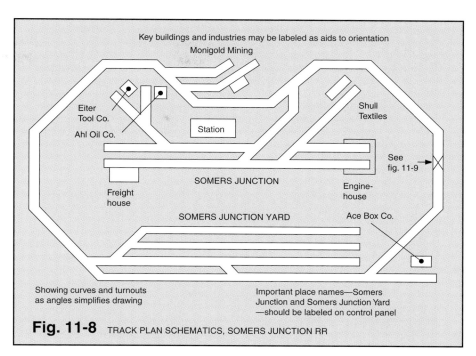

Fig. 11-8 TRACK PLAN SCHEMATICS, SOMERS JUNCTION RR

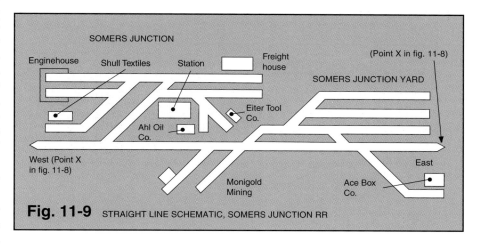

Fig. 11-9 STRAIGHT LINE SCHEMATIC, SOMERS JUNCTION RR

the switches, buttons, and other controls on hand when you design your panels, and to draw their full behind-the-panel outlines on your schematic, fig. 11-12, to make sure everything fits. Complicated items like multi-deck rotary switches can be pre-wired before you install them, but your panels will be easier to build and maintain if you leave room to work.

Wiring Control Panels

The control panel in fig. 11-13 illustrates a simple and effective method of construction. The panel frame or cabinet can be any wood, but the

panel face should be both rigid and thin enough to allow mounting the controls. In this example I've used 1/8" Masonite for the panel face; aluminum and Plexiglas are also suitable.

Figure 11-14 shows probably the most widely used method of painting the panel face. With the schematic laid out and the mounting holes drilled, you first paint the panel with a solid coat of a light color for the diagram lines, such as white, silver, or yellow. Allow that to dry thoroughly, then lay out the schematic with masking tape—you can use wider tape to designate main lines, and narrower

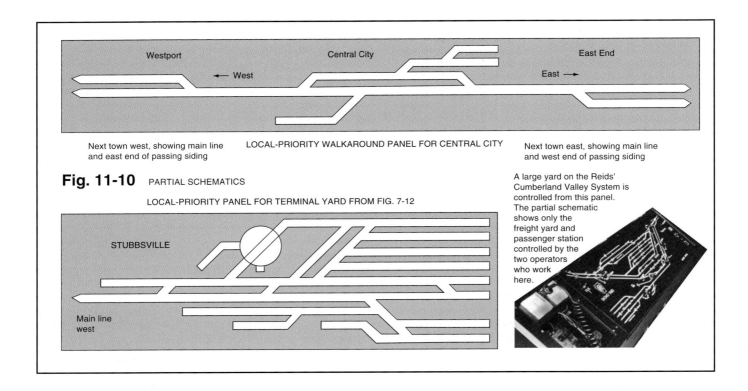

Next town west, showing main line and east end of passing siding

LOCAL-PRIORITY WALKAROUND PANEL FOR CENTRAL CITY

Next town east, showing main line and west end of passing siding

Fig. 11-10 PARTIAL SCHEMATICS

LOCAL-PRIORITY PANEL FOR TERMINAL YARD FROM FIG. 7-12

STUBBSVILLE

Main line west

A large yard on the Reids' Cumberland Valley System is controlled from this panel. The partial schematic shows only the freight yard and passenger station controlled by the two operators who work here.

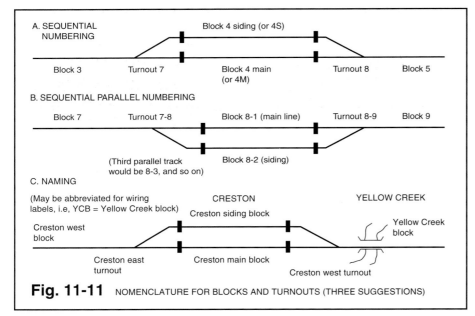

A. SEQUENTIAL NUMBERING

Block 4 siding (or 4S)

Block 3   Turnout 7   Block 4 main (or 4M)   Turnout 8   Block 5

B. SEQUENTIAL PARALLEL NUMBERING

Block 7   Turnout 7-8   Block 8-1 (main line)   Turnout 8-9   Block 9

(Third parallel track would be 8-3, and so on)   Block 8-2 (siding)

C. NAMING

(May be abbreviated for wiring labels, i.e, YCB = Yellow Creek block)

CRESTON

YELLOW CREEK

Creston siding block

Yellow Creek block

Creston west block

Creston east turnout

Creston main block

Creston west turnout

Fig. 11-11 NOMENCLATURE FOR BLOCKS AND TURNOUTS (THREE SUGGESTIONS)

tape for spurs. Now spray the panel with a darker background color, like green, gray, or black. Carefully peel up the masking tape to reveal the schematic.

To add lettering and labels apply decals or dry transfers. A variety of sizes and styles of dry transfer lettering is available at art supply stores; Chartpak and Letraset are two widely distributed brands. Model railroad manufacturers such as Walthers and Champion Decal offer dry-transfer and decal sets with useful control panel words spelled out. And don't overlook electronics supply outlets. They offer dry transfers with both alphabets and com-

mon control terms, such as Radio Shack set No. 270-201.

When all the lettering is in place, give the panel two or more coats of a clear sealing spray. This will bond the lettering to the panel and protect the panel face from wear. I'd choose a semigloss finish as a good compromise between easy cleaning and readability. Once that's completely dry you can mount the panel face on the cabinet and install the controls.

Working Inside

Hinging the panel face to the cabinet makes it easy to open the panel and work inside, fig. 11-15. If the panel face stands up close to the vertical when closed, or hangs past the vertical on an overhead panel, you'll need a catch or latch to hold it closed. Magnetic cabinet latches from the hardware store are a good choice.

Install terminal strips inside the panel to serve as junctions between the layout wiring and the wiring of the panel itself. The terminal strips make a convenient place to switch from heavy-gauge power wiring to lighter wires that will fit the control terminals. Terminal strips, especially the screw type shown here, also let you isolate the controls from the layout for troubleshooting.

Speaking of troubleshooting, you can avoid problems and make them easier to find if you keep the insides of your control panels neat and orderly. In fig. 11-15 I've gathered all the wires from the terminal strips into one cable running to the back side of the panel face, where they branch out again to the individual controls. I've used cable clamps to relieve the strain on the terminals and especially on the controls.

Note how the cable runs all the way across the panel between the last clamp on the frame and the first clamp on the face. That lets the wires twist rather than bend as the panel opens and closes, because wires are more likely to break in bending. An alternative is to make a hairpin bend in the cable, fig. 11-15 inset drawing. Stranded wire is more flexible than solid, making it the choice for this situation.

Panel Meters

Figure 11-15 does not include meters, but you may want to install a voltmeter and an ammeter for each cab to help you monitor performance. My experience is that meters don't matter much during normal operation, although they can show that a train is running properly on hidden track. They can help you identify short or open circuits when problems arise, and they are useful for testing locomotives. Figure 11-16 shows four ways to wire meters. The meters must be oriented to the correct polarity, fig. 11-16A, which means they must be connected between the speed control and the reversing switch. Most modern power packs are not made to be opened, so set the reversing switch on the pack to suit the meters, then add a new reversing switch on the control panel to control the train.

Figure 11-16B shows bipolar or center-zero meters that can be wired after

the reversing switch. They are harder to find than ordinary single-scale meters, and they aren't as sensitive for a given range because they can only use half their scales at a time.

In fig. 11-16C I've shown a method Don Hansen described in MODEL RAILROADER to wire single-scale meters for bipolar operation. The bridge rectifier corrects the polarity for the meters whichever way the train runs.

I've included fig. 11-16D for those who might want to add meters to a

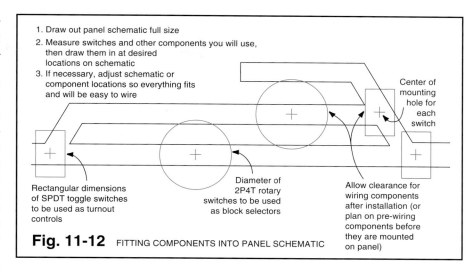

1. Draw out panel schematic full size
2. Measure switches and other components you will use, then draw them in at desired locations on schematic
3. If necessary, adjust schematic or component locations so everything fits and will be easy to wire

Center of mounting hole for each switch

Rectangular dimensions of SPDT toggle switches to be used as turnout controls

Diameter of 2P4T rotary switches to be used as block selectors

Allow clearance for wiring components after installation (or plan on pre-wiring components before they are mounted on panel)

Fig. 11-12 FITTING COMPONENTS INTO PANEL SCHEMATIC

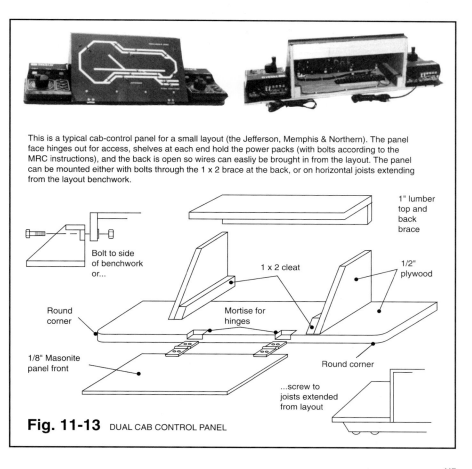

This is a typical cab-control panel for a small layout (the Jefferson, Memphis & Northern). The panel face hinges out for access, shelves at each end hold the power packs (with bolts according to the MRC instructions), and the back is open so wires can easliy be brought in from the layout. The panel can be mounted either with bolts through the 1 x 2 brace at the back, or on horizontal joists extending from the layout benchwork.

1" lumber top and back brace

Bolt to side of benchwork or...

1 x 2 cleat

1/2" plywood

Round corner

Mortise for hinges

Round corner

1/8" Masonite panel front

...screw to joists extended from layout

Fig. 11-13 DUAL CAB CONTROL PANEL

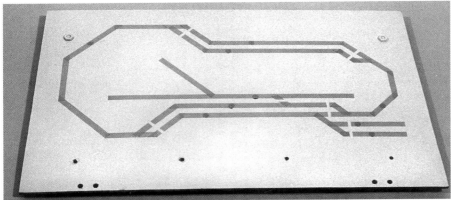

Fig. 11-14. DUAL-CAB CONTROL PANEL PAINTING. First cut out and drill the panel face, then spray paint it with the color you want for your schematic lines—this one is gloss white. Let the paint dry thoroughly, then lay out the schematic with strips of masking tape as in the left-hand photo. Spray the panel face with the background color—this one is a bright, gloss green—wait a few minutes for paint to set, then carefully peel away the masking as in the right-hand photo. Apply lettering with dry transfers, then seal the panel face with a clear spray.

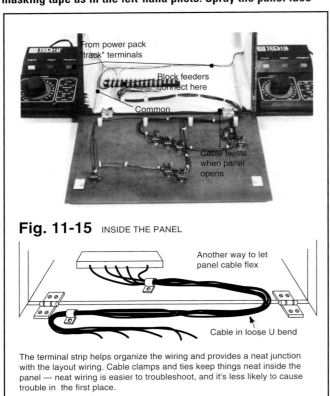

Fig. 11-15 INSIDE THE PANEL

The terminal strip helps organize the wiring and provides a neat junction with the layout wiring. Cable clamps and ties keep things neat inside the panel — neat wiring is easier to troubleshoot, and it's less likely to cause trouble in the first place.

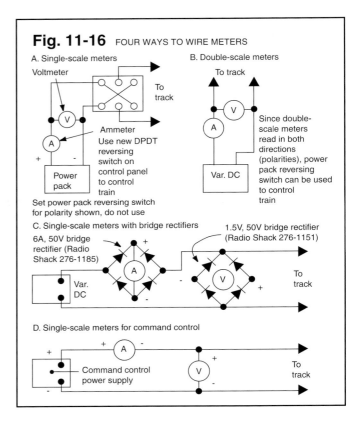

Fig. 11-16 FOUR WAYS TO WIRE METERS

command control system. In this case, however, the meters only serve to monitor the system as a whole or particular power supplies. They won't tell you much about the performance of individual locomotives, which should be tested in conventional DC operation before you install their command control receivers.

Test As You Go

My last recommendation on wiring control panels: Connect just one wire at a time. Test each connection or control immediately before moving to the next. This ensures that each addition is working properly as you go. and that any problem that appears relates to the last connection you made.

Even veteran model railroaders have trouble when they wire everything at once and then test. Besides, running a locomotive into each new block or over each route of a new turnout relieves the boredom of repetitive connections. After all, you certainly deserve to have some fun along the way.

In case of trouble...

'll repeat myself: The best way to take care of troubles is to make sure they don't happen in the first place, by working carefully and checking as you go. But we all make mistakes, and even something you've just installed can present a puzzling problem, so this chapter examines what to do when things go wrong. We'll look at simple test equipment you'll want handy, then I'll explain procedures for tracking down wiring problems.

Test Equipment

Test light. One of the most basic and useful items for your test kit is 16V or 18V bulb with alligator-clip on leads or test light with probes, fig. 12-1. You can connect it across the rails or across terminals on a switch or terminal strip, turn the power on, and see instantly whether you have current at that point. If the bulb lights brightly, the circuit's good; if it doesn't light, the circuit's open. There's a third possibility, too: The bulb may light, but only dimly. That likely indicates a short circuit, though you should confirm that indication with an ammeter reading as I'll explain.

Also in fig. 12-1 you'll see a molded plastic test light made by Campbell Scale Models. This has metal contact strips on the bottom so you can simply set it on the track and see if it lights—it's made for HO track but will work on other gauges. This is handy for checking track circuits but not so good with switches and terminal strips, so you'll need a test light with alligator clips too.

Clip leads. Clip leads or test jumpers, lengths of wire with alligator clips on each end, should be in your test kit too. The ones in fig. 12-1 are available at Radio Shack and other electronics stores. They're useful for making temporary connections either to discover if something works before you wire it permanently or to discover if something would work if you had wired it differently. You can also use them to extend the leads of a test light or other test equipment.

Panel meters. We learned how to install panel meters in Chapter 11. They will be valuable test instruments ready for use at any time. Figure 12-2 shows how they can help you by indicating normal operation, opens, and shorts. The ammeter is also useful when breaking in a new locomotive: You should see the motor's current drain drop as the mechanism runs more freely.

With a command control system the meter indications will be different than in fig. 12-2. In normal operation the voltmeter should always show the designed constant track voltage of your particular system. The ammeter will show the combined current drain of all locomotives on live tracks. However, the meters won't help you distinguish between shorts and opens. They'll give the open indication in either case, because the built-in electronic circuit breakers (ECBs) of command control systems instantly turn off the track power when a short circuit occurs.

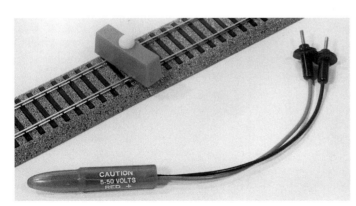

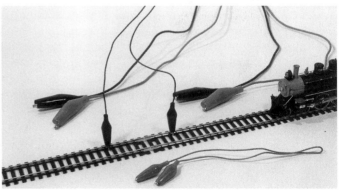

Fig. 12-1. TEST LIGHTS AND CLIP LEADS. The most basic equipment for layout troubleshooting includes test lights and clip leads. The Campbell Scale Models track test light with rail contacts shown here will light to show voltage on the rails, and the

Radio Shack low-voltage test light with probe can make a similar test at any location. The clip leads, lengths of wire with alligator clips at both ends, can be used to make temporary connections and to bridge around suspected open circuits.

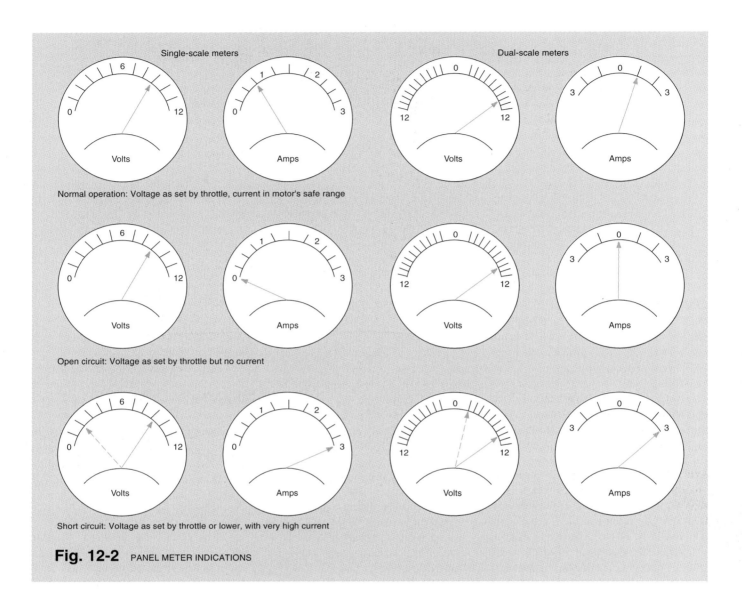

Fig. 12-2 PANEL METER INDICATIONS

An ammeter in a command control system may be useful for indicating a marginal overload, as when locomotives are using current in excess of the rating for a given power supply. This can degrade the control system's performance without tripping the ECB. Usually in a case like this you'll also see the track voltage indicated by the voltmeter dropping below the system's designed constant output, causing trouble with the transmission of control signals and erratic operation. Later I'll explain how to solve this problem.

Multimeter. A multimeter or VOM (for Volt-Ohm-Meter), fig. 12-3, is a portable test instrument that reads AC and DC voltage, DC polarity, resistance (ohms), and current (amps) over different ranges. Its controls let you switch from one function to another, and you read the needle on one of several scales depending on the function you've selected. It's up to you to read the right scale for a given test, so be sure to study the manufacturer's instructions.

A multimeter represents the most expensive single item you'll need for model railroad troubleshooting, but an adequate meter for our purposes costs only $30 or less. Here are ways that you'll use it, fig. 12-4.

To read voltage: First select AC or DC voltage in a range greater than what you expect to find, such as 0–30V if you're looking for 12V. Touch or clip the meter's leads to two sides of a circuit, as to two rails or the two terminals of a power supply, and read the voltage on the appropriate scale for the range you've selected.

To read a DC voltage the meter's positive lead must be connected to the positive side of the circuit (explained in the next paragraph). To read DC polarity: The meter leads are identified as positive (red lead) and common (black lead). Set the meter to read DC voltage of an appropriate